For Reference

Not to be taken from this room

D1367741

Radicals and Militants

Radicals and Militants

An Annotated Bibliography of Empirical Research on Campus Unrest

R
016.378
K355r

Kenneth Keniston
in collaboration with
Mary-Kay Duffield
Sharon Martinek

Lexington Books
D.C. Heath and Company
Lexington, Massachusetts
Toronto   London

Library of Congress Cataloging in Publication Data

Keniston, Kenneth.
  Radicals and militants.
   1. College students—United States—Political
activity—Abstracts. I. Title.
LA229.K46   378.1'98'108   72-11689
ISBN 0-669-85381-X

Copyright © 1973 by D.C. Heath and Company.

All rights reserved. No part of this publication may be reproduced or
transmitted in any form or by any means, electronic or mechanical, including photocopy, recording, or any information storage or retrieval
system, without permission in writing from the publisher.

Published simultaneously in Canada.

Printed in the United States of America.   4 3 4 1 2

International Standard Book Number: 0-669-85381-X

Library of Congress Catalog Card Number: 72-11689

The John J. Wright Library
LA ROCHE COLLEGE
9000 Babcock Boulevard
Pittsburgh, Pa. 15237

For My Mother

Acknowledgments

The preparation of these abstracts was made possible by a grant from the Ford Foundation for the study of youth. Sharon Martinek abstracted many studies independently; her abstracts served as a check on both accuracy and emphasis. Mary-Kay Duffield heroically edited the abstracts, verified the accuracy of countless figures and facts, and responded to innumerable queries of the editor. Sylvia Wishingrad Rifkin typed and retyped the abstracts with exemplary patience and good cheer.

Introduction

When I set out to abstract the available literature on student activism, radicalism, and the institutions where protests occurred, I little realized the scope of the task. Over the years, I had collected a number of published and unpublished works on these subjects, and I had noticed that authors "reviewing the literature" were not familiar with valuable studies. For this reason it seemed useful to try to locate and abstract the research on student political activities since the Second World War. What I did not realize was that my search would end up with more than 300 narrowly "empirical" articles and books, with countless more that surely failed to come to my attention.

I had expected that reviewing this research would show a "progressive" trend from primitive hypotheses, tested in elementary ways, to ever more sophisticated, theoretically based studies. This expectation turned out to be unfounded. Activism research has not in general built upon previous work; most researchers have started more or less from scratch; the comparability of any two studies is usually very tenuous. The traditional image of scientific research is of a ladder, with each study building on, amplifying, qualifying, or clarifying earlier research. With regard to student activism research, a better image would be that of a widening puddle. For example, two of the best studies—the Flacks-Neugarten and Block-Haan-Smith studies—were among the first undertaken. Both were conducted in the mid 1960s, but neither has since been rivaled in quality, range, methodological sophistication, or theoretical depth.

In much of the research reviewed, the level of methodological and theoretical sophistication is not very high. Taking the literature as a whole, it is notable how rarely elementary distinctions have been made, and to the detriment of the results. To cite one crucial example, the theoretical literature on activism counterposes two apparently opposite theories: that of intergenerational continuity and that of intergenerational conflict. Few writers have noted that exactly the same kind of data may be used to support both points of view. Those who argue for intergenerational continuity very often use correlational analyses of the socio-political position of parents and children. They find that if parents are ranked on a left-right spectrum, and their children are ranked on the same spectrum, there is a significant correlation between the two ranks. Such correlations are used to support the intergenerational continuity hypothesis. But if instead of correlating parental and filial data, we calculate the absolute discrepancies between parents' and children's socio-political views, we find especially marked discrepancies between left-wing activists and their parents. As a group, conservative students come from conservative families and have few political differences with their parents; but radical students more often come from liberal families and thus have more discrepant outlooks. Such discrepancies can be used to support the intergenerational conflict hypothesis. Few have gone on to ask the next question: Why is it that conservative parents tend to have equally conservative children, while liberal parents tend to have children whose politics are to the left of their parents'?

A few researchers like Block, Haan and Smith, Braungart, or Lewis and Kraut have asked direct questions about intrafamilial conflict of students with different political views. Overall, the results point to greater overt conflict in the families of left-wing students than in the families of right-wing students. Yet even this result is open to two divergent interpretations. One, propounded for their "activist" group by Block, Haan and Smith, is that the open expression of intrafamilial conflict (at least up to a certain point) is an index of family health, showing an ability to deal openly with the disharmonies that are inevitable in any family. The other interpretation is that reports of family conflict indicate deep-seated student resentments that originate in the family but are later "acted out" in the political arena. Here again, little research has attempted to explore and clarify the implications of these two interpretations of the same data.

Students have always protested about one thing or another; and during the 1960s they protested about a great many diverse issues. Another common failing of much research stems from not considering the issues over which protests arose. It is fairly obvious intuitively—and demonstrated empirically by A. Astin et al's research—that students who protest over the quality of food in the dining hall tend to be rather different from those who protest the war in Vietnam, racism on or off campus, and so on. Only a few studies, however, emphasize the importance of the issues at stake, much less explore the possibility that movements focused on different issues recruit different kinds of students. The more typical researcher refers globally to "activists" or "protesters," without noting the possibility that conflicts between his findings and those of other studies may be due to the fact that quite different issues were salient for the protesters he studied.

The student movement was a social movement, and social movements unfold, grow, and die according to complex laws of their own. Activists in the civil rights movement or at universities like the University of California at Berkeley were a vanguard. The first of their kind in many decades in America, they had a number of characteristics that distinguished them rather clearly from politically inactive students. But as student protests spread, were publicized by the media, and on many campuses became almost routine, the distinctiveness of the protester vis-à-vis his inactive classmates began to diminish. Characteristically, research conducted in the late 1960s shows less marked differences between activists and nonactivists than does earlier research, and this fact is sometimes used to conclude that the early findings were incorrect. But of course the conclusion need not be accepted. The divergence in "first-generation" and "second-generation" protestors—or between "vanguard" and "mass movement" activists—is probably best interpreted as a reflection of the dispersion of student protest within any given college and amongst the more than 2,500 institutions of higher education in America. Only a few investigators like Flacks and Mankoff or Dunlap and Gale have addressed themselves to this issue at the level of individual students, and only A. Astin's group has gathered evidence on institutional dispersion.

Another key distinction is between students who *profess* a set of beliefs (e.g., radicals) and students who *act* in the name of those beliefs (e.g., radical activists). From the beginning, it was obvious that these two groups did not overlap perfectly. For example, hundreds of thousands of students supported the goals of the civil rights movement; yet few were personally involved in any activity that expressed this support. In 1964, a majority of Berkeley's 27,000 students supported the goals, and a large minority the tactics, of the Free Speech Movement; yet less than 1000 were arrested in the Sproul Hall sit-in. In general, attitudinal support for any given student protest issue tends to be larger than the number of students truly active in protests. But until very recently, few researchers have bothered to examine the problematic relationship between political beliefs and actual participation in any socio-political activity.

Conversely, the simple fact that a student is "active" politically does not mean that he necessarily holds the same views as all other students who are active in the same way in the same cause at the same time. Here anecdotal and autobiographical accounts, not abstracted in this book, provide the best examples of the variety of motives and convictions that can impel a student to take part in a protest. James Kunin's *The Strawberry Statement*, for example, is a lively instance of the very mixed motives with which he entered into the "liberation" of five Columbia University buildings in 1968. Yet once again, much research treats "activists" as if they were all uniformly radicals in political conviction and had approximately the same motives in taking part in protests and demonstrations.

It remained for Kerpelman and others to remind us that many students do not put their money where their mouths are, much less their "bodies on the line." A few researchers have begun to investigate the apparently separate determinants of holding a given set of beliefs and acting on them. Kerpelman argues, for example, that many of the characteristics attributed to left activists are in fact also those of right-wing activists and moderate activists as well. More intellectually able, well integrated, and initiating students are more likely to act in the name of their beliefs—whatever these beliefs may be—than students possessed of lesser abilities. Doress, in his studies of Boston University activists, Cowdry and Keniston at Yale, Lewis and Kraut, and a handful of others began to explore this complex interaction between beliefs and behavior. But most studies simply neglect it, often juxtaposing results drawn from a study of students who have common beliefs with findings based on students who took a common action without noting the difference in who was being studied.

Another controversy that runs throughout the literature is that between "sociological" and "psychological" variables. At least a few authors seem to consider these two levels of explanation mutually exclusive or antithetical. Some researchers have argued that since demographic (sociological) factors appear to explain much of the difference between active and inactive students, there is no need for involuted psychological interpretations. Psychologists have replied that psychic factors, ranging from "radical political consciousness" to family upbringing patterns and levels of moral reasoning, should play a primary role in any explantion of student political activities. The obvious point that "background" (sociological) factors interact with attitudinal, characterological, and dispositional (psychological) factors has been made by relatively few. And a bare handful of studies examines the interaction between "sociological" factors such as religion or social class and "psychological" factors such as styles of family interaction.

Still another problem has plagued much activism research. In the early 1960s, it may have been adequate to classify students' political beliefs on a single spectrum running from far left to far right. In the latter part of the decade, however, the student movement developed internal ideological conflicts, even as it enlisted a more diverse group of students. At this time, it should have become increasingly clear that a simple left-right spectrum was inadequate to characterize the great diversity of political beliefs held by left-wing students. To be sure, a research technique such as asking students to label themselves on a continuum that runs from left to right has the great virtue of simplicity. But by 1968, it had the vice of glossing over the growing likelihood that any two self-labelled "radicals" would hold very different beliefs and behave in very different ways.

A few studies conducted during the late 1960s and in 1970 began to explore systematically these ideological splits within the student left. Studies at Kent State, Columbia, Yale, Chicago, and elsewhere showed clearly that "radicals" held a variety of diverse and even incompatible views. Perhaps the most critical of these schisms within the student movement was the attitude toward "revolutionary violence" as opposed to "due process." From 1967 on, no disputes were more bitterly waged than those over the proper role of confrontation, resistance, disruption, and violence, on the one hand, and legalism, due process, and working through "legitimate channels" on the other hand. But whether "radical" students whose beliefs inclined to either one or the other of these positions differed in other ways is not really known. Similarly, except for Watts' early studies of Berkeley dropouts and activists, we know little about the differences between dissenters who expressed themselves in a "hippie," "counter-culture," "new-life-style" mode and dissenters whose focus was on more specific socio-political rather than psycho-cultural issues.

The concept of "activism" is surely no less complex than that of "radicalism," especially as the range of tactics considered legitimate broadened in the late 1960s. Early on, Block, Haan and Smith proposed a distinction between "contructivists," "activists," and "dissenters," and demonstrated that the three types of student had widely divergent backgrounds. But few have followed up, much less refined, this early distinction. Instead, everything from writing one's congressman through peaceful picketing to illegal building seizures has been termed student activism, with the not too surprising result that the "activists" of one study turn out to be very different from the "activists" of another. "Activism indices" included behaviors that were seen by many students as totally incompatible—e.g., canvassing in a local election and trashing stores during street demonstrations. That this lack of specificity with regard to the meaning of "activism" muddied the waters was shown by Aron with a large group of University of Chicago students, where he found that there were at least four distinct and nonoverlapping modes of socio-political action. But since these modes have not been distinguished in most research, we know almost nothing about the factors that drew students to such different actions as legal protests or illegal disruptions, to drugs and new life styles or political actions.

Perhaps the most neglected topic is the process and persistence of what came to be known as "radicalization." Most studies were "static"—conducted at one particular point in time and focused on identifying the qualities of students who at that time held "radical" beliefs or were involved in "activism." But simply to study the special characteristics of radicals, especially during a campus crisis, does not necessarily tell us much about the process of becoming a radical. For example, some radicalism is "hereditary"—premised on the accepted radicalism of parents. Other radicalism is "instant"—somehow catalysed by events and issues that change the student's socio-political views. The most important questions from an historical and social point of view have rarely been asked: Through what processes and set of influences did students, as individuals and a group, move gradually toward a more "radical" and "critical" position in regard to many prevailing American practices and policies? What kinds of people are most susceptible to radicalization, and by what kinds of influences? To what extent did "radicalization" persist beyond the immediate events that inspired it? Under what circumstances did it disappear?

Impressionistic, biographical, and autobiographical studies provide far richer leads to such questions than the empirical research reviewed here. The only long-term followup study, conducted by Maidenberg and Meyer, found very high levels of persistence of radicalism five years later in students who had been "radicalized" at the time of their arrest in the Free Speech Movement demonstrations at Berkeley in 1964. But the 1964-69 era coincided with a time of increasing radicalization for virtually *all* students from such institutions as Berkeley. This fact permits us to interpret the persistence of FSM radicalization in two different ways. It may show that radicalization by events such as the FSM arrests is relatively permanent in and of itself. Or it may merely show that the natural tendency of "instant radicals" to return to their former stance after the crisis was in this instance counteracted by the increasing ideological radicalism of their Berkeley peers. In the end we know very little about the factors that led to persistence and attrition of radicalization.

Even more important, few have studied the factors that make for "radicalization" in the first place—e.g., the extent to which they involve a differential "readiness to be radicalized," or a special exposure to "radicalizing events," or friends and peers who encourage or support radical views, or some combination of these and other factors. Data collected by Barton and his colleagues at Columbia suggest that any answer will be extremely complex. For example, those who witnessed the police riot during the Columbia demonstrations were indeed more "radicalized" than those who did not; but those who witnessed police violence were, in the first place, far more likely to be supporters of the radicals' positions. Research at the University of California at Santa Barbara suggests tentatively that attitudes toward the war played an extraordinarily prominent role in the "radicalization" of other attitudes. And Mankoff suggests that at the University of Wisconsin, repeated encounters with the violence of public authorities contributed to radicalization. But none of these studies provides more than the beginning of an account of the interacting factors that contributed to the leftward shift of American students in the 1960s.

The bulk of the research on student activism was conducted at a relatively small number of institutions, most of which are among the most selective and publically visible colleges and universities in America. Partly for this reason, studies of institutions—and in particular the research of A. Astin et al.—provide a useful antidote to the widespread impression that by 1968-70 *most* students had become radical activists. Astin and his colleagues show that the selectivity of any institution vis-à-vis students applying for admission, along with other measures of institutional "quality," is highly related to the incidence of protests at that institution. Thus, the Berkeleys, Harvards, Oberlins, Reeds, Wisconsins, Columbias, and Chicagos of America experienced the earliest and in many cases the most dramatic protests.

But there are more than 2,500 colleges and universities in America. The President's Commission on Campus Unrest estimates that 1.5 million students were involved in demonstrations at the time of the most massive student protest in American history, the Cambodia-Kent-Jackson protests in 1970. But that leaves approximately 5 million students who were not involved. Studies of institutions further show that in no year from 1960-1970 did a majority of all institutions experience protests over war and race-related issues. In 1968-69, for example, Earth Day brought out more students in demonstrations than did war and racial issues. Such data serve to qualify the media-conveyed image of all American campuses seething with political unrest from Berkeley 1964 to Kent and Jackson State 1970.

The close relationship between the selectivity and "quality" of an institution and the incidence of protests obviously raises the possibility—often put forward as fact—that student protest was primarily "caused" by some characteristic of high-selectivity colleges and universities. Thus, for a time it was a favorite claim of right-wing politicians that "campus permissiveness" was the prime cause of student protests. Some radicals, too, charged that the complicity of American higher education with racism and imperialism was a prime factor in protests. Extreme right and extreme left have often agreed in blaming the college for campus unrest.

The existing data allow us to test these claims. Admittedly, there are complex methodological and political questions about how institutional data should be interpreted. But taken together, studies on the relation between institutional characteristics and protests make clear that, once we take into account the characteristics of the students enrolled in any college, the characteristics of the college environment itself make virtually no difference in determining the percentage of students involved in protests.[a] In brief, then, it appears to be the characteristics of the students who come together on a campus, not the nature of the campus itself, that are most predictive of the proportion who became involved in "activism."

These abstracts should make clear that anyone seeking clear answers, expecting neat comparability between studies conducted at different colleges, convinced of the inevitably "progressive" nature of social science, or unwilling to make distinctions, will be acutely frustrated by the literature on activism, radicalism, and the institutions where protests have occurred. But in defense of this research, the circumstances under which it was conducted must be remembered. Activism research has almost always been what David Riesman has called "firehouse" research—the alarm bell rings, the researcher slides down the greased pole, rushes to the fire, and begins collecting data. A study initiated at the very moment when protests begin to boil over allows no time for leisurely analyses of prior research or careful preparation of interview schedules, questionnaires and psychological tests, which alone could ensure an orderly and progressive accumulation of results. Given research planned in 24 hours in the midst of some apocalyptic campus event, one can sometimes only admire a researcher's ability to obtain reasonably adequate measures of relatively important variables. And it is surely not accidental that the studies I consider the most valuable were all conducted in a more leisurely way, not as an immediate response to a specific campus crisis, but a part of broader inquiries into the role of youth in social change, student development, or the general characteristics of student protest and activism.

As anyone willing to read through these abstracts will realize, it is not possible to summarize the research in any simple way; nor will I attempt a summary here. A large number of interpretive summaries are already available—

---

[a] If instead of considering the percentage of students involved in protests, we consider the absolute *number* of protests, then of course larger institutions tend to have more protests. As a result, all of those features generally associated with largeness (impersonality, large class size, absence of coherent school spirit, etc.) are directly associated with the number of protests on any campus. But these findings merely prove that the more students congregated on a given campus, the greater the likelihood that there will be enough of them to mount a protest about something.

many of them based in part upon a familiarity with some of the literature here abstracted. They offer many broader hypotheses, interpretations, and speculations about the student movement in America and abroad during the 1960s. As the debate about the significance of student movements continues, it will hopefully make use of, though not be tied to, the kind of empirical research reported here. Empirical research can never finally conform a given interpretation, for alternative explanations are always possible. But research can at least eliminate grossly implausible or simple-minded interpretations, pointing to the need for a complexity of interpretation that does justice to the actual complexity of the people and the events being interpreted.

For example, the "oedipal rebellion" thesis, although still favored by some critics of the student rebellion, receives no support from the research conducted to date. And I suggested above that the intergenerational continuity vs. intergenerational conflict debate requires restatement in the light of existing research. The argument that American colleges and universities are to blame for the protests that occurred on their campuses (and overflowed their boundaries) turns out to be implausible compared with the hypothesis that the characteristics and convictions of students, confronting real events in the real world, were the primary catalysts for student protests. The conflict between the "sociological" and the "psychological" explanations of student protest turns out to be a pseudoconflict, and one in principle resolvable by more sophisticated research methods. Precisely because research bears on debates like these, the tedious task of collecting and abstracting this research seemed useful.

The question that necessarily remains unanswered as of early 1973 concerns the decline and future of student activism. Since the spring of 1970, there has been a steady decrease in student protests, even in the face of provocations far more outrageous than the Cambodia invasion. Throughout 1971 and 1972, campuses were increasingly quiet, some commentators agreeing with Kingman Brewster that the tranquility was "eerie" and perhaps ominous, others suggesting that students were returning to the smug, security-seeking silence of the 1950s. No data exist which can fully explain the decline of the student movement after its climax at Cambodia-Kent-Jackson.[b] But Yankelovich's repeated polling of students (not abstracted here) points to what he terms an "unlinking" of the political and cultural aspects of the student revolt. Thus while political activity diminished, dwindled, and to all intents and purposes ceased, the "cultural critique" of American society that was mounted on campus in the 1960s appears to have continued.

---

[b]Clearly many factors are involved. I have elsewhere suggested that the student movement's confrontation with the violent rhetoric and, to a lesser extent, the violent deeds within its own ranks played a role in the decline of that movement. So, too, what Coles calls the "weariness of social struggle" may have been important not merely for individuals but (through vicarious participation) for a whole generation. The continuing escalation of the air war in Indochina despite many years of campus protests led many students to question the efficacy of all political action. And so on.

My own reading of the moods of students as of early 1973 agrees in essence with Yankelovich's argument. I see no massive return to the self-satisfaction and complacency of the 1950s. On campuses where protests were most prevalent during the 1960s I find no renewed enthusiasm for the foreign and domestic policies of the federal government, and little excitement about the possibility of meaningful social change through existing political institutions. On the contrary, dissatisfaction with the policies of this country seems extremely widespread, though less vocal. Even as protests and political actions are on the decline, however, we continue to see a "cultural revolution"—a questioning of many of the traditional value assumptions of American society, but one that increasingly takes private, psycho-cultural shape rather than public socio-political form.

The 1960s thus seem to have brought in their immediate wake not a "return" to traditional, tried-and-true American beliefs and practices, but increased cynicism about these beliefs and practices. The "new privatism" of the early 1970s is premised more on despair than on any conviction that all is well with the body politic. To understand this despair, recall that students being considered for admission to college in 1973 were born in 1955. They lived out their childhoods and came to political consciousness during a period when the three Americans most admired by young people (Martin Luther King, John F. Kennedy, and Robert Kennedy) were assassinated, when the country was involved in the most divisive war in its history, during which campus protest was a constant topic discussion (in June 1970, deemed the nation's "number one problem"), and when the faith of Americans in the credibility of government and the efficacy of organized political effort was deeply eroded.

In oversimplified summary, the activists of the 1960s were active largely out of indignation. They had been brought up to believe in the validity and realizability of a long series of American ideals: domestic justice, equal access to the rewards and dignity that American society offers, social change through existing institutions, America as a peaceloving, nonaggressive nation. But these beliefs were constantly attacked both by events and by the mounting critique of the existing American society. Those who grew up during the 1960s therefore arrived in late adolescence with far less capacity for indignation, with far less conviction in the effectiveness of their actions in effecting meaningful social change. Having been brought up not to expect very much, they are not readily disillusioned or outraged.

But this is not to say that the current younger brothers and sisters of the activists of the 1960s are enchanted by American society. Indeed they are probably even less convinced that hard work is rewarded, even more skeptical about such basic institutions as the nuclear family, even less certain about the usefulness of political action. Precisely because they were reared in an era in which many cherished social and political illusions were undermined, they seek salvation in some small private sphere over which they can have more certain effects and control. Yoga, Zen, Jesus, macrobiotics, rural communes and a variety of essentially small-scale and "privatistic" endeavors flourish; so even does studying in order to earn the wherewithal to find some personal security in an uncontrollable world.

Predictions about future student behavior are in principle impossible, since how students act depends not only on the characteristics of students, but on inherently unpredictable events in the wider world. Yet as of early 1973, it seems safe to conclude that a great deal of the sense of outrage, indignation, and determination to "implement and renew" the liberal, peaceloving, democratic tradition in America has gone underground amongst the 1970 equivalents of the activists of the 1960s. If this is true, then it may be the greatest domestic toll of that era. Any nation that has lost the hope, corroded the political idealism, and undermined the capacity for ethical outrage in its young has lost a significant part of its future.

New Haven, Connecticut

February, 1973

Explanatory Notes

The abstracts that follow are highly condensed and selective, in some cases compressing 500 pages into a page or two. In preparing these abstracts, I have been influenced both by the author's own emphases and by my sense of the findings that bear most directly on important theoretical questions or empirical issues. Another reader would obviously have chosen other findings for emphasis.

The research abstracted here is but a tiny portion of the total literature on student activism, campus unrest, and the meanings of the "youth revolt" in the industrialized nations. To keep the bibliography within manageable limits, I have included only empirical studies from 1945 on that report new findings on young American activists or radicals, or on the institutions where protests have occurred. An "empirical study" is defined as any study that employs systematic techniques for gathering information and attempts to report its results in a relatively dispassionate manner. Specifically excluded are studies of single individuals and reports based solely upon experience with patients, biographies and autobiographies, polls and surveys of student opinion, interpretive articles that present no new data, histories of the student movement, research conducted in other countries, and analyses of specific incidents at specific institutions. Institutional studies included here thus always involve comparisons among several institutions.

Every effort has been made to insure accuracy. Many of the studies were abstracted independently by myself and by Sharon Martinek; a comparison of the two abstracts showed remarkable consistency. In all cases, questionable points have been checked back against the original source. Despite these precautions, however, errors have certainly crept into abstracts that report tens of thousands of findings. The reader should therefore *consult the original reference* before citing any findings reported here.

As a guide to further reading, I have indicated my subjective estimate of the significance of the more important studies by using asterisks preceding the reference. Three studies, taken as a whole, have been marked ***. I think these studies are mandatory reading for anyone who would be familiar with activism research. A rating of two asterisks (**) conveys my judgment that the research is extremely important; one asterisk (*) indicates that I consider the study very valuable. Unstarred studies often make interesting points or present new data, but seem to me to deserve a somewhat lower priority in reviewing the literature.

A standard format has been used in abstracting. Under "SETTING" is given the year that data were gathered, the institution or location of the study, and any events that effect the results. The next heading, "SUBJECTS" or "INSTITUTIONS," indicates the numbers and special characteristics of the people or institutions studied, the representativeness of the sample, and other such matters. Percentages in parentheses, e.g., (78%), indicate the response rate;

"N = 127" indicates the number of subjects or institutions in the *final* sample actually studied. Under "METHODS," I have indicated how data were collected, the major areas about which information was gathered, key variables or classifications, and any complex or special statistical techniques employed. The "RESULTS" section summarizes the major findings of the study, often with an indication of the author's own conclusions. The final section, "COMMENTS," gives a brief indication of the importance of the study and any special strengths or limitations.

To avoid redundancy, a general introduction was prepared for several large studies that have produced many publications based on the same data and methods. These introductions are incorporated in the alphabetical listing and are referred to (e.g., as "A. Astin et al. Intro.") in other abstracts.

All abstracts have been repeatedly edited for concision. Detailed findings are neglected in favor of general ones, and important qualifications are often omitted. General conventions were adopted to shorten the abstracts. When authors calculate levels of significance, only findings significant at the $p = > 0.05$ level are reported without qualification; tendencies or trends are so indicated. The expression "vs." means "in comparison or contrast to"; thus the sentence "Activists major in social sciences, humanities (vs. agriculture, business administration)" indicates that activists are found significantly more often in the social sciences and humanities and significantly less often in agriculture and business administration. When findings apply only to one subgroup, that subgroup is indicated in parentheses immediately after the report of the finding. Thus the sentence "Radicals higher on OPI impulse expression (women)" should be read as "Female radicals, but not male radicals, score significantly higher on the Omnibus Personality Inventory measure of impulse expression."

The following abbreviations are used throughout the abstracts:

Glossary of Abbreviations

ACE	American Council on Education
ACESIF	American Council of Education Student Information Form
ACL	Adjective Check List
ANOMIA	Srole's Anomia Scale
AVL	Allport-Vernon-Lindzey Values Test
CORE	Congress on Racial Equality
CPI	California Personality Inventory
CUES	Pace's College and University Environment Scale
D	Rokeach's Dogmatism Scale
EAT	Astin's Environmental Assessment Technique
F	Adorno et al.'s F-Scale (Authoritarianism)
FSM	Free Speech Movement
GPA	Grade Point Average

I	Institution/institutional
I-E	Rotter's Internal-External Control Scale
N =	Final number studied
OPI	Omnibus Personality Inventory
(xx%)	Response rate in percentage
PEC	Levinson's Political-Economic Conservatism Scale
16PF	Cattell's 16 Personality Factors Test
r	Correlation
r'	Multiple correlation
SAT	Scholastic Aptitude Test
SES	Socioeconomic status
SDS	Students for a Democratic Society
SNCC	Student Nonviolent Coordinating Committee
S	Subject/student
SVIB	Strong Vocational Inventory Blank
VISTA	Volunteers in Service to America
vs.	In comparison/contrast to
YAF	Young Americans for Freedom
YC	Young Conservatives
YD	Young Democrats
YPSL	Young People's Socialist League
YR	Young Republicans

Radicals and Militants

Abstracts

1. Aiken, M.; Demerath, N.J. III; and Marwell, G. 1965. "Conscience and Confrontation." Christian Faith and Higher Education Institute, East Lansing, Michigan. Also in NEW SOUTH 21 (Spring 1966):19-28. See Demerath et al. 1970. A preliminary analysis of data gathered at the start of the 1965 SCOPE Project.

2. Ailey, John S. 1968. "Alienation among Oberlin College Students." Bachelor's thesis, Oberlin College. 21 pp. + App.

SETTING: 1967-68, Oberlin College, after demonstrations obstructing Navy recruiters.

SUBJECTS: 334 Ss (not random) completed initial questionnaire; 39 Ss involved in interview study.

METHODS: All Ss given Keniston's Cultural Alienation Scale, measures of radical activism, drug use, etc. Questionnaire factor analyzed, with 6 definable factors: cultural alienation, intensive drug use, violent confrontational political actions, 2 cultural commitment factors, and political liberalism. On the basis of cultural alienation scores, 9 male and 10 female high scorers, and 10 male and 10 female low scorers were selected for 1-1½ hour structured interviews.

RESULTS: Comparison of extreme Ss on cultural alienation shows differences on all other alienation scales except vacillation and self-contempt. Culturally alienated Ss more often define selves as radicals, readers of left-wing journals, participants in political demonstrations (especially illegal-coercive), and drug users. Interviews indicate that alienated Ss are nonchurch attenders (like mothers); are opposed to Vietnam war and to police-National Guard force; are less disapproving of black riots; believe citizens have less control over government; report parents have fewer strict rules and are more emotional and politically and civically active; report mothers more often gave up early ambitions; feel less close to fathers; have less strict sexual codes and less traditional definition of sex roles; are more uncertain about future plans; are more opposed to the draft; report more psychological change since high school.

COMMENTS: Primarily a study of cultural alienation. Major relevant finding is that cultural alienation is associated with radical self-label and participation in demonstrations.

3. *Allerbeck, Klaus R. 1968. "Alternative Explanations of Participation in Student Movements: Generational Conflict, Permissive Education, Revolt of the Privileged or Political Socialization: Some Results of a Cross-Cultural Analysis." Paper read at 8th World Congress of International Political Science Association, 1968, Munich. 12 pp. + App.

SETTING AND SUBJECTS: Data from Somers 1965; 1965 Harris Poll; Wisconsin Survey Research studies at University of Wisconsin (Madison) in 1966 and 1968; University of Cologne students in 1968 and 1969; German National Student Survey in 1968.

METHOD: Secondary data analysis to test generational revolt, permissiveness, revolt of privileged, and political socialization hypotheses.

RESULTS: Madison data show student-parent disagreement is associated with student support for activism only when father is conservative. German data show participation in demonstrations is tenuously associated with disagreement with father but strongly associated with father Social Democrat or Free Democrat (vs. Christian Democrat); student-parent disagreement not associated with student support for activism when father is conservative. German data suggest permissiveness hypothesis is invalid. Madison data show small but significant correlations between parental SES indicators and activism support, but in German data, activism-SES and activism-radicalism-SES correlations are 0 or negative. Madison data show that educated conservative fathers are no more likely to have activist offspring than uneducated conservative fathers. Author argues that this finding refutes "revolt of the privileged" hypothesis.

COMMENTS: Ingenious data analysis, using cross-cultural comparisons, to test theories of student revolt. Results support political socialization hypothesis, different structural conditions underlying student revolt in Germany and America.

4. ——. 1970. "Structural Conditions of Student Movements: The Student Community and the Student Role." Paper read at 7th World Congress of Sociology, 1970. Varna, Bulgaria. 19 pp.

SETTING, SUBJECTS, AND METHODS: See Allerbeck 1968.

RESULTS: German data indicate that identification with student role is associated with support for student movement; American data show association between vocational definition of education and anti-FSM attitudes. Multiple regression (1968 Cologne data) on support for student movement yields 4 main predictors: parents' liberalism, political climate of field of study, identification with student role, perceived cleavage between students and general population. Author concludes that "deviance on the social system level is not necessarily rooted in individual deviance, be it motivation or behavior."

COMMENTS: Cross-cultural paper that supports political socialization hypothesis, places secondary emphasis on self-identification as student (or nonvocational orientation) and perceived discrepancy between students and public.

5. *Angres, Salma. 1969. "Values and Socialization Practices of Jewish and Non-Jewish Parents of College Students." Master's thesis, Committee on Human Development, University of Chicago. Abstract, 3 pp.

SETTING, SUBJECTS, AND METHODS: See Flacks and Neugarten Intro. Sample contained 32 Jewish families, 38 non-Jewish families, and 6 families with 1 Jewish parent. Multivariate analyses used to explore relationship of child's activism, religion, and parent's sex with parent's values and socialization practices.

RESULTS: See Flacks 1965, Derber and Flacks 1968. Activists report more major and minor conflicts with their parents. With activism of child and sex of parents controlled, Jewish parents are more politically liberal, egalitarian, and intellectual, less religious and conventionally moralistic than non-Jewish parents. Jewish parents of nonactivists express especially high regard for friendliness and familial contacts. Overall, parents vary more by activism of child than by religion.

COMMENTS: Filial activism differentiates between parents more than sex or Jewish vs. non-Jewish differences; this suggests that activist vs. non-activist differences cannot be explained solely or primarily in terms of Jewish-non-Jewish differences.

6. Armistead, T.W. 1969. "Police on Campus and the Evolution of Personal Commitments: A Survey of Nonstrikers' Attitudes during a Berkeley Confrontation." ISSUES IN CRIMINOLOGY 4 (Fall):171-84.

SETTING: Feb. 19-20, 1969, University of California at Berkeley, during student action springing from police violence against pickets supporting demands of Third World Liberation Front.

SUBJECTS: Questionnaires handed out in Sproul Plaza to nonstrikers; attempt at random sampling of crowd, N = 124 (26%).

METHODS: Brief questionnaire concerning reasons for presence in Sproul Plaza, previous involvement in strike, attitudes toward strike, police, and impact of police action.

RESULTS: 2/3 of Ss were present because of past or anticipated police action, Ss drawn largely by violence or possibility of violence; 33% of Ss want police off campus, 21% report increased strike support and hostility towards police, 5% increased strike support, 9% no change from previous strike support. Only 3% more opposed to strike and 1% more supportive of police. Data suggest that police violence and on-campus police presence increase strike support and that hostility to police tends to escalate disorder.

COMMENTS: Despite nonrandom sample, data suggest "radicalizing" effects of police presence and witnessing of police violence.

7. Aron, William S. 1970. "Radical Ideology on the University of Chicago Campus." University of Chicago: Community and Family Study Center. 24 pp.

SUBJECTS: Random sample of undergraduates and graduate students, N = 619 (92.5%), undergraduate, N = 190.

METHOD: Ss interviewed about levels of political activity and 77 attitudinal variables. Undergraduate and graduate responses reported separately.

RESULTS: Descriptive summary of Ss' attitudes. About 40% of undergraduates consider political revolution in U.S. possible; less than 7% approve recent bombings in N.Y.C.; 78% undergrads (67% grads) sympathetic to destroying draft board files; 14% undergrads (9% grads) approve violence to bring about social change. Most Ss are committed to nonviolent demonstrations, resistance, political participation, and political education. 81% undergrads (89% grads) desire more peaceful sit-ins in the future.

COMMENTS: A description of sociopolitical attitudes at a highly selective university. Data indicate widespread acceptance by most of University of Chicago students of positions earlier defined as "radical."

8. ———. 1971. "Ideology and Behavior as Components of Radicalism." Paper read at American Sociological Association, September 1971, Denver. 30 pp.

SETTING, SUBJECTS, AND METHODS: See Aron 1970. Factor analysis of 77 attitudinal items (varimax rotation) produced 5 factors. First 2 factors are termed "ideological anger" (advocacy of militant, violent tactics) and "Ideological dissatisfaction" (advocacy of basic social change with special focus on university). Factor analysis of 11 types of political behavior reported by Ss produced 5 factor scores: general activism (first unrotated factor), and 4 rotated factors: confrontation; social service action; rallies, marches, and pickets; and political campaign. Data analysis consists of cross-tabulations of high/middle/low Ss on "ideology" factors with high/middle/low Ss on "activism" factors.

RESULTS: General activism is associated with both ideological anger and ideological dissatisfaction. Author concludes that there "appears to be a certain [threshold] level of ideological commitment, above which the barriers to behavior are surmounted and the level of activism increases greatly," a pattern repeated in many results. Association of confrontation with ideological anger much higher than with ideological dissatisfaction. Rallies, marches, and pickets are strongly connected with dissatisfaction but more tenuously with anger. Political campaign is unrelated to anger but mildly related to dissatisfaction. High and low dissatisfaction Ss both are disporportionately involved in social service. Author stresses difference between activism and ideology.

COMMENTS: Labels of ideology factors are overly general, but valuable distinctions are made between 2 types of radical attitudes and 4 types of activism. Cutting points used to define high, middle, and low groups on activism and ideology may affect "threshold" results.

9. ***Astin, Alexander W., et al. Introduction.

SETTING: 1966-71, American higher education (American Council on Education Cooperative Institutional Research Program).

SUBJECTS AND INSTITUTIONS: Studies involve a sample of over 400 I's, stratified by region, type of control, size, selectivity, etc., with some types deliberately oversampled. By weighting this sample, a representative picture of American higher education is reconstructed. At each I, incoming freshmen are tested at the beginning of their freshman year; response rates are generally close to 100%. The number of freshmen studied each year is 200,000-300,000. By weighting this sample, a representative picture of Ss at all I's can be reconstructed.

METHODS: Data on each I include 15 dichotomous measures (type of I, level, race, control, geographic region, etc.); measures of enrollment and selectivity; 33 measures of college environment derived from Inventory of College Activities (ICA)/(e.g., concern for the individual student, permissiveness vs. strictness of college policies concerning drinking, aggressiveness in the classroom, etc.). In addition, 155 "freshman input characteristics" for each I are obtained by averaging Ss' scores for each I on each variable included in ACESIF, administered to incoming freshmen. Data concerning protests, etc., are obtained from I representatives (generally top- or middle-level administrators) at each I.

Data on each S is derived from ACESIF, includes background characteristics, current attitudes and opinions, high school experiences and behavior, educational goals and priorities, and other activities (content varies slightly from year to year). Mailed follow-up questionnaires in longitudinal studies generally involve repetition of items on freshman ACESIF, with new items oriented toward particular research focus.

Methods include cross-tabulation of dependent variables (e.g., incidence of protests of specified type) with I characteristics (e.g., size, selectivity, type of control); calculation of zero-order correlations between I or S characteristics and dependent variables; multiple regression analyses. Analyses of protests by I generally entail "control for student input," which involves first allowing freshman input characteristics (derived from average ACESIF scores for each I) to enter regression equation in order of decreasing F-ratios until reduction in residual sum of squares $p = > 0.05$, then examining partial correlations or F-ratios of I characteristics.

Samples of Ss or I's are systematically weighted for representativeness; follow-up studies are weighted to compensate for characteristics of non-respondents. In most regression analyses involving I characteristics, I size is not entered into regression equation before studying other I characteristics.

RESULTS: See A. Astin 1968, 1969, 1970a, 1970b, 1970c, 1970d, 1970e, 1971; Astin and Bayer 1971; Bayer and Astin 1971; Bayer, Astin, and Boruch 1970, 1971; Boruch and Creager 1971; Bisconti 1970; Bisconti and Astin 1971; Royer 1971.

COMMENTS: These are the most reliable and methodologically sophisticated studies of protests and characteristics in the literature, although the research is atheoretical. Data files are open to qualified investigators (with precautions taken to assure confidentiality). Further I studies should consider using ACE data rather than gathering new data of their own.

10. **Astin, Alexander W. 1968. "Personal and Environmental Determinants of Student Activism." MEASUREMENT AND EVALUATION IN GUIDANCE 1 (Fall):149-62.

SETTING: Fall 1966, late summer 1967, national samples.

SUBJECTS AND INSTITUTIONS: See A. Astin et al. Intro. Fall 1966: representative sample of about 200,000 Ss tested at stratified national sample of 236 I's. Summer 1967: follow-up questionnaire mailed to representative subsample of 60,000 Ss, N = 35,000 (60%). Data analysis on individuals conducted on weighted subsample of Ss, N = 4,336.

METHODS: See Astin et al. Intro. 1967 reports from Ss of involvement in protests against racial discrimination, Vietnam war, and college administrative policy. Data from I representatives concerning % student body involved in each type of protest. Types of protest used as dependent variables in 2 main multiple regression analyses: (1) Ss' participation in each type of protest; (2) % student body at each I involved in each type of protest. Regression 2 examines input characteristics first; then with freshman input controlled examines I characteristics.

RESULTS: Best predictors of Ss' involvement in racial discrimination protests are no religious preference, black, participation in high school demonstrations, liberal self-rating, mother a lawyer, and 17 other variables ($r' = 0.308$). In Vietnam war protests: participation in high school demonstrations, no religious preference, life goals including Peace Corps or VISTA, wine drinking in high school, mother a research scientist, and 30 other variables ($r' = 0.422$). Of college administrative policies: no religious preference, high originality self-rating, residence elsewhere than large city, arguing with other students in high school, liberal self-rating, and 18 other variables ($r' = 0.275$). Best predictors of % involved in racial discrimination protests: % black, mean liberalism self-label, % fathers lawyers, % no religion, % home in large city, and 31 other freshman characteristics ($r' = 0.887$); adding 2 I characteristics (verbal aggressiveness in class, public control) increases r' to 0.891. Vietnam war: % no religion, % National Merit Award winners, mean value on "achieving in a performing art," % parents Jewish, % not choosing Jewish as own religion, and 28 other freshman characteristics ($r' = 0.911$); adding 1 I characteristic (musical and artistic activity) increases r' to 0.914. Protests against college administrative policies: % mothers elementary school teachers, % home in suburbs, mean value on being outstanding athletes, low mean conservatism self-rating, low % in technical field (excluding engineering), and 24 other freshmen characteristics (r' = 734); adding 5 I characteristics (low classroom organization, snobbishness, religiousness, technical school, low classroom involvement) increases r' to 0.783. High zero-order correlations between I characteristics and % involved in protests disappear when freshman input is controlled. Author concludes that "environmental characteristics of of the institution seems to play almost no part in the emergence of . . . protest activity."

COMMENTS: One of the most reliable studies conducted; examines both S and I characteristics. Dependent I measure automatically controls for size of I. Note that predicting protest involvement of individuals is difficult, but predicting % involved at I's is extremely easy. Data indicate that I characteristics play almost no role in protests once student characteristics are controlled.

11. *____. 1969. "Campus Disruption, 1968-1969: An Analysis of Causal Factors." Paper read at American Psychological Association, September 1969, Washington, D.C. 11 pp. + App. Also in Korten, F.F.; Cook, S.W.; and Lacey, J.I., eds. 1970. PSYCHOLOGY AND THE PROBLEMS OF SOCIETY. Washington, D.C.: American Psychological Association.

SETTING, INSTITUTIONS, METHODS: See A. Astin Intro., 1968-69. Stratified national sample of 427 I's, usable responses from 382 (90%). Complete data available for 200 I's. Mailed questionnaire about kinds of protest experienced, tactics, protest tactics (disruptive and violent or disruptive only), and issues. Stepwise regression of I characteristics on 4 categories of issues (war-related protest, student power, student services, racial policies) with control for student input. I's responses ("legal" and "institutional") evaluated by stepwise regression to study relation of discipline to (1) tactics and issues, (2) I characteristics with tactics and issues controlled. Examination of changes in I's policies concerning racial policies and student power. Nonviolent, nondisruptive protests not studied.

RESULTS: In 1968-69, 22% of I's had a disruptive protest, 6.2% had a violent protest. Violence most frequent at private universities, sectarian universities, private nonsectarian colleges (vs. 2-year private colleges), and in protests over racial policies (vs. student services). Controlling for student input characteristics (e.g., % Jewish, irreligious, interested in music and art, etc.), I's with more protests are universities, coed colleges, and public colleges (vs. 4-year colleges, technical schools, liberal arts colleges, private nonsectarian colleges, and I's with high concern for individual students). War protests most common in universities, coed and public I's, in I's where environment is incohesive, where there is little faculty-student involvement in class and less friendly relationships, where students are not verbally aggressive in class, where there are permissive drinking policies, much school spirit, and emphasis on social activities. Legal responses to protest are highly related to violent tactics; with tactics controlled, to war-related issues; with student characteristics, issues, and tactics controlled, to location of I's outside of West and public I's. I discipline most common in protests over racial policies. Changes in racial policies related to race-related protests and to disruptive and violent tactics (not sit-ins). Student power changes unrelated to tactics but related to racial protests. Protests over racial issues unrelated to % blacks in student body but highly related to absolute number of blacks. Universities are changing at a slower rate than 4-year colleges in racial policies. Student power changes are occurring everywhere.

COMMENTS: An important empirical paper focused solely on violent-disruptive protests. Note that regression analyses do not control for size of I, which constitutes an alternative explanation to author's emphasis on impersonality.

12. ____ . 1970a. "Campus Activism 1970: Trends and Their Implications." Paper read at American Personnel and Guidance Association, 1970, New Orleans.

13. ____ . 1970b. "Campus Unrest, 1969-1970." American Council on Education, Washington, D.C. 5 pp. + App.

SETTING, INSTITUTIONS, METHODS: See A. Astin et al. Intro., 1969-70, stratified sample of 223 I's. Data derived from student newspaper accounts of protests. Correlations between each type of protest and selected I characteristics. Stepwise regression on each type of protest of college characteristics. Protests divided into 2 categories: against the I and others.

RESULTS: 2/3 of I's experienced protests in 69-70; typical I had 5. Most common protests concerned with issues not directly related to I, including Earth Day (44% of I's), moratoria, Cambodia (16%), Kent State (24%), and Jackson State (2%). 1/3 of I's had protests directed against I (most frequently involving issues other than Vietnam or black demands); 1/7 had protests over black demands; 1/10 over war-related issues. Twelve percent of I's had protests that resulted in arrests, 7% in destruction of property, 4% in personal violence. 2-year colleges had fewest protests. Regression analysis shows protests against I's related to university status, size, selectivity, midwest location, and % Ph.D.s on faculty. Noninstitutionally directed protests related to public control, % Ph.D.s on faculty, selectivity, size, private nonsectarian control, black college, southeast or western location.

COMMENTS: A preliminary analysis with no control for student input characteristics, showing high protest levels in 1969-70. Inference that environmental pollution was greatest concern for students in 1969-70 seems questionable.

14. _____ . 1970c. "Determinants of Student Activism." In Foster, Julian, and Long, Durward, eds. 1970. PROTEST! STUDENT ACTIVISM IN AMERICA. New York: William Morrow, pp. 89-101.

15. _____ . 1970d. "Research on Campus Unrest in the United States." Paper read at Social Science Research Council, September 1970, University of York, England. 11 pp.

SETTING, INSTITUTIONS, METHODS, AND RESULTS: See other papers by A. Astin, H. Astin, Bisconti, Bisconti and Astin, Bayer, etc.

COMMENTS: A useful brief introduction to ACE campus unrest studies.

16. *_____ . 1970e. "Some Effects of Campus Protests on Student Attitudes." Paper read at Research Advisory Committee, American Council on Education, 1970, Washington, D.C. 12 pp.

SETTING: 1968, 175 colleges and universities.

SUBJECTS: Basic data from over 25,000 Ss surveyed as freshmen in 1967 and again in 1968. Slight sampling bias toward more selective I's.

METHODS: See A. Astin Intro. Stepwise regression analysis conducted on follow-up responses to 15 ACESIF attitude items completed by same Ss in freshman and follow-up study. Freshman data (including all attitude items) first allowed to enter regression equation. With all possible variance explainable by freshman data controlled, follow-up attitudes were related to occurrence of 3 types of protest (war, race-related, and student power) and violence-nonviolence of protest.

RESULTS: Overall, Ss' opinions move in a more "liberal" direction in virtually all areas measured: Ss seek greater control over academic environment, see college faculty as less competent, hold less conservative attitudes about marriage, family, and women, etc. Race-related protests slightly increase belief that officials are too lax with protesters; student power protests related to moderate liberalization of attitudes about student evaluation of faculty, college censorship of student publications, and behavior of campus officials in dealing with student protests. War-related protests and violent-non-violent protests have no major effects on the attitudes measured.

COMMENTS: Methods of data analysis used do not permit analysis of possible attitudinal polarization; show generalized trends. Most important findings are (1) that most freshman-sophomore attitude changes can be predicted on the basis of freshman characteristics, (2) that campus protests have only marginal impact on overall student attitudes, (3) that clear evidence exists of "liberalization" of freshmen from 1967-68, most of which is unrelated to occurrence or type of protest.

17. *____ . 1971. "New Evidence on Campus Unrest, 1969-1970." EDUCA-
TIONAL RECORD 52 (Winter):41-46.

SETTING, INSTITUTIONS, METHODS, AND RESULTS: See A. Astin Intro., A. Astin 1970b. At 4-year I's with protest (80%), average number of incidents was 7. War- and race-related protests show largest relative rates of increase. Noninstitutionally directed protests most frequent at I's of high prestige; Kent State protests most frequent in public I's; Jackson State protests in black I's. Southwestern location negatively related to all protest types except Earth Day. October Moratorium related to academic quality, November Moratorium to size. Size more important than quality in protest over facilities, student life, war-related issues; size and quality equally important in racial protests. Author argues that all types of protest are more frequent in larger, more selective I's because they attract more protest-prone students, hence providing "critical mass" of protesters; and because large, selective I's emphasize graduate work, show little concern for individual students, promote alienation and depersonalization.

COMMENTS: See A. Astin 1970b. Less discussion method, more extensive discussion and analysis of data than earlier paper.

18. Astin, Alexander, W., and Bayer, Alan E. 1971. "Antecedents and Conse-
quents of Disruptive Campus Protest." MEASUREMENT AND EVALUA-
TION IN GUIDANCE 4 no. 1 (April):18-30.

SETTING,INSTITUTIONS, METHODS: See A. Astin Intro., A. Astin
1969.

RESULTS: See A. Astin 1969. Violent and disruptive protests more likely
in I's with high ability, Jewish or nonreligious, and politically liberal
students. Protest issues and tactics not related to % students who demonstrated in high school. R' of student input characteristics with disruptive
tactics = 0.49, with violent tactics = 0.40. Protests over Vietnam (r' = 0.57)
can be predicted better from student input characteristics than can protests
over student services, student power, or racial policies.

COMMENTS: See A. Astin 1969. Good discussion of I susceptibility to
protests.

19. **Astin, Helen. Introduction.

SETTING: Spring 1969, 22 I's that had recently experienced protests. See
H. Astin 1969b.

SUBJECTS: 488 undergraduates of whom 255 had completed the ACESIF
at the beginning of their freshman year (usually one year before). Data
linkages made for these 255 Ss.

METHODS: Ss divided into 4 groups: random N = 185, nominated protesters, N = 83; nominated antiprotesters, N = 81, nominated leaders (student government, etc.) N = 97, unidentified, N = 42. Black students in
each: random, 4%; protesters, 36%; antiprotesters, 6%; leaders, 12%.
Correlation of left political self-label with participation in recent protest: +
0.28; with antiprotester: − 0.16. Faculty and administration samples also
studied.
    Interview included demographic data, socioeconomic background,
reasons for choice of I and attitudes toward it, goals of recent protest,
influence on protest of outside groups, effects of media, hypothetical
responses to protest, least acceptable forms of protest, changes anticipated
as a result of protest, and protest issues expected to arise in next 5 years.
All Ss given ACL.

RESULTS: See H. Astin 1969a, 1969b, 1970, 1971a, 1971b; H. Astin and
Bisconti 1970.

COMMENTS: An intensive study, incompletely analyzed, of Ss involved in or affected by 32 different protests. Note low correlation of political self-label and activism measures. Invaluable retrospective data.

20. Astin, Helen S. 1969a. "Selected Highlights of Interview Data on the Campus Unrest Study." Unpublished paper, Bureau of Social Science Research, Washington, D.C. 9 pp. + App.

SETTING, SUBJECTS, AND METHODS: See H. Astin Intro.

RESULTS: Descriptive summary of differences between 4 main groups. Males in each: random, 59%; protesters, 69%; antiprotesters, 80%; student government leaders, 71%. Protesters and campus leaders more often Jewish. Median ages: random, 19; protesters, 20; antiprotesters and leaders, 21. Socioeconomic background data: protesters come from lowest SES families (parental income, education, and occupational status); antiprotesters have highest SES (e.g., 28% parents over $30,000 income). Protesters are most critical of college, administration, curriculum, academic program and faculty; give more vocational reasons for choice of college; report highest % headed toward Ph.D. or Ed.D.; have most liberal-permissive sexual attitudes; report greatest drug use and favoring of marijuana; most often admire others for social-humanistic-individualistic reasons. Parental political orientation of protesters generally liberal, left, or far left; of leaders and control group, conservative; of antiprotesters, very conservative. Fewer protesters see positive changes resulting from protest than do members of other groups. Dissatisfaction with university is the reason most often cited for protest, and goals of protest are most often related to university governance. Administrators most likely to view outsiders as involved in protest, to see news media as inflammatory, and to agree with antiprotesters that force is needed to stop demonstrators. But 13% of students and 3% of faculty find no form of protest unacceptable if protest goals are furthered.

COMMENTS: Valuable data deserves reanalysis for whites and blacks only. Present findings, which contradict much of the literature, are difficult to interpret because 36% of protesters are black. Incidental findings support political socialization hypothesis.

21. *____. 1969b. "Themes and Events of Campus Unrest in Twenty-Two Colleges and Universities." Bureau of Social Science Research, Washington, D.C. 202 pp.

SETTING: Spring 1969.

INSTITUTIONS: 22 I's which were part of the general research program of ACE, had experienced organized protest during 1968-69, and served diverse populations. Sample included 7 4-year liberal arts colleges (2 not coed), 12 universities (7 private), 2 black colleges, 1 technological I.

METHODS: A complete chronology of key events and episodes, major participants, central issues, goals of protest and outcome at each I was compiled by 7 editors of student newspapers, 8 outside campus consultants, 7 local faculty or graduate Ss. Interviews conducted with key protest leaders, antiprotest leaders, student government leaders, random students, protest-supporting faculty, other faculty, and administrators. Profiles of the 22 I's compared with representative national I profile. Data include ACESIF on entering freshmen, EAT, scores on perceived environmental characteristics of colleges. Report consists mostly of summary of each protest and detailed documentation of 6 protest incidents.

RESULTS: Compared to national sample, I's studied generally had higher selectivity, higher high school grades of entering freshmen, higher % National Merit recognition, higher scientific and "enterprising" orientation, lower social orientation (% degrees in education, nursing, social work, and social science). Environmental descriptions of protest I's emphasize independence, permissiveness, academic competitiveness, snobbishness, musical and artistic activity, and lenient administrative policies re drinking, aggressive behavior, and heterosexual activities. Ss' family income and parents' education was higher than national average, religious backgrounds and preferences more Jewish, less Catholic, more "other" and "none." Ss place less stress on monetary value of college, oppose college control of off-campus behavior, do not believe colleges are too lax on student protest and are more involved in protest before arriving in college (especially against Vietnam war). They have high educational aspirations, with low % planning careers in business or engineering and high % in art, law, or scientific research; their life objectives less often stress financial gain, more often stress helping others and developing a philosophy of life.

Three major themes of protests were student power, special treatment for minority students, and university's independence from government control, especially war-related research, etc. Protests were largely nonviolent, most often led by black student organizations and SDS. % students involved ranged from 1-38%, generally under 7% for more active forms of protest. Student power protests more common at less selective I's, black demand protests most common at private I's. Black demands more often led to violent protests and involved larger %s of student body.

COMMENTS: A valuable study because of careful documentation of specific protest incidents, emphasizing enormous complexity of action and counteraction, and because of statistical data showing differences between protest sample and national sample. Sampling bias is probably toward a sample that is more representative of American I's than are most I's experiencing protests.

22. ____. 1970. "Profiles of Students During the 1968-1969 Campus Protest Activities." Unpublished paper, Bureau of Social Science Research, Washington, D.C. 4 pp. + App.

SETTING, SUBJECTS, METHODS: See H. Astin Intro. Analysis of student data using multiple regression analysis with freshman data and protest study data as independent variables, protest study characterizations and attitudes as dependent variables, N = 255.

RESULTS: (Dependent variable followed by major predictor variables in order of declining F-ratio.) *Being an organizer, leader, or active participant in protest*: black, protest activities meaningful experience, not engineering major, English major, left political orientation, grew up in city, high change (ACL). *Actively opposing campus protest*: extracurricular experiences shaped protest attitudes, low liability (ACL), won science contest in high school, published poems or short stories in high school, had no meaningful experiences in college. *Nominated protester*: black, protest activities meaningful experience, left political orientation, did not grow up in small town or farm, wants to participate in Peace Corps or VISTA. *Nominated antiprotester*: punitive approach to protest, extracurricular activities most meaningful, engineering major, not divorced or separated, did not win musical contest in high school. *Nominated campus leader*: law career, preprofessional, member fraternity, racism did not shape attitudes, being successful in business not life goal. *Left political orientation*: Vietnam war shaped attitudes, participated in high school protest, ghettos shaped attitudes, did not win speech debate in high school, nonpunitive approach to protest. Other variables on which multiple regression was performed: protest activity most meaningful college experience, self-predictions of political involvement in 15 years, nihilistic view of life in 15 years, lack of meaningful college experience.

COMMENTS: A valuable study flawed by grouping black and white student protesters. Note low correlation of political self-identification and protest participation. Data indicate importance of distinction between political orientation and activism. Comparisons not made between left, center, and right activists, actives and inactives. Factors other than political orientation predict protest involvement better than do political orientations.

23. _____ . 1971a. "Demographic Characteristics of Black and Non-Black Students." Unpublished paper, Bureau of Social Research, Washington, D.C. 3 pp.

SETTING, SUBJECTS, AND METHODS: See H. Astin Intro.

RESULTS: Black Ss constituted 15%, white Ss 82% of sample. Compared to whites, blacks were older, had less-educated mothers and fathers, had lower parental income, held more scholarships and received more loans, more often played organizer's role in protests.

COMMENTS: Points to major differences between black and white Ss; suggests that blacks should have been separated from whites in analyses of data.

24. *_____ . 1971b. "Self-Perceptions of Student Activists." JOURNAL OF COLLEGE STUDENT PERSONNEL 12 no. 4 (July):263-70.

SETTING, SUBJECTS, AND METHODS: See H. Astin Intro. Of 488 Ss, 451 completed ACL.

RESULTS: Compared to random Ss, protesters and antiprotesters are higher on need achievement, dominance, autonomy, exhibition, and aggression; lower on nurturance, abasement, and counseling readiness scale; describe selves as more intelligent, hard-working, forceful, strong-willed, aggressive, autocratic, individualistic, opinionated, skeptical, self-centered, self-confident, less self-punitive, anxious, etc. Compared to random Ss, antiprotesters higher on endurance, less erratic, more self-controlled. Compared to random Ss, protesters lower on personal adjustment and self-control, less optimistic, indicate greater argumentativeness, disorder, and rebelliousness. Protesters higher than student leaders on aggression; lower on personal adjustment, self-control, and nurturance.
    Analysis by sex and group on selected adjectives: male protesters more adventurous, active, and idealistic; male antiprotesters more reliable and moderate. In general, male protesters more spontaneous and uninhibited, male antiprotesters more planful and cautious. Female antiprotesters more like random group than like protesters. Female protesters more autono-

mous, aggressive, dominant, and exhibitionistic (like male protesters), but also higher on counseling readiness and anxiety (unlike male protesters). Campus leaders of both sexes closer to protesters than to random group or antiprotesters. Protesters' scores similar to those of "creative professionals."

When compared to random Ss, all 3 activist groups (protesters, campus leaders, and antiprotesters) are characterized by high need achievement, autonomy, dominance, exhibition, and low subordination and self-criticism. Protesters differ from other active Ss in being more adventurous, individualistic, spontaneous, risk-taking, desirous of variety, impulsive, and in conflict with others.

COMMENTS: One of the few studies that compares left, center, and right activists with random Ss on campuses where protests have actually occurred. Note overlap of characteristics of all activists in this study with findings of other studies concerning left activists only. Valuable data deserve more powerful statistical analyses.

25. _____. and Bisconti, A.S. 1970. "The Interviewing Experience: A Survey of Interviewers who Participated in the Study of Campus Unrest. Unpublished paper, Bureau of Social Science Research, Washington, D.C. 17 pp.

SETTING, SUBJECTS, AND METHODS: See H. Astin Intro.

RESULTS: A chronicle of the difficulties encountered by interviewers as a result of April 17, 1969 article in NEW LEFT NOTES attacking study. More negative responses from protesters than from random campus leaders, antiprotesters, faculty, or administration. Major problems cited by Ss are distrust of ACE and BSSR, fear of FBI or CIA, concern about authenticity of researchers. Despite this, 82% of protesters were friendly, 67% relaxed (vs. 23% suspicious).

COMMENTS: Reflects problems caused by the mistrust of research by some radical activists.

26. Auger, Camilla; Barton, Allen; and Maurice, Raymond. 1969. "The Nature of the Student Movement and Radical Proposals for Changes at Columbia University." THE HUMAN FACTOR (Journal of the Graduate Sociology Student Union, Columbia University) 9, no. 1 (Fall):18-40.

SETTING, SUBJECTS, METHOD: See Barton 1968. Original Barton sample supplemented by second questionnaire to arrested Ss, members of

Strike Coordinating Committee, and sample of Students for Restructured University. Third questionnaire distributed to all Ss during fall 1968 registration. Twenty interviews with student groups on campus. Total N = 1,889. Comparisons between participants, supporters, and opposers; arrestees and all Ss; groups classified according to support of goals/tactics; and pre- vs. postpolice bust attitudes toward sit-ins.

RESULTS: Shift among demonstrators pre- vs. post-demonstrations from focus on stopping gymnasium construction to emphasis on restructuring university. Forty-seven percent of student body supported building seizure, 54% supported later strike; 25% defined selves as participants, 31% supporters, 35% opposed (8% actively).

No relationships between activism and age, sex, father's occupation, or income. Activism associated with nonreligious parents (vs. Catholic), on- or near-campus residence, part-time jobs (vs. full-time), rejection of grading system, and major in humanities, social sciences, architecture, social work, graduate school (vs. business, engineering, library science). Most supporters opposed definition of the university as base for social action. Arrested Ss distinctively support interdisciplinary programs, student-faculty course design, more student power in major faculty decisions, community control over university expansion, sociopolitical goal orientation of university.

COMMENTS: See Barton 1968. Note absence of SES-activism association at a highly selective college, strong association of activism with major field and school.

27. Baird, Leonard L. 1969. "A Study of Student Activism." Unpublished paper, American College Testing Program, Iowa City, Iowa.

28. ____. 1970. "Who Protests: A Study of Student Activists." In Foster, Julian, and Long, Durward, eds. 1970. PROTEST! STUDENT ACTIVISM IN AMERICA. New York: William Morrow, pp. 123-33.

SETTING: April-May 1964, freshman data collected from 31 colleges; spring 1965, sophomore data from 29 colleges.

SUBJECTS: 12,432 freshmen studied in spring 1964. Spring 1965 follow-up, N = 5129, male N = 2295 (43%).

METHODS: 5-item activism scale: college political group or campaign; off-campus politics; worked in or organized campus-oriented student movement; demonstrations on civil rights, states rights, free speech, etc. 3 levels of activism: > 3 items = activist (2.7% men, 2.5% women); 1-3 items = moderate activists (21.6% men, 24.5% women); no items = inactive. Freshman data include self-ratings on common traits, goals and aspirations, extracurricular activities, Vocational Preference Inventory, Nichols and Holland Potential Achievement Scales, personality and value orientations, D, academic vs. vocational orientation, interpersonal competence measures. Sophomore follow-up includes socio-political activities during first year and nonacademic achievement scales.

RESULTS: Activists are more socially ascendent, capable, sensitive and gregarious, aesthetically talented and expressive and independent (women high on achievement needs, perseverance, and artistic ability, men high on self-confidence). Activists desire a central role in political affairs, have a life goal of helping others and developing meaningful philosophy, families provide unusual intellectual resources and wide experiences. Activists report more nonacademic high school leadership, speech and writing, high on preference for aggressive, social, enterprising and artistic occupations (men low on technical preference, women high on intellectual and scientific). Activists also high on potential achievement in leadership, literary work, art, speech, and drama (women high on science), on general competency measures, indirect measure of "preconscious processes," academic orientation and interpersonal competency. No relationship of activism and high school CPA or family income, or dogmatism.

Follow-up: Activists more likely to be in fraternities, not to dropout, work, or be in psychotherapy; high on all measures of nonacademic achievement, especially leadership and social service. Self-reported GPA unrelated to activism.

COMMENTS: Hard to compare with other studies, because definition of activism includes traditional campus leadership activities, not merely left- or right-wing activism. High fraternity membership, etc., indicates that these are often S government, YR and YD types.

29. *Barton, Allen H. 1968. "The Columbia Crisis: Campus, Vietnam and the Ghetto." PUBLIC OPINION QUARTERLY 32 (Fall):333-52.

SETTING: May 1968, Columbia University, a few weeks after the "liberation" of 5 CU buildings in protest over construction of gymnasium near surrounding black community and CU affiliation with military research group.

SUBJECTS: 1061 (55%) faculty members at the Morningside Campus (excluding Barnard and TC); 1977 undergraduates, graduates, and professional Ss at the Morningside campus (55% of 20% random sample).

METHODS: Questionnaire surveying opinions on goals and tactics of demonstration, S-faculty power and decision-making; perceptions of police, faculty and administration; general and specific satisfactions with university; actions during demonstration; draft status; attitudes toward war and political candidate. Somers' 1965 questions used when possible to facilitate comparisons between Berkeley and Columbia.

RESULTS: 51% faculty, 58% Ss support main protest goals; 10% faculty, 19% Ss support tactics. Faculty support is related to junior rank. Ss generally left of faculty. Most students believe police action involved excessive violence, but this belief is dependent upon whether S saw force used or not.

Seeing police use force is related to demonstration attitudes (8% strongly anti saw force used vs. 57% strongly pro). Judgments of "brutality" of police action explainable by interaction of pro/antidemonstration attitudes with saw-force-used/did-not-see-force-used. Police action increased acceptance of sit-in and polarization among both Ss and faculty: faculty agreement that sit-in was "probably or definitely justified" increased from 14% to 31%; S agreement from 23% to 42%; "undecided" dropped among faculty from 11% to 3%; among Ss from 14% to 3%. Increase in strike support greatest among those who saw police use force (faculty up from 28% to 53%; Ss up from 31% to 60%). But pre/postbust attitudes on protest issues changed very little. Support of strike never equalled majority of Ss or faculty, but was found only in the majority of the self-selected group who saw force used.

Strong criticism of administration from all factions: dissatisfaction index highly associated with strike support for all groups. Strike greatly increased and improved faculty-student interaction, but worsened relations with administration for both faculty and Ss.

Attitudes toward demonstrations and strike goals strongly related to opposition to Vietnam war but unrelated to draft status. High correlation between war opposition and support for poor and blacks. Most popular S presidential candidates were McCarthy, Rockefeller, R. Kennedy. Support for antiwar candidates uncorrelated with draft status.

COMMENTS: A preliminary report. Most interesting results involve "radicalizing effects" of police action on strike support (but not on attitudes toward protest issues), selective perception of police violence according to sit-in support, and the absence of relationship between draft status and other issues. Good data on radicalization due to events.

30. Bayer, Alan E., and Astin, Alexander W. 1969. "Violence and Disruption on the U.S. Campus, 1968-1969." American Council on Education Research Report, 4, no. 3 (August):1-46. Also in EDUCATIONAL RECORD 50 (Fall):337-50.

SETTING, SOURCE, AND METHODS: See A. Astin Intro., A. Astin 1969. New categories discussed: off-campus issues, secondary issues, substantive I changes (in racial policies, increased student power and curriculum, ROTC, or recruiting).

RESULTS: See A. Astin 1969. Violent or disruptive protests most common in private universities (vs. public universities), public or private nonsectarian 4-year colleges (vs. church-related I's), large I's, and highly selective I's; least common in 2-year I's (especially private). 1/3 of violent protests involved personal injuries; occupation of building most frequent nonviolent tactic. 3/4 of protests were over student power issues, next most frequent were off-campus problems (Vietnam, civil rights, labor and community problems); protests over student minorities are most associated with violence. In response to violent protests, 1/2 of I's called police, 1/2 had protesters arrested, 1/4 had them indicted. In response to nonviolent disruptive protest; 12% of I's called police, 7% used legal action, 11% reprimands, 5% expelled or suspended Ss. Negotiation occurred at 83% of nonviolent, 62% of violent protests. About 1/2 of violent protests and 1/3 of nonviolent protests received national press coverage. Some faculty support at 30% of I's with violent, disruptive protests. Racial policy changes made at 55% of I's with violent, 11% disruptive protests. Changes in student power were likely to be independent of protest. Substantive changes not resulting from protest were made at 80% of I's with violent protest, 89% with nonviolent protest and 63% with no protest.

COMMENTS: Largely descriptive account, focusing on issues, incidents and outcomes of violent-disruptive protests.

31. _____. 1971. "Campus Unrest 1970-1971: was it really all that quiet?" EDUCATIONAL RECORD 52 (Fall):301-313.

SETTING: See A. Astin, et al. Intro. 1970-71 survey of 425 representative colleges.

INSTITUTIONS: Questionnaires mailed to I representatives, 369 responses (87%) from I's sampled in 1968-69 ACE study (A. Astin 1969).

METHODS: Reports of protests, protest issues, severity (disruption and violence) of protests. Most questions and definitions same as A. Astin 1969.

Data linked to Is' characteristics, including private/public, 2-year/4-year/ university, size, selectivity, etc. Comparisons of 1969-69 and 1970-71 data.

RESULTS: Severe protests declined from 22.4% of all I's in 1968-69 to 19.6% in 1970-71. 43.1% of all I's experienced some protest (including nondisruptive) in 1970-71. Compared to 1968-69, protests were down in private nonsectarian colleges (from 42.6% to 19.7%) and in private and public universities; up in 2-year private colleges, Roman Catholic colleges, and 2-year public colleges. But private universities still have the most protests and 2-year private colleges the fewest. Characteristics associated with number of protests include university (vs. 2-year I's) and size (but for universities, moderate size is associated with protests). Selectivity strongly associated with severe protests for universities, mildly associated for 4-year colleges, and inversely associated for 2-year colleges. All correlates of protest and severe protest lower than in 1968-69. Percentage of I's experiencing severe protests declines in most categories, especially building occupation and interruption of school functions. Increase in protests involving general opposition to U.S. military policy and I services; decline in protests concerning draft policy, on-campus recruiting, military research, ROTC, special educational programs for minority groups, special admissions policies for minority groups, local community problems, and I procedures.

I's with severe protests report declines in civil action, discipline against Ss, negotiation with Ss and public-faculty support. National press coverage of severe protests declined from 40% in 1968-69 to 10% in 1970-71, with no coverage whatsoever at low or low-intermediate selectivity I's. Fewer I changes made in 1970-71, perhaps because changes that become the focus of protest were already most common in I's experiencing severe protests. Authors emphasize persistence of high level of protests, shift to less "visible" I's.

COMMENTS: Decisive evidence of dispersion of protests in 1970-71, manifest by lessening frequency of protests at large, high-selectivity universities and increasing frequency at small, low-selectivity 2-year and 4-year colleges, and overall drop in correlation between severe protests and I characteristics.

32. _____ ; and Boruch, Robert F. 1970. "Social Issues and Protest Activity: Recent Student Trends." American Council on Education, Office of Research Reports, 5, no. 2, (Washington, D.C.).

33. ____. 1971. "College Students' Attitudes toward Social Issues: 1967-1970. EDUCATIONAL RECORD 53 (Winter):52-59.

34. Bisconti, Ann S. 1970. "Events in Protest: Preliminary Findings in the Analysis of 103 Protests Based on Campus Newspaper Reports." American Council on Education, Washington, D.C. 19 pp. + App.

SETTING AND INSTITUTIONS: See A. Astin Intro. Sept. 1-March 1, 1970. Subsample of 103 protests (all directed against the I) at 67 I's.

METHODS: Coding scheme for data derived from campus newspapers: (1) sequence of events; (2) issues and changes; (3) additional information; (4) newspapers' bias. Reliability checked by sending compilations of newspaper studies to administrators; 66% of administrators returned compilations; 5 returns resulted in corrections. Three issues and changes: (1) minority groups; (2) other aspects of academic life; (3) university policy on war-related and social issues. Events in each protest coded sequentially to permit later analysis of antecedents and consequences of each type of events. See Bisconti and Astin 1971.

RESULTS: Rallies, picketing, marches most common incidents (245 times in 68 protests). Presentation of demands associated with racial issues, rallies and marches with war-related and social issues, petitions with academic issues. Violence arose in 24 protests, disruption in 59. Racial protests most disruptive, had most impact on campus activities, and were most successful. Efforts to communicate with protest leaders occurred in 84 protests, were least common in war-related and social issues protests, which also resulted in fewer changes. Off-campus police on hand in 16 protests, arrested persons in 11. Campus police on hand in 1/5 of protests, especially war-related. Typical sequence of events involves nondisruptive dissent, communication and disruption; if violence and change occur, they occur later. Usually campus police come before violence and off-campus police after. SDS involvement related to war and social protest; black student, and college presidents involvement to racial protests; trustee involvement to academic life protests. SDS and white students most associated with violence. Injuries mostly from police. Student involvement greatest in protests with violence, police, and arrests. Longer protests tend to involve more violence, disruption, police, punishment, off-campus participants, and SDS. College newspapers most proprotest on academic and war-related issues; no bias found on racial issues.

COMMENTS: A preliminary report with detailed discussion of coding methodology. Some findings not in line with earlier research; e.g., whites more associated with violence than blacks. See Bisconti and Astin 1971 for further data analysis.

35. *____, and Astin, Alexander W. 1971. "Protest Behavior and Response on the U.S. Campus." Unpublished paper, American Council on Education, Washington, D.C. 149 pp.

SETTING, SUBJECTS, AND METHODS: See Bisconti 1970. This paper, eventually to form part of a book, summarizes and discusses data from A. Astin 1970a, 1970b, 1971, and further analyzes data described in Bisconti 1970. Detailed discussion of coding, research methodology, reliability of newspaper reports, etc. Initial presentation of data cross-tabulates precipitating factors, effects on campus activities, participants, protest leadership, attitudes of campus newspaper, types of events occurring, etc., for all protests, and separately for racial, academic and student life, war-related and social issue protests. Sequential analyses first identify dependent variable (e.g., violence); all coded events occurring before dependent variable are used as independent variables for multiple regression. Tables describing regression analyses are unusually complete. Sequential multiple regression analyses performed on 20 dependent variables; nonsequential analyses on 9 variables.

RESULTS: Extraordinarily complex results, too detailed to summarize.

COMMENTS: Methodologically the most complex study in the research literature, employing multivariate statistics and sequential analyses for each of a large number of protest events. Results and data analysis would be more intelligible if variables were empirically grouped, and with further analysis of temporal antecedents of protests that can be considered to play a causal role.

36. Blau, Peter, and Slaughter, Ellen. 1971. "Institutional Conditions and Student Demonstrations. SOCIAL PROBLEMS 18 (Spring):475-87.

SETTING: 1967-68.

INSTITUTIONS: 155 I's (100%) from a population of 1000+ accredited 4-year I's, stratified and weighted for representativeness.

METHODS: Personal interviews with 2 top administrators at each I, data on student demonstrations in 1967-68 from assistant to president. Two major variables: (1) number of demonstrations in 1967-68, (2) issues. Index of protest seriousness with 4 categories (no demonstrations, only internal issues, only external issues, both internal and external issues). Multiple regression analysis used to examine the effects of I conditions, administrative computer use, faculty size, student intellectualism, student ratings of faculty, free computer time and innovation, on the index of serious protests.

RESULTS: Serious protests most likely at I's with large faculties, but r of faculty size and demonstrations is reduced when other variables are controlled. With size and student intellectualism controlled, extensive use of computers for administration purposes and high aptitude student body increase likelihood of demonstrations; student evaluation of teaching and the establishment of new departments and similar innovations decrease probability of demonstrations. With all of these variables controlled, faculty emphasis on teaching (vs. research) is unrelated to protests. Authors argue that size is important because large I's are impersonal, make students more alienated; and because a "critical mass" is available in large I's.

COMMENTS: Good study of the role of I size (measured solely by faculty size). Excellent discussion. Note absence of relation between faculty research orientation and protests when size, etc., are controlled.

37. ***Block, Jeanne, et al. Introduction.

SETTING: 1965-67 University of California at Berkeley; San Francisco State College; Peace Corps trainees.

SUBJECTS: 2 groups from UCB, 1965-66: FSM: undergraduate arrestees remaining on campus, N = 111 (44%), and cross-section: undergraduates present at UCB at time of FSM, N = 231 (52%). Supplemented by small samples from UCB political organizations including YD, YR, and conservative groups, N = ? (50+ %). Two groups from SFSC, Spring 1967: activists: members of "student organizations committed to positive social action," mostly educational reform, N = 95 (20%), and cross-section, N = 296 (52%). Separate analyses for UCB and SFSC showed redundancy of findings and legitimized pooling the 2 data sources. Peace Corps volunteers being trained in various California locations, N = 220 (34%). Total N = about 1000.

METHODS: 5 basic types defined on the basis of number of social service activities, number of protest activities, and fraternity-sorority membership: inactives (0 protest, 0 social service, not fraternity-sorority, N = 237); conventionalists (not members of right-wing groups, 0 social service, 0-1 protests, fraternity-sorority members, N = 80); constructivists (1+ social service, 0-1 protest, N = 239); activists (1+ social service, 2+ protests, N = 112); dissenters (0 social service, 2+ protests, N = 260).

All Ss given basic demographic and background questionnaire, ACL for self and ideal, Block Child-Rearing Practices Report (26-factor survey of parents' child-rearing practices, attitudes and relationships with children; evidence of validity of Ss' reporting presented), questions concerning agreement with each parent and each parent's influence on a variety of issues, and Kohlberg Moral Judgment Test (written responses to moral dilemmas reliably scored into 3 levels of moral development, with 2 stages at each level: (1) Premoral (instrumental relativism); (2) Conventional (personal concordance, law and order); and (3) Principled (social contract, individual principles).

RESULTS: See Block 1968, Block et al. 1969, Haan et al. 1968, Haan and Block 1969a, 1969b, Haan 1972, Smith et al. 1970.

COMMENT: Overall, the most complex, in-depth, broad-gauged and informative of the activism studies in the literature. Moral development results especially notable.

38. **Block, Jeanne H. 1968. "Rebellion Re-Examined: The Role of Identification and Alienation." Paper read at Foundations' Fund for Research in Psychiatry Conference on "Adaptation to Change," June 1968, Puerto Rico. 49 pp.

SETTING AND SUBJECTS: See Block et al. Intro.

METHODS: Of 909 Ss who had rated selves on 8-point political self-label scale, 147 Ss selected with scores $>$ 1 S.D. above mean on radical end of scale. Of these liberal-radical students, discontinuity group defined as $>$ 3 points left of parents on political scale and $>$ 1 S.D. below mean on measures of agreement with and influence from parents (N = 40, male N = 25), and continuity group defined as $<$ 4 points from parents on political preferences and not $<$ mean agreement with and influence from parents (N = 59, male N = 37). 4 Ss not classifiable. Analysis compares continuity and discontinuity groups, also discontinuity and conventionalists (both middle-class groups with politically conservative parents). Special focus on parental socialization variables.

RESULTS: Continuity vs. discontinuity group. Self-descriptions and ideals: continuity males describe selves as more responsible, masculine, orderly and practical; discontinuity as doubting, shy, self-denying, rebellious, stubborn, worrying, etc. Ideals of continuity group more "straight," those of discontinuity group more "hippie"-like. Continuity group shows more principled moral reasoning than discontinuity group. Child-rearing practices: continuity parents encourage reflection, curiosity, questioning, expression of both positive and negative feelings, individuation of child, rational discussion of issues, are most active sociopolitically, most often discuss contemporary problems at home, are better educated (fathers more than mothers). Discontinuity parents emphasize appearances, concerned about impressing others, are suppressive and unresponsive, use many prohibitions and punishments, are less well educated, (mothers more than fathers). Continuity group fathers vocationally more concerned with people, discontinuity group fathers with products.

Conventionalists vs. discontinuity group. With parental political conservatism and social class held constant, discontinuity is stimulated by psychological manipulation of child to achieve parents' goals and expectations, guilt and anxiety induction, insulation and suppression of child, vacillating and conflicting parental behavior and values. Parents of conventionalists more encouraging to children, derive greater satisfaction from parent role, have more explicit expectations, duties and responsibilities for children, have warmer and more affectionate parent-child relationships. Author concludes that rebellion against (conservative) parental values is more likely when parents are intolerant of individuality, immature and self-serving in definition of parent and child roles, do not provide rational explanation, coherence and structure.

COMMENTS: A study that holds sociopolitical self-definition constant and examines "rebellion" within liberal-radical group. Discontinuity group most "hippie"-like, continuity group more "straight." Discontinuity women are especially conflicted, anxious, and self-doubting as compared to all other groups.

39. **____; Haan, Norma; and Smith, M. Brewster. 1969. "Socialization Correlates of Student Activism." JOURNAL OF SOCIAL ISSUES 25 (November):143-77.

SETTING, SUBJECTS, METHOD: See Block et al. Intro.

METHODS: Socialization practices of Ss' parents are major focus of analysis. Ego functioning index uses Loevinger ego levels: opportunistic (low), conformist, conscientious, autonomous, integrated (high). Q-sort for each S performed by researchers, Q-sort items rated on ego level. Data analysis involves 5 types, 2 sexes, 2 parents and 26 child-rearing factors.

RESULTS: Activists: somewhat negative parent-child relationships, parental emphasis on independence, responsibility and early maturity, de-emphasis of achievement and competition, suppression of aggression, tolerance of child's secrecy and privacy needs, little anxiety induction and intrusive control. Activist women report more troubled parent-child relationships than activist men. Dissenters: Strongly negative parent-child relationships, parents have permissive or laissez faire attitudes in some areas but controlling attitudes in others, little emphasis on independence and maturity, stress achievement, competition, and children's self-expression, but oppose secrecy and privacy needs of children. Both sexes are characterized by strongly negative portraits of parents, picture of incoherent and inconsistent child-rearing. Conventionalists: positive parent-child relationships, parents are emotionally involved, stress socially appropriate behavior, independence, achievement and obedience within clear structure and varied disciplinary techniques. Parents suppress sex but tolerate aggression, have highly differentiated sex role expectations for children. Overall picture of filial identification with parents who adhere to traditional societal values in a caring, consistent context. Constructivists: positive parent-child relationships, but relatively low parental involvement in parental roles. Emphasis on nonphysical punishments, anxiety induction, restriction of self-assertion in child. Inactives: Neutral parent-child relationships, parents worry about children's health, are emotionally uninvolved, inhibit self-expression, display strong conformity concerns, use anxiety to control children, and do not encourage independence.

Dissenters' parents score highest on opportunistic ego level, inactives' highest on conformity; activists highest on conformity-conscientious and conscientious-autonomous. In general, activists' parents reach highest ego levels, dissenters are lowest, others between.

Study of parental child-rearing practices, comparing conventionalists and activists of same social class, for nonJewish Ss only yields results virtually identical to results without control for social class and religion. Authors conclude that social class and religion "cannot be invoked to explain the divergences in child-rearing orientations that were found to discriminate the 2 activist subgroups." "Permissiveness" characterizes socialization practices of dissenters, but demand for "responsible and mature behavior" characterizes parents of activists. Authors warn against generalizing about *all* politically active students.

COMMENT: A difficult, complex and important study. Highly differentiated and coherent account of child-rearing in the several groups studied;

evidence that socialization variables override social class and religion; subtle analysis of permissiveness issue.

40. Blume, Norman. 1971. "Young Republican and Young Democratic College Clubs in the Midwest: A Study of Variables Related to Club Activity." YOUTH AND SOCIETY 2, no. 31 (March):355-65.

SETTING: Spring 1969, 12 states in Midwest.

INSTITUTIONS: 155 (73%) YD clubs, 203 (75%) YR clubs at 152 private, 82 public, 4 combination I's. Sample of I's judged representative.

METHODS: Political activity index measured extent of clubs' support for their 1968 presidential candidate. Panel of 10 (5 YR and 5 YD) presidents from all types of I's rated 16 campaign activities on scale from 1-10, least to most effort. Respondents' scores at each I were averaged.

RESULTS: Activity scores of clubs higher in public I's (vs. private, Catholic, Protestant), in I's with enrollment > 1000, in I's in towns with population > 2000. Activity unrelated to mean SAT score, or to dormitory (vs. commuter) status.

COMMENTS: Study suggests that the I conditions that foster traditional political activity are similar to those that foster protest.

41. Boruch, Robert F., and Creager, John A. 1971. "A Note on the Stability of Self-Reported Protest Activity and Attitudes." Unpublished paper, American Council of Education, Washington, D.C. 12 pp.

SETTING: 1968-69, Washington, D.C.

SUBJECTS: Ss recruited through newspaper advertisements at public state university, N = 97, private coed university, N = 62, community college, N = 43.

METHODS: Ss given ACESIF twice at 1-week intervals. Data analyzed to assess stability of responses. Ss used aliases except at community college.

RESULTS: Test-retest r's of involvement in high school protests against military policies vary from 0.76-0.93, against racial policies from 0.54-0.74, against administration policies from 0.29-0.59. At community college (no aliases), significant retest decreases in reports of high school protest. Ss' predictions of future protest involvement show test-retest r's of 0.73-0.86; no systematic shifts in direction. Attitudes toward protest issues show test-retest r's ranging from 0.52-0.90; self-reported liberalism most reliable. Authors underline unreliability of Ss' reports of past activities, predicted future activities and current attitudes; argue that Ss understate past protest involvement when anonymity is not assured.

COMMENTS: A useful methodological study that indicates unreliability of many key variables in activism research.

42. Bowers, William J. 1971. "Trends in College Campus Deviance." COLLEGE STUDENT SURVEY 5, no. 1 (Spring):20-30.

SETTING: Spring 1966, 97 colleges and universities across the country.

SUBJECTS: 690 Ss who had attended same schools since freshman year. Freshman data available from same Ss in 1963.

METHOD: Tabulation and comparison of 1963 and 1966 data on Ss' approval of and engaging in various types of "deviant" conduct.

RESULTS: In 1966, 10% of seniors had taken part in "student uprising, riot or mob action," 2.4% had engaged in deliberate civil disobedience, 20.3% had participated in a social protest, demonstration or march. Civil disobedience is almost entirely confined to "top-ranking" schools; protest participation is twice as common in "top-ranking" I's.

COMMENTS: In 1966 protest activities are highly associated with "top-ranking" schools.

43. **Braungart, Richard G. Introduction.

SETTING: 1966-67, samples of SDS and YAF members surveyed at national conventions of SDS in Ohio and of YAF in Pennsylvania. Other data collected from Ss at Pennsylvania State, Temple, University of Pittsburgh, University of Maryland, Harper University, SUNY Binghampton, City University of New York, Brooklyn College, University of Pennsylvania, Johns Hopkins, Carnegie-Mellon.

SUBJECTS: Student members of SDS, N = 236, YR, N = 114, YD, N = 108, YAF, N = 206. "Apolitical" control group, N = 557, (40% Jewish), students in introductory sociology classes at CUNY, Maryland, Pennsylvania State, and Temple.

METHODS: Questionnaire covering GPA; social class; ethnicity; religion; family politics; future careers; authoritarian/authoritarian-democratic/ democratic parental decision-making (= father/mother/both parents make decisions); family argumentation (frequency with which S argued with parents over civil rights, distribution of wealth in America, and American foreign policy), ethnicity (high = entirely Anglo-Saxon, North European or Irish, low = any mixture of East Europe, South Europe, African, or West Indian), degree of identification and closeness, as child and at present, with mother and father. Data analysis involves comparison of group means for 5 groups, often separately by sex; multivariate path analysis on dependent variable of political identification, based on scale indicating approval of 16 national political figures ranging from (far left) Gus Hall, Mario Savio, Staunton Lynd and Norman Thomas to (far right) Barry Goldwater, William Buckley, Jr., Robert Welch, and George Lincoln Rockwell. Correlations of political identification scale with group membership = +0.83.

RESULTS: See Braungart 1966a, 1966b, 1969a, 1969b, 1970a, 1970b, 1970c, Westby and Braungart 1970a, 1970b.

COMMENTS: The large groups of right, center, and left activists and an inactive control group, together with sophisticated and theoretically-informed data analyses, make this an outstanding study.

44. _____ . 1966a. "SDS and YAF: Backgrounds of Student Political Activists." Paper read at the American Sociological Association, September 1966, Miami. 22 pp. Also in YOUTH AND SOCIETY 2, no. 4 (June 1971):441-57.

SOURCE, SUBJECTS, AND METHODS: See Braungart Intro. This paper contrasts SDS and YAF on items about high school experiences, parental support for political activity, present and past church attendance, parental politics, annual income, father's occupation, education, and ethnic background. No tests of significance.

RESULTS: SDS Ss appear to be reacting against authority as indicated by attitudes toward high school, family, and church officials. SDS political ideology is generally consistent with political identification of parents. YAF Ss conform both politically and institutionally. Data interpreted to support status-inconsistency hypothesis with regard to both extreme groups, based on "lower ethnic status" of SDS and "relatively high income homes" of YAF.

COMMENTS: Support of status-inconsistency theory questionable, especially for SDS, since definition of "low status" ethnicity makes most Jews low status, and "ethnicity" disappeared from path analysis reported in Braungart 1969a and 1969b.

45. ____ . 1966b. "Social Stratification and Political Attitudes." Unpublished paper, Pennsylvania State University.

46. *____ . 1969a. "Family Status, Socialization and Student Politics: A Multivariate Analysis." Ph.D. dissertation Pennsylvania State University. 357 pp.

SETTING, SUBJECTS, METHODS, AND RESULTS: See Braungart Intro., 1969b. Most of the results of the thesis are reported in published articles by Braungart or Westby and Braungart. The thesis is the best single discussion of methodology, use of multiple path analysis and testing of alternate theoretical models. Three main methods used: (1) tabular control technique using chi-squares and gammas; (2) amended Simon-Blalock casual analysis technique to determine the theoretical model of best fit; (3) multiple path analysis. Unanalyzed results in appendix show that SDS is highest of all groups on father exercised little control when S was younger, on family political discussion, on unhappy parents' marriage, on S's dissatisfaction with relationship with parents, on infrequency of talking about personal problems with parents.

COMMENTS: An outstanding study because of the size and nature of the sample and the sophistication of the analysis. Helps disentangle influences of class, religion, family politics, etc. on student activism.

47. *____ . 1969b. "Family Status, Socialization, and Student Politics: a Multivariate Analysis." Paper read at American Sociological Association, September 1969, San Francisco, California. 85 pp. Also in AMERICAN JOURNAL OF SOCIOLOGY 77, no. 1 (July):108-130.

SETTING, SUBJECTS, AND METHODS: See Braungart Intro., 1969a. Separate path analyses for total student sample, activists only, and control group only. Three levels of variables distinguished: independent (class, religion, ethnicity, family politics); intervening (family argumentation and family decision-making); dependent (political identification based on candidate preferences).

RESULTS: For entire sample, path analysis shows high social class, none or Jewish religion, left-wing parent politics directly affect Ss' (left) political identification. None or Jewish religion affects intervening variables of high family argumentation and democratic decision-making. Of intervening variables, high argumentation alone exerts an independent effect on (left) political identification, $r'^2 = 0.288$. For activists only, family politics, class, religion, and argumentation directly affect political identification, religion affects family (democratic) decision-making, which affects political identification, $r'^2 = 0.387$. For control group only, family religion and politics affect political identification, $r'^2 = 0.162$. Ethnicity removed from all analyses for statistical reasons. Strongest single effect is of family politics on S's political identification in all analyses.

COMMENTS: See Braungart 1969a. Measures of family argumentation and family decision-making may be unreliable, which clouds the conclusion that these are not strongly related to family politics, religion and class, etc., and do not strongly determine political identification.

48. _____. 1970a. "Parental Identification and Student Politics: An Empirical Reappraisal." Paper read at American Sociological Association, September 1970, Washington, D.C. 18 pp. Also in Manning, Peter K., and Truzzi, Marcello, eds. 1972. YOUTH AND SOCIOLOGY. New York: Prentice Hall, Inc.

49. _____. 1970b. "Parental Identification and Student Politics: A Research Note." Revised version of paper read at American Sociological Association, September 1970, Washington, D.C. 18 pp. Also in SOCIOLOGY OF EDUCATION 44, no. 4 (Fall 1971):463-73.

SETTING, SUBJECTS, AND METHODS: See Braungart Intro. Analysis of "parental identification" (closeness to mother and father) measures.

RESULTS: Overall tendency towards consistent rather than differential parental identification. SDS alienation from both parents is higher than for any other group; selective identification with mother most common among YD males and females. Lowest identification with mother found among SDS males and YAF females. SDS males characterized by no change between childhood and present attitudes toward father, but greater decrease than in other group in closeness toward mother. All SDS groups rate past and present attitudes toward both parents, regardless of S's sex, as less close than any other group. Author concludes there is no support for

THE JOHN J. WRIGHT LIBRARY

"special closeness with mother" theory of radicalism, for radicals are more alienated from both parents.

COMMENTS: No evidence of a distinctive "protest-prompting family constellation," if the constellation is measured by avowed closeness to one or both parents.

50. ____ . 1970c. Status Politics and Student Politics: An Analysis of Left and Right Wing Student Activists. Paper read at Research Institute of the District of Columbia Sociological Society, May 1970, College Park, Maryland. 18 pp. Also in YOUTH AND SOCIETY 3 (December 1971).

SOURCE, SUBJECTS, AND METHODS: See Braungart Intro., 1966a.

RESULTS: SDS Ss exhibit upper-middleclass origins relative to low religious, political and ethnic status; YAF Ss exhibit lower class origins relative to high religious, political and ethnic status. Radical students on both left and right exhibit more extreme status strains than moderate or apolitical youth; but family political status is the strongest predictor of student politics.

COMMENTS: Emphasis on status inconsistencies as explanatory seems questionable. See comments on Braungart 1966a.

51. ____ , and Braungart, Margaret M. 1971a. "Administration, Faculty and Student Reactions to Campus Unrest." Paper read at American Sociological Association, September 1971, Denver. 16 pp. + App.

SETTING, INSTITUTIONS, METHODS, RESULTS: See Urban Institute 1970. After May 1, 1970, 32% of incidents were disruptive, 8% violent. Mediation most frequent response. Serious protests lead to harsher responses. Violent incidents led to administrators using mediation (44.4%), student marshals (44.4%), off-campus police and arrests (38.9%), National Guard (16.7%), expulsion of students (13.9%), suspension of students (11.5%). Major internal issues: administrators from I's with violent incidents list school regulations, black demands; administrators with incidents but no violence and with no incidents list black demands, school regulations. Administrators from schools with no incidents most likely to believe punitive measures are appropriate for all types of unrest.

COMMENTS: See Urban Institute 1970.

52. ____. 1971b. "Social and Political Correlates of Protest Attitudes and Behavior among College Youth: A Case Study." Unpublished paper, University of Maryland.

SETTING: Spring 1968, Pennsylvania State University.

SUBJECTS: Random sample of undergraduates and graduate students, N = 745 (93%).

METHODS: Major dependent variable: nonparticipation, wish to participate but did not participate, participation in a demonstration. Data on sex, year in college, major, GPA, type of housing, SES, party identification, importance of politics, factual political knowledge, membership in political organizations, frequency of political discussion with friends, political change since entering college. Data cross-tabulated.

RESULTS: Participation in and wish to participate in demonstrations related to liberal arts major, (trend toward) off-campus housing, "independent" political preference, high political interest, high political information, membership in campus political organization, frequent political discussions with friends, change in political attitudes during college. No relationships found with SES, GPA (but trend for demonstrators to be very high *or* very low), sex, year in college. Authors suggest importance of broadly "psychological" factors in determining protest.

COMMENTS: A recent study that fails to replicate many pre-1967 findings.

53. Brown, S.R., and Thomas, D.B. 1971. "Public Response and Private Feeling: Reaction to the Kent State Situation." Paper read at American Educational Research Association, February 1971, New York City. 36 pp.

SETTING: May 1970, Kent State University (after killings).

SUBJECTS: Group 1: Data gathered by students in political analysis class to N = 228, including 94 Kent State students, faculty, administrators, staff members, and student National Guardsmen. Group 2: Juniors and seniors, N = 53 in political science class.

METHODS: Group 1: 75 statements concerning student unrest, violence, rebelliousness, and Kent State incident. Group 2: Items drawn from "a number of scales designed to measure radicalism-conservatism."

RESULTS: Group 1: Statements factor analyzed, resulting in 2-factor solution. Factor I: positive loadings; rage at killing, sadness, anger, fear, judgment that it was cold-blooded murder; negative loadings, approval of violence against students, justification of National Guard ("This is what it may take to keep our country free"). Factor II: positive loadings: antiviolence, working in established framework, support for rules of the game, reform and change; negative loadings: justification for violence, rejection of system. All students who witnessed shooting and all but 2 students on campus at the time score very positive on Factor I.

Group 2: First 2 factors involve "radical vs. conservative" and "moderate" [liberal] positions. 50-adjective Q-sort administered to 6 highest-scoring Ss on factors 1 and 2: each S described approximately 30 persons or objects. Detailed analyses of perceptual spaces of 2 representative radicals and moderates presented. Higher self-ideal congruence among moderates than radicals. Tendency for radicals to polarize good objects and bad objects, whereas for moderates, disliked figures are orthogonal to bad figures. Authors conclude that to a radical a National Guardsman represents someone opposite to his ideals, whereas to a moderate he is simply irrelevant.

COMMENTS: Study limited by sampling and unusual methods of data analysis. Important chiefly because it demonstrates, in the highly charged Kent State situation, the orthogonality of the "liberal-nonviolent-work-through institutions" position and the radical vs. conservative position.

54. *Cherniss, Cary. 1971. "Personality and ideology: A Personological Study of Women's Liberation." Predissertation thesis, Department of Psychology, Yale University. Also in PSYCHIATRY, 35, no. 2 (May 1972):109-25.

SETTING: 1969-70, Yale University.

SUBJECTS: 12 active members of Women's Liberation (WL) compared with matched control group of 8 nonwomen's liberation women.

METHODS: Intensive unstructured clinical interviewing, 4-6 hours per S, focusing on developmental history, current feelings, impact of WL, and researcher-interviewee relationship.

RESULTS: Author stresses distinctive lifestyle of WL Ss: alloplastic, emphasizing autonomy and self-control, action, assertion, and achievement, self-esteem, sense of specialness, and interest in the dramatic. Family backgrounds suggest distinctively strong mothers, relative absence of conflict with fathers, a "colorful male" (usually not father) in the background. Development entails intense social estrangement during adolescence. Involvement in WL results in problems previously experienced as personal being redefined as sociopolitical, redefinition and more sympathetic view of mothers, increased criticism of prevailing definitions of female sexuality, marriage and nurturance, strong sense of community with other women in movement, and growing sense of anger at perceived female oppression. Author stresses quasi-therapeutic effects of consciousness-raising groups, analogies to psychotherapy and group therapy.

COMMENTS: An intensive clinical study of a small group of WL members, especially valuable for the hypotheses it generates concerning the effects of membership in Women's Liberation.

55. *Christie, R.; Friedman, L.N.; and Ross, A. 1969. "The New Left and Its Ideology: An Exploratory Study." Paper read at American Psychological Association, September 1969, Washington, D.C. 5 pp. + App.

SETTING: September 1968, freshmen orientation week at Columbia.

SUBJECTS: Background information questionnaire distributed to 700 incoming freshmen; 254 completed questionnaires. Of these, 153 recruited for study, paid $3.00.

METHODS: Items designed to measure New Left attitudes, regardless of whether "psychedelic left," Marcuseans, Debrayists, etc. Sixty-two items included in preliminary New Left scale. Part-whole correlations used as measure of consistency.

RESULTS: Mean part-whole correlation for best 30 items = 0.50. Mean interitem correlation = 0.475. Self-reports of activity in civil rights and peace movements before coming to college and choice of left-wing presidential candidates highly associated with New Left scale. Authors conclude there is a highly consistent ideological frame of reference among members of the New Left in this sample of unacculturated (to Columbia) freshmen.

COMMENTS: See Gold et al. 1971. An excellent preliminary report of an exploration of the ideology of the New Left.

56. Clarke, J.W., and Egan, J. 1971. "Social and Political Dimensions of Campus Protest Activity." Paper read at Florida Academy of Sciences, March 1971, Melbourne, Florida. 18 pp.

SETTING: 1969, Florida State University

SUBJECTS: 380 students (63%). Sample judged representative.

METHODS: Self-defined political orientation; "political alienation" defined by 5 items involving rejection of or cynicism toward present political system, classified from proximate (= party officials) to distant (= Constitution). Ss classified into apathetics (16), passive (203), conventional activists (72), legal demonstrators (65), illegal demonstrators (14).

RESULTS: No significant relationship of level of political activity with parent income, GPA, sex, marital status, fraternity affiliation and college class; but no illegal demonstrators come from lower income families. College of Arts and Science Ss more likely to demonstrate; Ss in Schools of Social Welfare and School of Education unlikely to do so. In vocationally oriented fields like engineering, business, etc., activism is nonexistent. Jews, irreligious, and males most active. Progressive decrease of parental support from apathetic to illegal demonstrators (e.g., 56% of illegal demonstrators' parents disagree with their political views).

Linear relationship between left political self-identification and involvement in demonstrations. But most demonstrators conceive of themselves as liberal or middle of the road, and 33% of radicals are not politically active. Political alienation highest among illegal demonstrators, next among legal demonstrators, other groups about the same. Analysis of proximate vs distant distinction shows greater activist alienation for proximate, some suggestion of curvilinear relationship.

COMMENTS: A recent study at a nonselective college that finds no SES correlates, higher levels of political cynicism and parental disapproval associated with left activism.

57. *Coles, Robert. 1964a. "Social Struggle and Weariness." PSYCHIATRY 27:305-315.

SETTING, SUBJECTS AND METHODS: See Coles 1964b.

RESULTS: Discussion of "weariness" or "battle fatigue" in black civil rights activists. Emphasizes problems in controlling fear, anxiety, and anger after prolonged, frustrating organizing work in Southern towns. Depression, loss of hope and purpose, silence, drinking, withdrawal from social contacts, and waning commitment to nonviolence are frequent symptoms of "weariness." Stresses precocious idealism of civil rights workers and role of guilt over wish to leave activism. Concludes that "weariness touches almost all the students who stay in the movement for any significant period of time," but views vulnerability to it as not predictable on the basis of previous background.

COMMENTS: An insightful, sympathetic account of the impact of prolonged social activism on black youth, which is potentially extendable to most committed activists.

58. *____ . 1964b. "The Protestors." In Coles, Robert. 1964. CHILDREN OF CRISIS. Boston: Little Brown, pp. 173-238.

SETTING: 1960-65, Southern civil rights movement.

SUBJECTS: Civil rights workers, largely black.

METHOD: Unstructured clinical interviewing and participant observation often involving prolonged relationships with Ss. Account, largely in Ss' own words, of 5 civil rights workers, 3 black and 2 white.

RESULTS: Empathic study of process of involvement in civil rights movement, family background, experiences in movement. Underlining of psychological themes and early experiences that were interwoven into civil rights activities. Author stresses that "there is no one kind of student—of either race—who typifies the activist. An enabling historical moment progressively came into the lives of all sorts of youths, . . . " He emphasizes factors that allow civil rights workers to persist in the face of fear and danger and stresses exhaustion and "battle fatigue."

COMMENTS: Clinical paper that provides a useful antidote to statistical presentations of "the activist" and a good account of the development and experiences of civil rights workers.

59. ____ . 1965. "Serpents and Doves: Non-Violent Youth in the South." In Erikson, Erik, ed. 1965. THE CHALLENGE OF YOUTH. New York: Doubleday Anchor, pp. 223-59.

SETTING, SUBJECTS AND METHODS: See Coles 1964b.

RESULTS: Interpretative account of civil rights workers and their opponents that emphasizes role of historical opportunity in bringing out latent psychological strengths of activists, stresses importance to civil rights workers of maintaining self-control and the psychological price this involves. Doubts usefulness of concepts of "normality" and "abnormality" (or of psychiatric terminology in general) in dealing with strengths and struggles of civil rights workers.

COMMENTS: Perceptive, sympathetic account.

60. ____. 1967. "Psychiatric Observations on Students Demonstrating for Peace." AMERICAN JOURNAL OF ORTHOPSYCHIATRY 37 (January): 107-11.

61. Collins, John N. 1970. "Student Participation in University Administration and Campus Disorder." Paper read at American Political Science Association, September 1970, Los Angeles. 20 pp. + App.

SETTING: May 1970, student strike.

INSTITUTIONS: 80 I's with enrollments of > 10,000, N = 45.

METHODS: Index of student participation based on (1) presence-absence of 2 or more voting student members on at least 1 major university committee dealing with important policy areas; and (2) students voting members of major deliberative body on campus. Protest activity reports derived from NEW YORK TIMES, other New York newspapers and Urban Research Corporation 1970d: 3 categories: none or minor protests; significant protests; extensive protests.

RESULTS: In 6 of 45 I's, > 2 students sit on central policy-making body. No clear relationship between student participation in deliberative body and intensity of protest but high student committee participation is related to low protest levels. Author notes need to qualify findings by studies of student input characteristics.

COMMENTS: Limited range of variables studied makes interpretation of findings difficult.

62. *Cowan, John L. 1966. "Academic Freedom, Protest and University Environments." Paper read at American Psychological Association, September 1966.

SETTING: 1964, data covers fall 1961-spring 1964.

INSTITUTIONS: 1,000 regionally accredited 4-year I's. Five respondents polled at each I: president, dean of students, chairman of faculty committee on student affairs, president of the student body and editor of student newspaper. Five replies obtained from 695 I's; at least one from 850 I's. Sample judged representative on sex, race, enrollment, curricular emphasis, type of control, and region.

METHODS: Each respondent completed 40 items estimating campus permissiveness regarding expression of unpopular viewpoints, invitation of controversial speakers, methods for expression of student opinion. Data on sociopolitical student groups, editorial freedom, student government, student participation in policy-making. Factor analysis of 40 items yielded 6 factors: controversial speakers (greatest % common variance), sociopolitical topics, acceptable speakers, civil rights activism, modes of expression, religious issues. I's classified into 10 types: large public, small public, private, Protestant and Catholic universities; private, Protestant, Catholic liberal arts colleges; teachers colleges and technical I's. Data analysis include comparison of I types on 6 factors; relationship of freshmen input data and EAT scores to 6 factors. Using input and environmental variables, multiple regression on controversial speakers and organized protest factor scores performed separately for 5 types of I's: public universities and technical schools; private nonsectarian I's; Protestant I's; Catholic I's; teachers colleges, and all I's.

RESULTS: Generally high levels of freedom reported, with Ss reporting more freedom than administrators on some controversial issues. Greatest freedom on controversial speakers factor found in large public and private universities (vs. teachers colleges and Catholic liberal arts colleges). Results for other factors are similar, except that Catholic universities are generally perceived as less free, private liberal arts colleges more free. Considerable variance within categories noted.

Multiple regression of freshmen input and enviornmental orientation for all I's on controversial speakers score indicate best input predictors are high student SES, I size and selectivity, low enterprising and artistic orientation. Multiple regression results for subsamples of I's differ markedly from results obtained with total sample. Highest r' (+ 0.695) obtained in private I's. For 65 I's where all 5 respondents agree on the level of freedom, higher r' is obtained. For all I's, $r' > 0.55$ obtained on militarism and civil rights protest, using freshmen input and environmental characteristics. For 65 I's with agreement between respondents, r' increases to > 0.79.

COMMENTS: An early study with a sophisticated methodology since employed in many other studies. Note high predictability of protests, using S and I characteristics in the early 1960s, and different predictors of I freedom, depending on type of I.

63. *Cowdry, R. William; Keniston, Kenneth; and Cabin, Seymour. 1970. "The War and Military Obligation: Private Attitudes and Public Actions." JOURNAL OF PERSONALITY 38, no. 4 (December):525-49.

SETTING: May-June 1968, Yale College.

SUBJECTS: Initial sample: 263 male seniors (58.4% of 450 random sample of half of senior class). Final sample: random sample of 200 in initial sample, N = 131 (65.5%). Final sample judged representative.

METHODS: Criterion of activism: signing/not signing strongly-worded antiwar resolution distributed at commencement. Attitude criterion: Vietnam Opinion Survey (Geller and Howard 1969) (antiwar vs. prowar). Four groups defined: signers (N = 49), antiwar nonsigners (with antiwar attitudes equal to those of signers, N = 25), moderate nonsigners (N = 36), prowar nonsigners (N = 21).

Demographic data, reports of early family atmosphere, 47-item ACL for self, mother, father; attitudes toward American society; alienation scales; reports of participation in sociopolitical activities (classifed as traditional, constructivist, protest); plans regarding military service; and information about Vietnam. Data analyzed using one-way analysis of variance, chi-squares, correlations, and factor analysis.

RESULTS: Demographic and background variables do not distinguish between groups or correlate with signing or antiwar attitudes. Correlation between antiwar attitudes and signing = + 0.57. Antiwar attitudes associated with self-described idealism, passionateness, nonconformity, low conservatism, determinedness, and realism, but these variables are not distinctively associated with signing.

Variables associated with *both* antiwar attitudes and signing: commitment to social action, high level of sociopolitical activities (especially protest), high importance contributed to community service and political activity, low importance to good academic standing and conformity in dress. Signers disproportionately plan to enter teaching, antiwar nonsigners to enter law, government, and politics, prowar nonsigners to enter business.

Compared to antiwar nonsigners, signers more often report happy family, parents' marriage solid, strong emotional bonds to father, low ACL discrepancy between mother-father and father-self. Variables distinguishing antiwar signers from antiwar nonsigners are almost identical to those distinguishing prowar signers from antiwar nonsigners. With opposition to war held constant, closeness to family, and in particular perceived similarity to father, predicts "consistency" of ideology and action.

COMMENTS: Finding that "consistent" Ss at both ends of the political spectrum resemble each other in socialization experiences more than either group resembles the "inconsistent" Ss underlines importance of distinguishing ideology and activism.

64. Crisp, Lloyd E. 1968. "Attitudes: Liberal versus Conservative, Degree of Self Distortion." Ph.D. dissertation, University of Denver.

65. Dan, Alice J. 1969. "Role Conflict and College Students' Empathy with Their Parents." Master's thesis, Committee on Human Development, University of Chicago. Abstract, 2 pp.

SETTING, SUBJECTS, AND METHODS: See Flacks and Neugarten Intro. Ss scored for "empathy" on the basis of accuracy of prediction of mothers' and fathers' value orientations and political attitudes, producing 4 uncorrelated measures of empathy.

RESULTS: Most results are concerned with role conflict. Incidental finding that there is no association between activism and any empathy measure.

COMMENTS: Activists are not better predictors of parents' real views than are nonactivists.

66. *Demerath, N.J. III; Marwell, G.; and Aiken, M. 1970. "The Dynamics of Idealism: Student Activism and the Black Movement." Unpublished paper, Department of Sociology, University of Wisconsin. 338 pp.

SETTING: June and fall 1965, SCOPE voter registration project in Alabama, Georgia, Florida, North Carolina, South Carolina, and Virginia. 1969 telephone follow-up. University of Wisconsin, Madison comparison group.

SUBJECTS: 256 (85%) SCOPE volunteers tested at Atlanta orientation sessions in June 1965. Some comparisons with UWM sample tested April 1965. Thirty-three black respondents excluded from data analysis. 120

males. Of white Ss, 166 (74%) completed follow-up questionnaire in fall 1965. In fall 1969, 40 telephone interviews (average 20 mins.) conducted with locatable Ss.

METHODS: Questionnaire concerned family background, demographic variables, motivations, political and social outlooks, expectations and attitudes concerning Southern experience. Report is largely descriptive; some correlations between a priori indices of variables like religiosity and liberalism; pre- and postsummer changes are analyzed.

RESULTS: Researchers were rejected by 1964 COFO Mississippi Summer Project and had difficulties in obtaining cooperation from 1965 SCOPE project. SCOPE participants were diverse, from upper middle-class college backgrounds (comparable to UWM sample), reported greater distance from parents than UWM sample though 60% of parents supported summer work, most parents liberal politically. Extremes of nonreligiosity and religious commitment overrepresented among volunteers. Eighty percent of volunteers plan postgraduate work, 33% aspire to Ph.D. Fifty-four percent volunteers see college purpose as value-definition and service, not occupational skill (vs. 15% UWM). Volunteers more "alienated" from American society, more ideologized and more leftist than UWM civil rights supporters. Many volunteers consider disarmament, end of Vietnam war, and civil rights in North as important as Southern civil rights work. Stated motivations for participation varied: preponderance of "helping others," but also personal improvement and discharge of moral obligation. Volunteers' concerns before summer focused on personal success, safety, ability to communicate, fear of violence. Few significant correlations between expectations and other measures.

Detailed narrative of volunteers' experiences in local organizing projects (mostly voter registration). Black high school students most supportive; relationships with whites were minimal, with blacks extensive. Large cultural gap between white volunteers and Southern blacks, even greater gap between volunteers and Southern whites. Most volunteers judged project and personal role successful, but would have preferred greater involvement in political education, community organization, tutoring, remedial education, etc. Correlates of perceived project failure include personal dissatisfaction with activities, lack of group cohesion, friction with co-workers (especially over sexual issues), inability to work with local black community.

After summer, volunteers reported less optimism about white Southerners, less faith in class struggle or Southern solution to racial problems, greater difficulties in working with blacks, greater assumption of cooperation from Southern blacks, lower judgment of sensitivity of permanent field workers in South, less rejection of violence, etc. (But overall support for nonviolence persisted.) Summer did not increase radicalization, but attitudes tended to crystallize and acquire depth as a result of summer's experience. Percentage undecided about future careers up from 10% to 17%; 23% of those in college in fall 1965 changed majors; relevance of college decreased significantly after summer. Evidence of "wrong-way culture shock" on returning North.

Follow-up Ss classified into alienated active (radicals); nonalienated active (reformists); nonalienated nonactive (disengaged); alienated non-active (dropouts). Low alienation associated with working or lower class background; alienation with middle-class background. Of radicals, N = 10, 6 were socialists before 1965, all males, all resist or oppose draft, 4 abandoned previous college teaching plans. Of reformists, N = 13, 4 (vs. 1 of all others) stayed in the South, and 4 of the 9 who left South felt guilty about it; 10 held full-time jobs, 12 had definite career plans. Disengaged, N = 10, had dropped out of the movement, 8 females, 4 married, all emphasize close interpersonal relationships. Only 4 dropouts were con-tacted, but this underestimates total. Overall, disillusionment has persisted and intensified in the 4 years since SCOPE.

COMMENTS: Rich anecdotal material and astute observations on the impact of Southern civil rights work upon white volunteers. Limited follow-up study suggests that pre-SCOPE characteristics persist and deter-mine long-term impact of SCOPE experience. Note 75% of follow-up were "nonradicals" after 4 years.

67. Denisoff, R. Serge, and Levine, Mark H. 1970. "Generations and Counter-Culture: A Study of the Ideology of Music." YOUTH AND SOCIETY 2 (September):33-58.

SETTING: 1968, Vancouver, British Columbia.

SUBJECTS: Secondary school students and dropouts, ages 13 to 19, N = 444. Parents of these Ss, N = 121. 36 teachers and administrators.

METHODS: Ss questioned to test 2 hypotheses: differentiations between generational units will be greater (1) than between intragenerational units, (2) in the sphere of rock music than in political attitudes.

RESULTS: Comparing students with dropouts and parents with teachers, no intragenerational conflict found on either politics or music. Comparing students and dropouts with parents and teachers, no political differences found (all tended to prefer the Liberal Party). But generational differences are highly significant in musical preferences. Ninety-six of adults prefer movie, classical, show, or religious music (vs. 12.5% of youths); 87.9% of youths choose rock music as their first or second choice (vs. 4% adults).

COMMENTS: Youth "rebellion" is seen as cultural not political. Note youth of students, predominantly middle and upper middle-class sample.

68. **Derber, C., and Flacks, R. 1968. "An Exploration of the Value System of Radical Student Activists and Their Parents." Paper read at American Sociological Association, August 1968, San Francisco. 72 pp.

SETTING, SUBJECTS, AND METHODS: See Flacks and Neugarten Intro. This report divides student Ss into 4 groups (high activism N = 34, medium activism N = 17, low activism N = 12, nonactivists N = 37) and analyzes relationship between activism and student and parental values. Value scores divided into high (top quartile), medium (middle quartiles), and low (bottom quartile) for cross-tabulations. F-tests on mean value scores.

RESULTS: Values that most distinguish activists (in order of declining F): humanism, intellectualism, low moralism, low materialism, authenticity, and romanticism. No relationship with interpersonal intimacy or career emphasis. Values most characterizing fathers of activists (in order): low moralism, humanism, intellectualism, authenticity. Values distinguishing mothers: low moralism, intellectualism, authenticity. In many or most cases, high and medium activist groups do not differ with regard to Ss' or parents' value scores. Most differentiating parental characteristic is high emphasis on self-expression (vs. moralism and self-control). Authors emphasize role of humanistic subculture in disposing to activism, identify 2 clusters of humanistic values: (1) individual development and self-expression and (2) ethical humanism; emphasize activists' and activists' families rejection of Protestant ethic.

For 51 activists only, factor analysis of 8 values produces 2 rotated factors: (1) romanticism, intellectualism vs. self-control; (2) humanitarianism, intimacy vs. career. Ss classified as high humanists if both scores above median, N = 15, low humanists if both scores below mean, N = 18, middle if other, N = 18. high humanists differ from low humanists in lesser conventionality, more creative aspirations, greater activism, egalitarianism-populism, political radicalism, identity diffusion, alienation from America, lower authoritarianism, less clarity of occupational choice. Humanism level unrelated to SES, demographic characteristics, all parental values. Authors point to the role of generation, exposure to student movement, and sex in determining whether predisposing family value context will lead to activism in child; predict that as student movement grows, family background and tradition will become less important predictors of activism.

COMMENTS: An important paper, especially notable for its excellent theoretical discussion.

69. Donaldson, Robert H., and Pride, Richard A. 1969. "Black Students at a White University: Their Attitudes and Behavior in an Era of Confrontation." JOURNAL OF SOCIAL AND BEHAVIORAL SCIENCES 15 (Fall): 22-38.

SETTING: 1968 (?), Vanderbilt University.

SUBJECTS: All black students at Vanderbilt contacted, N = 34 (68%).

METHODS: Complex questionnaire dealing with early background, psychological orientation (civic competence, efficacy, cynicism, racial stereotyping, distrust of whites, etc.) attitudes and perceptions of Vanderbilt (social distance measures, success orientation, etc.), and current behavior (traditional/protest political participation, group membership, etc.).

RESULTS: Presentation of Ss' scores on all measures. Cross-tabulations indicate that high SES is related to civic competence, efficacy and low cynicism; high family participation (in decision-making) related to high political efficacy; men more cynical than women; support for racial integration related to extremely high or extremely low SES, high family participation and female sex life; high civic competence related to traditional and protest political participation; high political efficacy related to traditional participation but not protest activity; cynicism highly related to protest activity. Distrust of whites related to exclusive association with blacks; militancy on black studies at Vanderbilt related to sex (male), integrated high school; high family participation.

COMMENTS: Small sample size and large number of variables make interpretation of and generalization from this study problematic.

70. Donovan, J.M., and Shaevitz, M.H. 1970. "A Study of Student Political Groups." Unpublished paper, Connecticut Mental Health Center, New Haven, 42 pp. + App.

SETTING: 1968 (?), University of Michigan, Ann Arbor.

SUBJECTS: Ss drawn from 3 groups: left-wing political group, right-wing political group, and fraternity. Exact N's and response rates not given.

METHODS: Names obtained from group leaders. Approximately 20 questionnaires completed by members of each group; 1-hour interviews with 10 members of each group. Informal observation of all groups.

RESULTS: Radicals are hostile to authority, closed-minded, impulse and action-oriented, little emotional contact between group members, personally cold and inflexible, rude to strangers, open about sex lives, adopt Marcusean "line," strongly oppose "coercive" university, exaggerate divergence from parents' views, parents often politically involved. Ss with most rigid left-wing parents are coldest and most mistrustful, report high school alienation from classmates and many early radical activities. Divided into "Ideologues" (inflexible, Marxist, cold, rebellious, ideological, anticompetitive) and "Humanitarians" (less rigid, genuine empathy and compassion, less political in high school).

Right-wing Ss are reserved, polite, correct, humorless, strongly proauthority, deferential, strict superegos, "shalt-not" morality, cold, and distant. Primary emphasis on individual freedom paralleled ideology of radical group, but conservatives respect university as proving ground. General parental support for political beliefs, powerful achievement orientation. Divided into "Birchers" (quasi-paranoid style, anti-communist, withdrawn, isolated, nonempathic, from small town and less wealthy families) and "Pioneers" (rugged individualists, strong desire for freedom, articulate, outgoing, interested in frontier).

Fraternity members also studied. Authors stress role of parental modeling and early experiences in defining political style and group membership, and argue that in each group, psychopathology takes the form of an exaggerated embodiment of the group ethic.

COMMENTS: Hypotheses about childhood experiences are highly inferential. Virtually the only study that presents a predominantly negative picture of radicals. Note differentiation of types within radical and right-wing groups.

71. **Doress, Irvin. 1968. "A Study of a Sampling of Boston University Student Activists." Ed.D. thesis, Boston University. 219 pp.

SOURCE: May 1966-Dec. 1967, Boston University.

SUBJECTS: 4 groups studied, all B.U. Ss, ages 18-31. 3 activist groups defined on the basis of sustained involvement in sociopolitical activities directed outside the academic community, time- and energy-consuming activities within 1 or more organizations or on an *ad hoc* basis. Right activists recruited from YAF and YC, N = 36; moderate activists from "liberal" YR and YD, N = 31; left activists from BU Civil Rights Coordinating Committee, SDS, and Students for Peace, N = 36. (Young Socialists' Alliance members refused to cooperate.) Control group of nonactivist volunteers (not random), N = 77.

METHODS: Shostrom's Personal Orientation Inventory, CPI, D, Riess' Moral Acceptability Scale (sexual permissiveness), Wallach's Risk-Taking Scale, ANOMIA, Stearn Study Social Background Questionnaire. Semi-structured interviews lasting about 1½ hrs. conducted with representative Ss from each group. Quantitative data analyzed by one-way analyses of variance between pooled activist groups and control groups, and between right, moderate, and left activists.

RESULTS: Compared to nonactivists, activists are higher on CPI scales measuring dominance, capacity for status, sociability, self-acceptance, intellectual efficiency, psychological mindedness; lower on Anomia; more often in "basic" (vs. applied) fields.

Comparison of 3 activist groups shows that left activists manifest lower D, higher sexual permissiveness, inner-directedness, self-actualizing values, existentiality, feeling reactivity, and intimate contact; higher achievement via independence and flexibility; higher % majoring in non-applied fields.

Interviews suggest that compared to right activists, left activists are more often upper middle class, less often downwardly mobile or poor; center activists are most affluent. Left activists most often off-campus, nonreligious, and have parents who had moved away from orthodox religion, least often choose power-wielding heroes, report more peer influence, less parental influence, more marijuana use. Parent-child relationships of left activists show great diversity, but nonactivist families are more lacking in overt conflict. Right activists most constricted sexually. Left activists talk openly about psychotherapy but view it as conformist and possibly self-indulgent. Left activists see activism as most personally valuable, future plans most vague, undecided, and noncareer-oriented.

Eleven significant differences between left activists and control group on personality scales vs. 3 significant differences for center activists and right activists. Compared to control group, left activists are higher on moral acceptability, self-actualizing value, feeling reactivity, dominance, capacity for status, self-acceptance, achievement via independence, intellectual efficiency, psychological mindedness, flexibility; lower on D. Negative findings include no higher GPA for activists, low D for left activists, no evidence that greater "psychological health" uniquely characterizes left as opposed to other activists. Author concludes that activists, regardless of ideology, are higher on intellectual efficiency (but not grades), less neurotic, less anomic, and function more effectively in personal and social milieux. Left activists compared to moderate and right activists are more autonomous of social-cultural past, less dogmatic, more often in "basic disciplines," possess qualities that favor achievement where independence is needed, more flexible and adaptable. Left activists differ from moderate and right activists in direction of greater self-actualization.

COMMENTS: Valuable study that separates activism and ideology, and studies the characteristics of activists of different ideological persuasions. Some, though not all, of the characteristics ascribed to left activists in other studies may be the characteristics of *all* activists, but within high activism groups, leftists are more flexible, autonomous, and independent.

72. Drew, David E. 1971. "Jewish Students Today: Radical or Conservative?" TRANSACTION (October):45-48.

SETTING, SUBJECTS, METHODS: See A. Astin Intro. fall 1969 freshman data: ACESIF. Comparison of the students of Jewish background (4.2% of total) with students from other religious backgrounds (Ss with no religious background excluded).

RESULTS: Compared to others, Jewish students more often have highly educated parents, report high on high school GPA, deemphasize financial gains of college, have higher degree aspirations, are in preprofessional and social science majors, career plans legal, medical, or undecided (vs. business), fathers more often businessmen. Jewish junior college students differ markedly from this pattern, with lower GPA, more business careers, more conservative attitudes. Jewish students report their parents less "deeply religious," show more movement away from religious origin (17% vs. 11% others), hold more liberal views on virtually all issues. Compared to non-Jewish women, Jewish women more often value performing in creative arts, favor liberalization of abortion and divorce laws, place higher value on raising a family, believe individual can do little to change society.

COMMENTS: Note similarity between profile of Jewish students and many profiles of activists.

73. *Dunlap, Riley, 1970. "Family Backgrounds of Radical and Conservative Political Activists at a Nonelite University." Published in revised version as "Radical and Conservative Student Activists: A Comparison of Family Backgrounds. PACIFIC SOCIOLOGICAL REVIEW 13 (Summer):171-81.

SUBJECTS: Radical activists N = 22 (88%), include 9 of 10 "core members" of SDS and 13 rank and file members; conservative activists are members of YAF, N = 23 (100%); random sample of 237 undergraduates, N = 202, (85%).

METHODS: Self-administered questionnaire mailed to random sample, delivered individually to SDS, YAF. Data concerning parents' party affiliation, political position, income, education, etc. Comparisons involve SDS, cross-section and YAF.

RESULTS: Party preference of parents (especially mother) differentiates SDS from YAF but not strongly from cross-section; SDS parents' politics are much more liberal. Compared to YAF and cross-section, SDS parents reported to have less interest in politics. Parental disapproval of S's political activity highest for SDS, lowest for YAF. No relationship between SDS membership and parental education or SES index. Author concludes that many previous generalizations about left activists do not apply to sample because (1) University of Oregon is nonelite I and/or (2) composition of radical movement has changed since mid-1960s.

COMMENTS: A sharply-focused recent study at a nonselective state university that supports the theory that the base of enlistment into the movement is changing.

74. *____ , and Gale, Richard P. 1971a. "Politics and Ecology: A Political Profile of Student Eco-Activists." Paper read at Pacific Sociological Association, April 1971, Honolulu. 27 pp.

SETTING: May 1970, University of Oregon.

SUBJECTS: Students active in each of 8 ecology organizations ("eco-activists") who claimed regular participation and involvement in environmental activities, N = 51, comparison group: of random sample of 300 Ss, N = 237 (79%). Third comparison sample of 22 University of Oregon SDS members studied in 1969. See Dunlap 1970.

METHODS: Data on political self-characterization, causes of environmental degradation, strategies for solving environment problems. Tabulations with no tests of significance.

RESULTS: Modal eco-activist self-label "very liberal," random sample "moderately liberal," SDS "radical left." No SDS Ss in 1970 eco-activist sample. Party preferences of eco-activists close to random sample, unlike those of SDS. Ninety percent eco-activists report previous political activity (not related to environment) vs. 68% random. Participation in demonstrations: 95% SDS, 83% eco-activists, 58% (of politically active) random Ss. Fourteen percent eco-activists blame "capitalism" for environmental problems, 50% blame social preoccupation with economic growth, 87% eco-activists (vs. 48% random) believe solution of environmental problems will entail significant changes in political-economic system; most random Ss see solution in "more people getting involved." Authors argue that eco-activists are like random sample in perception of causes of ecological problems, but more likely to feel basic social change is necessary to solve these problems.

Given flagrant ecological problems, 55% of eco-activists (vs. 19% random) indicate willingness to engage in illegal demonstrations leading to arrest. Authors suggest potential for radicalization in the ecology movement.

COMMENTS: This first study of student ecology activists locates them between random sample and SDS sample on a variety of issues, underlines their willingness to use militant tactics and their view that fundamental social changes are needed to solve ecology problems.

75. *_____ . 1971b. "Student Recruitment into the Environmental Movement: A Test of a Reformulation of Mass Society Theory." Paper read at Rural Sociological Society, August 1971, Denver. 25 pp. + App.

SETTING, SUBJECTS AND METHODS: See Dunlap and Gale 1971a. This paper distinguishes 3 groups: "core group" of 51 eco-activists; random sample of UO undergraduates, N = 237 (79%), divided into "followers," N = 117 (who had taken some action in behalf of the environment), "inactives," N = 120.

RESULTS: Compared to random sample, eco-activists have higher SES, but no difference in parental political preference, are more often nonreligious (but not Jewish), social science and natural science majors (vs. business, education, preprofessional or humanities), more often members of groups supporting conservation or wilderness preservation and of outing clubs, involved in intensive wilderness camping, have friends engaged in outdoor activities, and are children of parents involved in recreation and conservation organizations. Eco-activists more often foresee disaster unless ecology problems are solved, more often liberal-left, have high scores on Concern for Environmental Rights Scale. (See Dunlap and Rutherford 1971.) Followers got involved later in ecology movement than activists, largely because they heard about ongoing campaigns or visible problems (vs. activists, who attribute initial involvement to parental influence or to perceived deterioration in recreation areas).

Compared to followers, eco-activists are more distinguished from inactive population by membership in supporting secondary groups, perception of environmental strain, political outlook and environmental ideology.

COMMENTS: An ingenious application of empirical data to support a theory of political mobilization which argues that later recruits should differ from early recruits.

76. _____, and Rutherford, Brent M. 1971. "Concern for Environmental Rights among College Students." Paper read at Pacific Sociological Association, April 1971, Honolulu. 24 pp.

SETTING, SUBJECTS, AND METHODS: See Dunlap and Gale 1971a, 1971b. This paper deals with development and validation of Concern for Environmental Rights Scale.

RESULTS: Factor analysis of 8 environmental items suggests 1-factor solution. Scale scores are related to taking action on an environmental issue, participation in campus environmental organization, and willingness to engage in sit-ins for environmental rights.

COMMENTS: Report of the development of an ecological rights scale.

77. Epstein, Yakov M.; Suedfeld, Peter; and Bresnahan, Daniel M. 1971. "Reaction to a Campus Confrontation." JOURNAL OF APPLIED SOCIAL PSYCHOLOGY 1, no. 1 (January):57-65.

SETTING: Feb. 1969, Newark and New Brunswick campuses of Rutgers University, during and after 4-day occupation of university building at Newark by black students.

SUBJECTS: Day and evening Ss polled on both campuses on the first and last days of building occupation; New Brunswick day Ss polled 2 weeks after occupation. Data analysis conducted with 183 Ss matched for age, major, and political affiliation to equate 2 campuses: 2/3 male, 60% day Ss. Self-labeled activists N = 26, liberals N = 49, moderates N = 36, conservatives N = 29, 42 not classified.

METHODS: Data include attitudes toward black organizations and other issues. Comparisons of Newark vs. New Brunswick, day vs. evening, first vs. last day polls, and political self-identification.

RESULTS: Ss at Newark are more opposed to black student organization than are New Brunswick Ss. Evening Ss are more negative than day Ss toward black student organization and other militant-activist black groups. Newark and evening Ss favor harsher treatment of occupiers, but 73% of all Ss advocate negotiation. Evidence of polarization across time: increasing hostility to SDS and disappearance of initially neutral 17% on last day of conflict. 2 weeks later, even less support for SDS and increased support for YAF, Republicans, and Democrats.

Analysis of activists, liberals, moderates, and conservatives shows lower authoritarianism for activists, punitive response most advocated by conservatives. Activists differ more from liberals, moderates, and conservatives than these groups differ from each other.

COMMENTS: Nonrandom sampling may make comparisons unreliable. Results suggest black campus militancy increased opposition to blacks. Note trend toward both increasing polarization and opposition to leftists.

78. Everson, David H. 1970. "The Background of Student Support for Student Protest Activities in the University." PUBLIC AFFAIRS BULLETIN 3, no. 2 (March-April): 1-7.

SETTING, SUBJECTS, AND METHODS: See Miller and Everson 1970. Comparison of SIU responses with Berkeley responses (Somers 1965) and study of background correlates of militancy scale scores.

RESULTS: On 4 items where comparisons are possible, 1969 SIU Ss gave responses almost identical to 1964 Berkeley Ss. Militancy related to mothers' political values and high mothers' education (but not to fathers' politics or education), to religion for both parents (Jews high) and to Ss' future occupation (clergy, teaching, social work high).

COMMENTS: Socioeconomic variables largely in predictable direction in 1969. Note greater importance of mothers' than fathers' education and political beliefs.

79. ____, and Miller, Roy E. n.d. "Southern Illinois University Student Attitudes toward University Authority: A Profile." Unpublished paper, Public Affairs Research Bureau, Southern Illinois University, Carbondale. 99 pp.

SETTING, SUBJECTS, AND METHODS: See Miller and Everson 1970.

RESULTS: Descriptive account of students' desire for campus change, specific issues on which change is desired, strength of opinions on various campus issues, and political self-label (1% revolutionary or militant, 6% nonviolent radical, 30% liberal, 36% moderate, 16% conservative, 1% ultraconservative), feelings of alienation from personal involvement with the university administration, low sense of political efficacy on campus, etc. Graduate students and upperclassmen are more conservative, women are more alienated, less trustful, less efficacious and are somewhat more radical than men. Extensive discussion of study methodology.

COMMENTS: A descriptive study that indicates fairly high disillusionment in 1969 at a nonelite state university.

80. Ezekiel, Ralph. 1969. "Peace Corps Teachers in Ghana." Unpublished paper, cited in Angell, Robert C. 1969. PEACE ON THE MARCH: TRANSNATIONAL PARTICIPATION. New York: Van Nostrand Reinhold Co. p. 96. A secondary report of a study of 50 Peace Corps teachers tested during preduty training in U.S. and after Ghana service. Results indicate a shift toward greater internationalism, liberalism and antimilitarism.

81. Fenton, J.H., and Gleason, G. 1969. "Student Power at the University of Massachusetts: A Case Study." Bureau of Government Research, University of Massachusetts. 71 pp.

SETTING: Spring 1968 and 1969, University of Massachusetts; student power demonstrations and controversy in February 1968.

SUBJECTS: Spring 1968 N = 232; spring 1969 students N = 292.

METHODS: Spring 1968: 7-item student power scale used to define 2 extreme groups: prostudent power, N = 48 (21%); and antistudent power, N = 37 (16%); groups compared on demographic and attitudinal variables. Spring 1969: new and reliable scales developed for student power, black power, and New Left. Multiple regression conducted on each scale score with other variables, including items on scale.

RESULTS: Spring 1968: prostudent power Ss more often have poor relationships with parents, nonreligious, nonchurchgoers, or Unitarians, females, sophomores, below C+ average, father blue collar, mother Independent, father Democratic, high interpersonal mistrust, favor legalizing marijuana, making contraceptives available, stopping North Vietnam bombing, busing blacks, more often attend college because of "increased freedom," select extreme questionnaire responses. Antistudent power Ss more often graduate students, live at home, older, male, fathers small business or white collar, 4th generation or more Americans, fraternity-sorority members, engineering majors, both self and mother Republican. "Parents too permissive" higher for both extreme groups.

Spring 1969: comparison with 1968 shows general drift towards more leftist views in all areas measured. Multiple regression predictors on 3 scales. Student power: student power defined radically, support black UMass sit-in, female, freshman or sophomore, Vietnam war outgrowth of American imperialism, $r' = 0.52$. New Left: support more blacks at UMass, reject working within political system, support marijuana legalization, humanities or social science major, support student decisions on courses, Vietnam war outgrowth of American imperialism, nonfraternity member, $r' = 0.69$. Black power: blacks treated unfairly, identify with rebelling students, radical definition of student power, report personal activism, $r' = 0.64$.

COMMENTS: A recent study at a large public university that documents leftist shift between 1968-1969, demonstrates distinct correlates of student power, New Left and Black power attitudes.

82. Finney, Henry C. 1971. "Political Libertarianism at Berkeley: An Application of Perspectives from the New Left." JOURNAL OF SOCIAL ISSUES 27, no. 1:35-61.

SETTING: 1959, 1961, 1963, University of California at Berkeley.

SUBJECTS: All freshmen at UCB tested in 1959 (100%), retested in 1961 (74%). Analysis based on American males tested in 1959 and 1961, N = 792. Of these Ss, 159 retested in 1963.

METHODS: Ss given OPI in 1959, abbreviated OPI in 1961, data on political preferences, SES, attitudes toward university, success and achievement, grades, intellectual interests, leisure patterns and preferences. Data analysis focuses on 5-item scale of political libertarianism. Ss classified into 6 groups: nonchanging, consistent nonlibertarian, consistent libertarian, conservative change, liberal change, and inarticulate (greater than 2 "don't know" responses) on the basis of 1959-61 comparisons.

RESULTS: Overall increase in libertarianism between 1959 and 1961, which continues in 1963 subsample. Libertarian Ss more often Democrats, support Kennedy, oppose Joseph McCarthy, have high GPA, tend to be more knowledgeable politically and of higher status backgrounds. Liberal change associated with decreasing attachment to getting high grades, high status father's occupation, but not with other SES measures. Libertarianism and liberal change not associated with most measures of dissatisfaction with education, but related to high intellectual disposition (OPI), rejection of conventional achievment orientation, expectation of lower income than parents, high valuation of "creative and original" ideal job, opposition to "vocational training," other measures of rejection of conventional success-achievement orientation, willingness to study before quiz, rejection of "collegiate culture." High academic competence interacts with deprecation of grades to maximize libertarianism.

Author argues that findings support "New Left" theories of the sources of student activism. Paper contains excellent methodological discussion of distinction between composition and incidence inferences in studying class origins of student politics.

COMMENTS: Consistent with other early Berkeley studies, but author's extrapolations of 1959-61 Berkeley data to later student activism seem questionable.

83. *Fishkin, James, Keniston, Kenneth, 1971 and Mackinnon, Catherine, 1973. "Moral Reasoning and Political Ideology." JOURNAL OF PERSONALITY AND SOCIAL PSYCHOLOGY, in press, 18 pp. + App.

SETTING: May 1970, 10 major American universities.

SUBJECTS: 155 Ss interviewed, 120 completed moral reasoning measure, 75 completed slogan ideology measure, N = 75. Sample chosen "for heterogeneity."

METHODS: Ss completed 31-item slogan scale and Kohlberg Moral Dilemmas Test (Hahn et al.,1968). Ss classified as preconventional, N = 12, conventional N = 36, and postconventional, N = 27, according to moral reasoning scores. In addition, % moral reasoning scores calculated for each S on Kohlberg's 5 major stages of moral reasoning.

RESULTS: Factor analysis of slogan responses yields 3 varimax factors: violent radicalism, peaceful radicalism, and conservatism; factor scales also combined into general radicalism vs. conservatism and agreeing response set measures. Analysis of variance shows preconventional Ss distinctively high on violent radicalism, conventional Ss high on conservatism, postconventional Ss low on conservatism. Correlations of % moral reasoning by stage scores with ideology measures show stage 4 (law and order) moral reasoning positively associated with conservatism ($r = + 0.635$) and negatively associated with both radicalism measures. Multiple regression on ideology scores using % moral reasoning by stage and agreeing response set measure shows that 48% of variance of radicalism vs. conservatism can be predicted by % moral reasoning scores, 67% of conservatism scores can be predicted by using % moral reasoning and response set scores. Authors emphasize connection between law and order moral reasoning and conservative ideology, argue that nonconservative Ss are of 2 moral types, the regressed and advanced.

COMMENTS: An exploratory study that replicates in the realm of ideology what Hahn et al 1968 found in the realm of behavioral activism.

84. Fishman, Jacob R., and Solomon, Frederic. 1961. "Psychological Observations on the Student Sit-in Movement." PROCEEDINGS OF THE THIRD WORLD CONGRESS OF PSYCHIATRY 2 (June):1133-38.

85. ____. 1963. "Youth and Social Action: I. Perspectives on the Student Sit-in Movement." THE AMERICAN JOURNAL OF ORTHOPSYCHIATRY 33, no. 5 (October):872-82.

SETTING: 1960, Washington, D.C., nonviolent action group, an interracial student group involved in desegregating restaurants, picketing, and other civil rights activities.

SUBJECTS: 20 Ss: 9 black, 11 white, males and females, who were members of leadership group.

METHODS: Intensive clinical interviewing, individually and in groups; direct observations of demonstrations and group activities.

RESULTS: Authors stress catalytic role of 1954 Supreme Court decision, Martin Luther King as identity model, and Greensboro, North Carolina 1959 sit-in. A new social character is emerging among Southern blacks involving "prosocial acting-out" (related to image of what S believes parents "really" want him to do). Authors emphasize underlying resentment, anger and hostility, high moral purpose, nonintellectual and non-ideological orientation in activists.

COMMENTS: Psychodynamic interpretation of small group of black and white civil right activists. Major concepts are "prosocial acting-out" and importance of identification with fantasies concerning parents' "real" values.

86. ***Flacks, Richard, and Neugarten, Bernice. Introduction.

SETTING: 1965-1966, Chicago area.

SUBJECTS: Activists drawn from membership lists of SDS, April 1965 March on Washington, Illinois-Wisconsin AFSC, North Short Project for Open Occupancy, and SNCC Committee Chicago Project, N = 50 (90%), 23 males; Ss attend 26 different colleges; all parents resident in Chicago area and interviewed (93%). Control sample selected at random from directories of Chicago area colleges with effort to match type of college, neighborhood, sex, and religion, N = 50, 24 males. All control parents interviewed (92%).

METHODS: Data derived from 2-hour interviews with each child, mother, and father, including open-ended and closed-ended questions. Areas covered include political ideology, participation and attitude toward student movement; values; family life including child-rearing, parent-child conflict, etc.; rating scales and "projective" questions; 6-item activism index (students only) involving participation in rallies, picketing, being jailed for civil disobedience, work on projects for disadvantaged, canvassing, full-time social action work, officer in social action group. Activism index used to reclassify Ss (some Ss in original "activist" group fall below median on activism index). All interviews coded with reliability of ratings established. Value ratings include romanticism, intellectualism, authenticity, interpersonal intimacy, humanism, moralism and self-control, materialism, emphasis on career, etc.

Methods of analysis include comparisons of high, medium, and low activists with inactive Ss and their families, F-test on Ss and families categorized according to Ss' level of activism, correlations, and multiple regression. Focus of most analyses is on relationship of activism to background characteristics, Ss' and parents' value orientations and personality characteristics.

RESULTS: Angres 1969, Dan 1969, Derber and Flacks 1968, Flacks 1966, 1967a, 1967b, Goldsmid 1967, 1972, Kimmel 1967, Schedler 1966, Troll 1967, Troll et al. 1969.

COMMENTS: A very significant study, especially valuable for direct examination of parental values and personality characteristics, demonstration of close relationships between activism and family value climate, ingenious data analyses, and unusually strong theoretical and interpretive perspective.

87. **Flacks, Richard W. 1966. "The Liberated Generation: An Exploration of the Roots of Student Protest." Working Paper I: Youth and Social Change Project, University of Chicago. 52 pp. + App.

SETTING, SUBJECTS, AND METHODS: Study 1: See Flacks and Neugarten Intro. Only high activists, N = 37, and nonactivists, N = 34, compared. Study 2: 1967, University of Chicago, after sit-in by 500 students in administration building protesting sending class-rankings to draft boards. Ten days after sit-in, random sample of 65 members of sit-in organization contacted, N = 47 (74%), 35 student members of anti-sit-in group contacted, N = 23 (65%). Random sampling of 1 floor of largely freshman-sophomore male and female dormitories, N = 60 (78%), N sit-ins = 14. Analysis compares 3 activist groups (Study 1 activists; Study 2 members of sit-in group and dormitory sit-ins) and 3 nonactivist groups (Study 1 nonactivists, Study 2 antiprotesters and dormitory nonparticipants). Groups not combined for analysis. Not all findings consistently differentiate all activist from nonactivist groups. No tests of significance.

RESULTS: Activists define themselves as upper middle class (but nonactivists somewhat more so), more often report higher family incomes—only Study 2—professional fathers, both parents highly educated (but Study 1 fathers also more likely to have only high school education), mothers employed in high status occupations, Jewish families and recent immigrant stock, grandparents more educated and white collar, Ss from large cities, define selves, fathers, and grandfathers as Democrats or left-wing. On specific attitudes like bombing North Vietnam, student protests, civil disobedience, HUAC, Lyndon Johnson, Goldwater, etc., Study 1 activists' fathers are highly liberal (sons even more so); both parents are politically active. But on most issues, attitude differences between activists and fathers are greater than differences between nonactivists and fathers.

Activists place higher value on ideas, art, music, national, and international betterment; lower value on career, marriage, family, and religion. Parents of Study 1 activists have generally the same values, but place more stress on career and marriage. Activists more often have indefinite occupational plans, plan careers in college teaching and the arts. Study 1 activists report higher high school class rank and higher GPA (not as marked in Study 2), place much greater emphasis on values of romanticism, intellectualism, humanitarianism, and lower value on moralism and self-control. Activists more often rate parents "mild," "soft" (differences marginal), "lenient" and "easy." Parents of Study 1 activists tend to rate selves permissive, less likely to intervene strongly if child dropped out of school or had an affair. Activist males plan higher-risk behavior vis-à-vis draft.

COMMENTS: A study notable for its strong theoretical perspective, 3 different samples, and data obtained directly from parents of activists. Author sees student activists as socialized by "deviant" families whose values they incorporate; stresses extent to which activists "implement and renew" parental values.

88. *____ . 1967a. "The Liberated Generation: An exploration of the Roots of Student Protest." JOURNAL OF SOCIAL ISSUES 23, no. 3 (July):52-75. Condensed version of Flacks 1966 with the same theoretical introduction and conclusions, but much less data (21 tables reduced to 5).

89. ____ . 1967b. "Student Activists; Result, Not Revolt." PSYCHOLOGY TODAY 61 (October):18-23.

SETTING, SUBJECTS, METHODS, AND RESULTS: See Flacks and Neugarten Intro., Flacks 1966, Derber and Flacks 1968. This article presents family data and classifications of values not employed in Flacks 1966. Activists are characterized by atypical humanistic values in family culture, which contrast with dominant middle-class emphasis on self-control. Activists' parents higher on humanism, much lower on self-control, higher on romanticism, intellectualism, authenticity (sensitivity to hypocrisy and wish for self-knowledge and understanding), and humanitarianism. Activists' parents do not differ fron nonactivists' parents in emphasis on career, although children differ. Low traditional morality vs. high expressiveness appears to be the "core of value differences" between families of activists and nonactivists. No significant differences between parents' emphasis on material values and filial activism, although students are antimaterialistic.

A second sample was asked to choose from 22 "isms" the 3 with which they most identified. Humanism and existentialism choices differentiate activists from nonactivists.

COMMENTS: Further analyses of parental value data referred to in Flacks 1966. Note emphasis on close relationships between moralism/self-control and nonactivism for both parents and their children.

90. *Foster, Julian, and Long, Durward. Introduction.

SETTING: 1967-68.

INSTITUTIONS: 1,251 colleges and universities (47% of which are in ACE sample of colleges and universities). Reponse rates highest for liberal arts colleges (61%) and teachers colleges (59%), lowest for junior colleges (35%), and miscellaneous, theological, professional, technical, and fine arts schools (30%); increase with size of I. 515 I's reported some protest.

METHODS: Presidents completed questionnaire on occurrence, type, and extent of protest, issues, tactics and responses. Data analyzed in 2 X 2 tables, usually controlling for some I variable.

RESULTS: See Long 1970, Foster and Long 1970, Long and Foster 1970, Hassenger 1970.

COMMENTS: Despite rudimentary data analyses, valuable data, generally congruent with other recent I studies.

91. ____. 1970. "The Dynamics of Institutional Response." In Foster, Julian, and Long, Durward, eds. 1970. PROTEST! STUDENT ACTIVISM IN AMERICA. New York: William Morrow, pp. 419-46.

SETTING, SUBJECTS, AND METHODS: See Foster and Long Intro.

RESULTS: Prior to protests, most I's indicated discussions of issues; 14% had no discussions. 304 I's reported knowledge that protest was to occur; 96 I's were unaware. Protests often triggered by acts of the administration. Issuing statements used by 26% of the administrations (6% supportive of tactics; 26% critical of issues; 28% supportive of issues). 54 I's gave specific warnings to protesters, 195 issued general warnings (judged least effective), 38 called local or city police, 4 called state police. Injuries most often involved students resisting arrest or expulsion (11 I's) and police (9 I's). Counterprotesters sometimes used by administration. 58 I's brought civil charges or inflicted on-campus penalties. Harsh punishment was most successful in private, conservative residential I's. During protests, 54% of I's took initiative in negotiating with students. More study groups appointed before protest than after, but 218 policy changes reported after protests. Most common concession was establishment of black-ethnic studies. Protests associated with prior institutionalized student power. Small minority felt protests hurt the administration or the I, or damaged relations with community.

COMMENTS: Largely descriptive account with emphasis on administrative strategies for dealing with protests.

92. Frank, J.D., and Nash, E.H. 1965. "Commitment to Peace Work: A Preliminary Study of Determinants and Sustainers of Behavior Change." AMERICAN JOURNAL OF ORTHOPSYCHIATRY 35 (January):106-119.

SETTING: 1963, workers in peace movement.

SUBJECTS: Ss solicited through liberal magazines explicitly seeking individuals who became active in peace movement after "critical episode." 92 Ss, 20% under age 25, 5% over age 55.

METHODS: Open-ended questionnaire focused on determining characteristics of "critical episode."

RESULTS: Highly educated, professional, established Ss, 17% devote most or all of their time to peace work; 37% no religion, 30% Unitarian or Quaker; predominantly nonconformist; liberal domestically and internationally; self-doubting; 40% have undergone psychotherapy; 76% describe their families as atypical; many report early history of nonconformity.

"Sensitizing experiences" detached Ss from former reference groups, often involve intense emotional confrontation with threat of thermonuclear war. Fear and anger reported at time of "crucial episode," but also increase in positive feelings upon entering peace work, heightened self-esteem, conviction of rightness, reduction of unpleasant feelings, desire for new information, and increased involvement with other issues like race relations, poverty, etc.

COMMENTS: See also Frank and Schonfield 1967. A self-selected sample of older respondents that precludes generalizations about the general role of "critical incidents" as catalysts for activism. Note pattern on long-standing nonconformity, self-doubt (high % psychotherapy). Contributes to understanding one process by which individuals become activated.

93. *____ . and Schonfield, J. 1967. "Commitment to Peace Work II: A Closer Look at Determinants." AMERICAN JOURNAL OF ORTHOPSYCHIATRY 37 (January):112-119.

SETTING, SUBJECTS, AND METHODS: See Frank and Nash 1965. A more quantified analysis of determinants of change toward peace work, degree of attitude change, and duration of activity change.

RESULTS: Women report influencing agent more often personal, men more often impersonal. Parents concerned over the welfare of minor children and convinced of futility of civil defense are most sensitive to change. Degree of attitude change related to youth (Ss under 25 most changed, though their families were more opposed than families of older Ss). Extent of attitude change is related to reported intensity of emotion at time of crucial incident and to changing friends thereafter. Persistence of increased activity is related to support by family, regardless of age (56% of Ss whose families opposed activity reduced or dropped it) and, for males only, to shift in friends.

COMMENTS: See Frank and Nash 1963. Study relevant to an understanding of the process of activation. Persistence of activity change (retrospectively) is related to support by family and (for men only) to change of friendships following critical episode.

94. Freeman, J.L. 1969. "Parents It's Not *All* Your Fault, but . . . " JOURNAL OF PERSONALITY 31:812-817.

SETTING: Spring 1968, Vanderbilt University.

SUBJECTS: 10% sample of undergraduates and graduate students, N = 328 (?%), N males = 232.

METHODS: Questionnaire examining Ss' political attitudes, opinions, activities, family and educational background. Report uses S's "degree of political interest" and "degree of activism" (demonstrator/nondemonstrator) as dependent variable.

RESULTS: For male Ss only, political interest and activism are related to amount of reported home political discussion. For both sexes, high political interest is associated with parental liberalism, activism is related to parental liberalism on civil rights and, to a lesser extent, on economic issues.

COMMENTS: A brief report that supports political socialization hypothesis. Author's view that "women get their politics from men" while men get theirs from their families is not supported by other studies.

95. Gales, K.E. 1966. "A Campus Revolution." BRITISH JOURNAL OF SOCIOLOGY 17 (March):1-19.

SETTING: March 1965, University of California at Berkeley.

SUBJECTS: Representative sample of graduates and undergraduates, N = 439 (83%).

METHODS: 1/2 hour structured interview, conducted by students, on attitudes toward FSM, socioeconomic, political and religious background, political ideology, etc. Approval/disapproval of FSM used as major dependent variable. Many questions indentical to those used by Somers 1965.

RESULTS: Retrospective questions show increase in approval of FSM and polarization as measured by more extreme responses. FSM support associated with nonfreshmen status, social science, physical science or humanities major (vs. business administration, engineering, or architecture), high GPA (checked on college records), independent living arrangements (vs. fraternity), agnostic or Jewish (vs. Protestant) religion, favoring permitting Communists to teach in public schools. Little relationship between family SES and FSM support, but extremely high and extremely low SES students tend to favor FSM. FSM support associated with paternal religion Jewish, political party liberal Democrat, political agreement and frequent political discussion with parents; but disagreement with parents on religion and intellectual ideas slightly associated with FSM approval. FSM support associated with generally liberal or left political attitudes, but unrelated with dissatisfaction with education at Berkeley.

COMMENTS: Essentially a follow-up and replication of Somers 1965. Note polarization of attitudes, trend to curvilinear relationship between FSM support and family SES, absence of relationship between FSM support and educational dissatisfaction.

96. *Gamson, Z.F.; Goodman, J.; and Gurin, G. 1967. "Radicals, Moderates and Bystanders during a University Protest." Paper read at American Sociological Association, August 1967, San Francisco. 11 pp. + App.

SETTING, SUBJECTS, AND METHODS: See Gurin 1971, Study 3. Within each of 3 activity levels, stable and increased interest groups distinguished: stable means past interest in student control of university, increased interest means little previous interest. 6 final groups: increased interest bystanders, N = 25, stable bystanders, N = 16, increased interest moderates, N = 40, stable moderates, N = 17, increased interest activists, N = 26, stable activists, N = 27. Data reported in tabular form for each of 6 groups. Results presented largely in 18 tables, mostly uninterpreted.

RESULTS: See Gurin 1971, Study 3. Activists are antivocational, high GPA, high intellectualism and academic achievement, social science majors, likely to have Jewish and Democratic parents. Moderates disproportionately humanities majors. Bystanders most often science-math majors, least involved in activism-supporting subcultures, generally isolated.

Stable activists are characterized by absence of obstacles that might prevent them from acting on their beliefs. Increased interest (vs. stable) activists seem more conflicted, less at home with themselves, more involved in personal identity questions, most likely of all S groups to report crises in college, to have considered dropping out, to have used counseling service. Moderates face conflict between family background and impact of university and national-international events, more often from Protestant, Republican backgrounds, report major differences with parents. Increased interest bystanders most uninvolved, anti-student-power, seniors, seem to have a temporary interest in passing events. Stable bystanders show discontinuity with past, lack of social support for activism at university, closed, tense, rigid, anxious, quiet personalities.

Authors argue that, with student power attitudes held constant, continuity with past, social support, and open flexible personality predicts stable activism; conflict with self, peers and parents decreases activism.

COMMENTS: Enormously rich data source, barely scratched. Multivariate statistics and comparisons with antistudent-power Ss would be useful. Study indicates that with ideology held constant, personal conflict and familial discontinuity is an obstacle to activism; for many Ss, psychological, social, and familial conflict is a consequence of activism.

97. Gastwirth, Donald. 1965. "Why Students Protest." Unpublished student paper, Department of Psychology, Yale University.

SETTING: 1964, Yale University, after demonstration protesting nonpromotion of popular philosophy professor.

SUBJECTS: Leaders, followers, and nonparticipants in demonstration.

METHODS: Interviews with all Ss focusing on attitudes toward issues, academic interests and performance, religious affiliations.

RESULTS: Leaders and highly involved students most often in philosophy or related fields, better students, more knowledgeable about issues, active in civil right and peace movements, more liberal; leaders disproportionately deacons of university chapel. (University chaplain noted for activism.)

COMMENTS: An early exploratory study broadly consistent with other early research on activists. Note influence of university chaplain.

98. **Gaylin, Willard. 1970. IN THE SERVICE OF THEIR COUNTRY: WAR RESISTERS IN PRISON. New York: Viking Press. 344 pp.

SETTING: 1968-69, 2 federal prisons.

SUBJECTS: 26 imprisoned war resisters (4 black), none of whom resisted for religious reasons. Of 22 whites, 10 Catholics, 12 Protestants.

METHODS: Intensive, prolonged nontherapeutic psychoanalytic interviews of each S, often over a period of 1 year or more.

RESULTS: Detailed presentations of interviews with 6 Ss, stressing reactions to prison, family background, relationship to interviewer, etc. Individual accounts largely uninterpreted. As a group, Ss show high degree of ego strength and disproportionately severe superego; are quiet, contemplative, introspective, nonhostile, highly service-oriented. 20/22 whites are eldest sons. Most striking psychological similarity in Ss is ambivalent, contradictory image of father, who was both loved, admired and respected yet perceived as a figure of neglect, abandonment, weakness or rejection. Ss identify with positive paternal image, are ready to lead, do for others, and sacrifice; are protective and understanding of the weak. Author stresses impact of uncertainties, brutalities and irrationalities of prison system upon resisters, almost unanimous conversion of Ss from nonviolence, serious questioning by Ss of efficacy of resistance.

COMMENTS: A humane, in-depth study of imprisoned war resisters that refutes many stereotypes and emphasizes psychological diversity of resistors.

99. Gelineau, Victor A., and Kantor, David. 1964. "Prosocial Commitment among College Students." JOURNAL OF SOCIAL ISSUES 20 (October): 112-30.

SETTING: 1960-61, Harvard University and Radcliffe College.

SUBJECTS: 300 student volunteers who worked directly with patients on chronic psychiatric wards, compared with nonvolunteers. Intensive interviews with 20 students in 1960, 28 in 1961.

METHODS: Instruments include sociological background information, reports of student motivation, AVL, occupational plans and preferences, general value orientations and selected psychological characteristics. Data presented in nonstatistical form with emphasis on types and theoretical discussion.

RESULTS: Compared to nonvolunteers, volunteers have same parental income, but more often from Eastern urban, highly educated professional families, disproportionately public school, disproportionately Jewish, less religious than parents who in turn are less religious than nonvolunteer parents, no differences in GPA. 1/3 of volunteers had prior interest in mental health profession. Fewer volunteers are considering business, law, or natural science. Volunteers place more emphasis in discussing future work on service, personal contact and creativity, less on independence, income, or prestige. Volunteers score lower on AVL economic, higher on theoretical and aesthetic. Five types of volunteers distinguished on the basis of interviews and questionnaires: (1) professional or career testing, (2) political-ideological, (3) social, (4) moral, (5) existential. "Political-ideological style" involves intellectualized moral indignation, rejection of professionalism and of Establishment, criticism of adult I's, constant pressure on hospital administration in favor of patients' rights, etc. "Existential" style primarily concerned with exploration of experience, self-concern, the need to experience patients and the hospital intensely, need for direct and "human" encounters with patients.

COMMENTS: An early description of mental hospital volunteers that is similar to later pictures of activists; political-ideological type is like later radicals, existential type like later hippies.

100. *Geller, Jesse D., and Howard, Gary. 1969. "Student Activism and the War in Vietnam." Paper read at American Psychological Association, September 1969, Washington, D.C. 56 pp. Also appears as "Some Sociopsychological

Characteristics of Student Political Activists" in JOURNAL OF APPLIED SOCIAL PSYCHOLOGY, 2, no. 2 (April-June 1972): 114-37.

SETTING: Spring 1968, Yale University, after October 1967 circulation of draft refusal pledge.

SUBJECTS: Undergraduate signers of a draft-refusal pledge contacted, N = 38 (74%); compared with random undergraduate nonsigners, N = 39 (69%).

METHODS: Data on socioeconomic background, SAT and GPA, activism index (16 different sociopolitical activities), political self-label, Vietnam Opinion Survey (34 pro- and antiwar statements), Vietnam Information Survey (34-item measure of knowledge of Vietnam facts), I-E, D, Importance of Activities Questionnaire, Stein's Self-Description Questionnaire. Purposes of research concealed from Ss.

RESULTS: Compared to nonsigners, signers are more often older, social science and humanities (vs. natural sciences) majors, choose humanitarian-expressive occupations, active in social service and religious organizations, Jewish, high SES, high father's education, high general activism, antiwar, knowledgeable about Vietnam, radical, value love and sexual relationships, friendships, political and community activities; disvalue fraternity membership, good academic standing, extracurricular activities, high grades, dress conformity; married, engaged or going steady, describe selves as succorant, sentient, and nurturant, not deferent, achievement-oriented, counteractive, or playful. No differences found on year in college, type of secondary school, self-reported academic standing, SAT, high school class rank, predicted and actual GPA, extracurricular activities, political, artistic-intellectual and athletic interests, birth order, type of city, area of origin, parents' political party, D or I-E.

COMMENTS: A study of draft refusers at a selective college, notable for findings of greater activist stress on interpersonal intimacy, rejection of "Protestant ethic" and traditional male characteristics.

101. Gergen, K.J., and Gergen, M.K. 1970. "Higher Education: Missing in Action." Paper read at American Psychological Association, September 1970, Miami. 11 pp.

SETTING: Pre-May 1970, 40 randomly selected I's.

SUBJECTS: 1200 faculty members, 60 college and university presidents, 5,000 Ss of whom 42% had been engaged in antiwar protests.

METHODS: Questionnaire involving demographic characteristics, educational setting, Ss' attitudes on war and related issues, definition of "key issues" facing the country, and involvement in various forms of protest. Report includes description of Ss' reports of impact of Vietnam war on them, description of antiwar protesters (presented without comparative data), and stepwise multiple regression on participation in antiwar demonstrations, all other variables apparently allowed to enter equation in order of decreasing weights.

RESULTS: Effects of war (based on student and faculty reports): influenced Ss to disengage themselves from higher education, produced widespread fragmentation and intergroup hostility within college community; lowered faith in system of higher education; is detrimental to Ss' mental and emotional welfare.

Antiwar protesters tend to be male, white, high parental education, high SES, 12% Jewish, 29% no religion, 50% uncommitted to 2-party system, 45% New England college, disproportionately from moderately to very selective colleges, 70% B average or better, 70% plan post-BA studies, 50% plan Ph.D., 40% social sciences, 25% humanities, 15% natural sciences, 49% advocate immediate unilateral withdrawal.

Multiple classification analysis on subsample of 2582 Ss. Predictors of antiwar activism in final equation (beta weights): previously demonstrated for civil rights (0.27); opposition to war (0.20); dislike of Nixon (0.16); key issue is morality of war (0.11); white (0.10); high degree aspiration (0.60); low importance attributed to success of war (0.06); attend nonsectarian school (0.60); etc. Regression analysis produced no relationship with religion, political party, father's education, sex, self-reported GPA, major, year in school, school size, and selectivity, sex composition of school. Multiple regression with opposition to war as dependent variable: both religion and political party account for significant variance, with Jews and nonreligious, Democrats, Independents, and radicals more opposed.

COMMENTS: Important study with reliable data from large sample at time of intense antiwar feeling. Report does not make clear whether variables were allowed to enter regression equation in order of highest correlation. If so, then the surprising finding that demographic variables like religion, parents' social status, parents' political beliefs, and school selectivity are irrelevant to protests may be the result of previous control for highly correlated behavioral and attitudinal variables. In the absence of a clearer description of statistical procedures, the study's findings cannot be clearly interpreted.

102. *Gold, Alice R.; Friedman, Lucy N.; and Christie, Richard. 1971. "The Anatomy of Revolutionists." JOURNAL OF APPLIED SOCIAL PSYCHOLOGY 1, no. 1 (January):26-43.

SETTING: Fall 1968, fall 1969, Columbia College, New York University.

SUBJECTS: Group 1: 145 members of introductory psychology class mostly sophomores and activists, tested in early spring 1968. Eighteen percent later arrested in building occupation, N = 26, vs. 19% of Columbia College. Group 2: 153 Columbia freshmen tested in fall 1968. See Christie et al. 1969. New Left radicals may have been underrepresented. Retested in fall 1969. Group 3: Introductory psychology class at Columbia College, tested April 1969, N = 220. Group 4: Introductory psychology students at Washington Square Campus of NYU, tested April 1969, N = 404.

METHODS AND RESULTS: Group 1: Given traditional moralism scale (from F-scale), Machiavellian tactics (duplicity), Machiavellian cynicism (distrust), and negative view of the world scale. Comparisons between arrestees and nonarrestees. Ss extremely high on traditional moralism not arrested (significant); arrestees lower on Machiavellian tactics, higher on Machiavellian cynicism (trend). Group 2: Divided into 3 types by self-reports of extracurricular sociopolitical activities: none (no activity, N = 53); passive (signing petitions, donating money, tutoring, N = 36); active (participating in demonstrations, marches, antiwar organizing, etc., N = 40). Ss given scales administered to Group 1 plus New Left scale. Factor analysis of items yielded 5 varimax factors: New Left philosophy, revolutionary tactics, Machiavellian tactics, Machiavellian cynicism, traditional moralism. Actives significantly higher than passives and none on New Left philosophy, revolutionary tactics, and Machiavellian cynicism; lower on Machiavellian tactics and traditional moralism. Only New Left scale differentiates passives from none. Retesting of Group 2 in fall 1969 shows general increase on revolutionary tactics scores, strongly correlated with increased activism. Groups 3 and 4: Classification and scales administered as with Group 2. Actives higher on New Left philosophy, revolutionary tactics. Discrepancy score of Machiavellian cynicism minus Machiavellian tactics strongly related to activism. When groups were "purified" by analysis of preferred presidential candidates, relationship of activism with Machiavellian cynicism minus Machiavellian tactics becomes more marked. Traditional moralism negatively related to activism in all groups.

Authors conclude that radical activism requires absence of traditional moralism, New Left philosophy, Machiavellian cynicism, and repudiation of Machiavellian tactics. Whether activity ensues then depends upon belief in revolutionary tactics.

COMMENTS: A valuable recent study clearly distinguishing separate attitudinal dimensions that are related to behavioral activism. Note key role attributed to belief in revolutionary tactics, and differentiation of 2 components of Mach scale: tendency for activists to be high on distrust-cynicism but low on approval of duplicity.

103. Goldsmid, Paula. 1967. "Dimensions of Political Ideology: Student Activists and Their Parents. M.A. thesis, Department of Sociology, University of Chicago. 52 pp.

104. ____. 1972. "Intergenerational Transmission of Political Attitudes: The Effects of Conflict and Exposure to Politics." Ph.D. dissertation, University of Chicago.

105. Goldsmith, Jeff C. 1971. "Collective Behavior in an Academic Community: A Case Study." Bachelor's thesis, Reed College. 24 pp. + App.

SETTING: 196(?), Reed College, after tuition boycott to protest non-reappointment of certain younger faculty members.

SUBJECTS: Random sample of Reed College freshmen, N = 154 (?%).

METHODS: Ss divided into 3 groups: withdrawals (from college, N = 15), boycotters (who did not register, N = 58), and registered freshmen (N = 81). OPI Scale scores for these Ss gathered 3 months earlier. Data presented only in graph form. Largely an interpretative-sociological-historical account of changes in the Reed College community as a backdrop and cause for boycott.

RESULTS: Compared with students who did not boycott, boycotters are significantly higher on OPI Scales measuring theoretical orientation, autonomy, religious liberalism; lower on response bias. Also trend for boycotters to be higher on thinking introversion, aestheticism, and complexity.

COMMENTS: Incomplete presentation of data makes evaluation of study difficult. OPI results parallel those reported in earlier studies at Berkeley.

106. *Goodman, J. 1968. "Alienation and Commitment in Contemporary America: Speculations from a Study of Student Activists at the University

of Michigan." Unpublished paper, Department of Sociology, University of Chicago, 107 pp.

SETTING, SUBJECTS, AND METHODS: See Gurin 1971, Study 3, Gamson et al. 1967. Ss divided into 2 categories: activists, N = 46 (25%), who sat-in and took part in at least 1 other event during UM sit-in; others, N = 136 (75%). Male activists further divided into 3 groups: stable activists, N = 12; activated activists, N = 15; nonparticipants, N = 25.

RESULTS: Differences between 3 groups unrelated to SES, parental liberalism, permissiveness, and sociopolitical involvement. Stable activists have lowest parental education and income, stable and activated activists have more nonreligious and urban parents. Stable activists' families not usually liberal or humanitarian but most well read. Stable activists closer to mother than father, both parents permissive, both parents least religious. In freshman data, stable activists report high theoretical, aesthetic, and social concerns, high conflict with parents over life values (chronic with mothers and increasing with fathers), many high school conflicts with parents and others, etc. Activated activists are more attached to mothers, report less past conflict, but increasing present conflict with family. Nonparticipants began college with conventional backgrounds and aspirations, but somewhat greater awareness, intellectuality and commitment to social values than typical students. By senior year, they show less self-confidence, more self-criticism, more political liberalism, greater unconventionality, and more value change. In general, nonparticipant group shows greater change and ongoing conflict.

Author interprets activism in general as involving continuity only with regard to "basic values" of family; discontinuity present in both stable activists and activated activist groups, who start from parents' values, but go well beyond them to a more active and radical position.

COMMENTS: Thoughtful analysis on a tiny subsample of University of Michigan seniors. Study useful in differentiating between subtypes *within* activist group. Good discussion of differing processes of activation and radicalization.

107. Gore, P.M., and Rotter, J.B. 1963. "A Personality Correlate of Social Action." JOURNAL OF PERSONALITY 31:58-64.

SETTING: 1962 (?), black college in Florida.

SUBJECTS: Ss in introductory psychology course, N = 116, males = 62.

METHODS: Measures included I-E, Marlowe-Crowne Social Desirability Scale, measures of SES and religious preference. Four weeks after initial testing, Ss asked to indicate interest in civil rights rally, signing petition calling for immediate integration of all Florida facilities, joining silent march through capital for immediate integration, or joining Freedom Riders group. Items assumed to involve increasing risk; each S assigned to category of highest risk.

RESULTS: Significant relationship between internal control and willingness to commit self to risky social action. Nonsignificant trend relating high social desirability to low commitment to social action. Both high and low risk-taking are associated (trend) with low SES.

COMMENTS: Definition of "highest risk activities" questionable. Generalizability limited.

108. **Gottleib, David; Gold, Carol Hancock; Baker, Keith; and Bellevita, Christopher. 1971. "VISTA and Its Volunteers." Office of Educational Opportunity. Project B99-4902, Pennsylvania State University. 169 pp.

SETTING: Data collected in 1970-71 from VISTA volunteers and no-shows of 1965-69.

SUBJECTS: Questionnaire sent to 10,801 former VISTA volunteers from 1965-69; and to 12,209 "no-shows" (persons accepted for VISTA who did not finally enlist). N = 3,878 (36%) volunteers; N = 4,053 (33%) no-shows. Return rate increases with recency of service.

METHODS: Lengthy questionnaire includes demographic data, description of VISTA work, attitudinal items, evaluations of VISTA work, motivations for involvement in VISTA, assessment of impact of VISTA, current activities, future plans, specific attitudes toward VISTA. Data presented in tabular form without tests of significance, infrequent comparisons between volunteers and no-shows, no correlational analysis, no grouping of items or Ss apart from volunteer/no-show distinction. No study of nonrespondents. Essentially a descriptive study with emphasis on policy recommendations for future VISTA planning.

RESULTS: Demographic data: few differences between volunteers and no-shows. Volunteers' modal age 21-22, fewer Protestants (more Jews and others) than in general student population, low religiosity, almost entirely white caucasians, 59% single (especially males), 10% had less than college education, most had high status parental occupations, modal parental income about $12,000, about half from cities of $> 250,000$ (including suburbs), disproportionately liberal arts and social science majors. After VISTA, ex-volunteers and no-shows become students or are in BA and post-BA occupations. Majority plan to get or have post-BA education. Volunteers and no-shows both shift from liberal arts to law, medicine, and education. Compared to no-shows, volunteers report earning capacity has become less important. No-shows are as involved in social change programs as are ex-volunteers, but ex-volunteers head toward more altruistic and nonmaterialistic careers.

Major motivations of volunteers involve doing meaningful and relevant work, helping poor, helping others, fighting social injustice, doing useful work while making life decisions. Youthfulness of volunteers associated with emphasis on meaningful and relevant work motivations, helping poor, and doing useful work while making life decisions, testing courage of convictions, "getting away from what I was doing," and "giving myself a chance to mature." Most important reasons for leaving VISTA involved returning to school, personal-family obligations, discouragement and frustration, natural end to assignment. More recent volunteers less often left to return to school. Discouragement and frustration related to brevity and to recency of service. Seventy-six percent believe VISTA helped fulfill need for relevant involvement, but % declines with recency and brevity of service, and with youth. Older, longer, and earlier volunteers report greatest impact on local area and on society. More recent volunteers are more activistic, less patient with traditional I processes, less accepting of institutional restraints, more critical of VISTA.

Current attitudes and values: younger, male, and more recent volunteers are most radical, alienated and bitter, as reflected, e.g., in attitudes toward government-sponsored social change programs, where 59% of 1969 volunteers are suspicious, 49% of under 20 male volunteers. Percent of volunteers who consider selves "revolutionaries" increases from 14% in 1965 cohort to 22% in 1969; % who report "being radicalized" up from 20% in 1965 to 33% in 1969. "Revolutionary" and "being radicalized" associated with youth and maleness. More than half of volunteers say they now feel more disenchanted with American society than before VISTA. Volunteers much more critical of VISTA than no-shows.

Politicization: clear trend from 1965-69 for both no-shows and volunteers to enter VISTA progressively more liberal or radical, less conservative or moderate. Pre-VISTA/post-VISTA increments in % labelling self "radical left" for volunteers by year: 1965, 13%; 1966, 16%; 1967, 13%; 1968, 21%; 1969, 26%. For no-shows, "radical left" increments are lower: 1965, 9%; 1966, 10%; 1967, 14%; 1968, 12%; 1969, 11%. Data indicate that VISTA experience is radicalizing, regardless of initial political position; and across time, increasingly more radicalizing. Regardless of age, cohort, or sex, volunteers are more likely than no-shows to report changes to the left in political attitudes and values. With age and sex controlled, volunteers much more likely to report selves now "revolutionaries" than no-shows.

Authors stress dangers of "overselling" VISTA, need to make explicit the political constraints and realities within which VISTA operates, dangers of romanticization of program; emphasize the "marked shift in the attitudes, values, and expectations of many American youths . . . toward activism, liberalism, pluralism, and politicization"; discourage a more professional orientation in VISTA as a way to prevent trouble; warn against VISTA becoming a youth-pacification agency.

COMMENTS: A descriptive study with invaluable and mostly unanalyzed data on overall shifts in student attitudes from 1965-69, along with specific demonstration of "radicalizing" impact of work with VISTA.

109. Graham, George Jr., and Pride, Richard A. 1971. "Styles of Political Participation: Want Conversion and Political Support among Adults and Students in a Metropolitan Community." Paper read at American Political Science Association, September 1971, Chicago. 43 pp.

SETTING: Late spring 1970, Nashville-Davidson County, Tennessee.

SUBJECTS: 11th grade Ss in stratified sample of 5 public and 2 private high schools, mean age 16.9, N = 558. In 180 families of Ss, adults over age 19 tested, mean age 42.6, N = 302.

METHODS: Questionnaire measures style of political participation (traditional, protest, mixed traditional and protest, ambivalent = uncodable or no participation), political attitudes, societal wants and political demands in 19 areas, conversion index (measuring positive responses on both societal needs and political demands), political attitudes, group memberships, etc. Ss are 50% traditional, 9% mixed, 7% protest, remainder ambivalent. Adults more traditional, rarely mixed or protest. Style of political participation is the major dependent variable in cross-tabulations; no tests of significance.

RESULTS: Compared to adults, Ss are more skeptical of democratic means, more supportive of individual rights, more distrustful of government authority, have similar societal wants (except for age-relevant items), less often convert societal wants to political demands. Among Ss, mixed style political participants are highest on individual rights, distrust of government, lowest on political conversion of societal wants, highest on change, citizens' duty, political efficacy, trust, lowest on futility, highest on group memberships, most involved in groups that talk politics and take issue stands. Protest Ss (50% black) low on individual rights, high on distrust of government authority, have few societal wants, low political conversion, low cynicism, trust, and group membership. Ambivalent-inactive Ss score low on individual rights, change, citizens' duty; highest on futility, low group membership. Data also reported for adults on all variables.

Authors argue that generational differences are mostly small, thus indirectly supporting family socialization hypothesis; suggest importance of group associations outside family in moving students away from adult commitment to democratic means; suggest that students press symbolic demands to which society does not respond, thus diminishing commitment to democratic means.

COMMENTS: A preliminary analysis of a rich data source that deserves much further examination. Results suggest distinctiveness of "mixed" political participation S group, which most resembles activists in college studies.

110. Graham, Robert H. 1968. "The Community of Scholars at the University of Wisconsin." Unpublished paper, University of Wisconsin. 61 pp. + App.

SETTING: December 1967, University of Wisconsin, Madison; after Dow Chemical demonstrations in October 1967.

SUBJECTS: Ss and faculty divided into left-wing Ss, N = 5, and faculty, N = 4, and right-wing Ss, N = 3, and faculty, N = 5.

METHODS: Personal interviews focusing on demographic factors, socio-politcal views, views on Vietnam, preferred political candidates, etc., views of the university and the Dow demonstration.

RESULTS: Presented largely in the form of quotations from interviews, especially about responses of each group to demonstration. Right-wing faculty members tend to have longer tenure at university, left-wing students and faculty members disproportionately Jewish.

COMMENTS: Numbers too small to permit generalization, but general findings are consistent with those of other researchers.

111. *Greene, D.L., and Winter, David G. 1971. "Motives, Involvement and Leadership among Black College Students." JOURNAL OF PERSONALITY, 39, no. 3 (September):319-32.

SETTING: Nov. 1969, Wesleyan University.

SUBJECTS: Paid black undergraduates recruited through Wesleyan Afro-American Society, N = 38.

METHODS: Ss tested in groups, asked to write stories to 4 TAT-type pictures. TAT pictures contained mostly black figures. TAT stories scored for achievement, affiliation, and power. Factor analysis of ratings of Ss by 3 knowledgeable members of Wesleyan Afro-American society produced 2 factors: (1) active within black community vs. willing to work within system; (2) pragmatic.

RESULTS: Ss high on Factor 1 score significantly lower on N affiliation. Compared to Ss from South, N = 17, Ss from North are roughly equivalent on SES, intact family, etc., on factor ratings and on need ratings, but Northern Ss show high correlation between Factor 1 and N power, while Southern Ss show high correlation between Factor 2 and both N achievement and N power. Ss who are leaders, influential or active in Black Repertory Theater score higher on N power than inactives. Authors conclude that militancy among Northern (but not Southern) blacks is associated with high N power.

COMMENT: Generalizability limited by small sample size, but approach deserves replication. Differences between blacks of Southern and Northern origin points to importance of socializing culture in determining how underlying motives are expressed in concrete sociopolitical attitudes and actions.

112. **Gurin, Gerald. 1971. "A Study of Students in a Multiversity." Office of Education, Project 5-0901, University of Michigan. 532 pp.

SETTING: 1962-67, University of Michigan.

SUBJECTS: 2 cohorts: all freshmen entering the University of Michigan in the fall of 1962 and of 1963 given 2-hour questionnaire during orientation week, N = 2250 each year (95%). In second freshman semester, 450 Ss in each cohort were given further questionnaires. Ss in 1962 cohort retested at the end of sophomore and senior year, N = 1900 (78%); Ss in 1963 cohort retested at the end of senior year. In each cohort, intensive interviews with approximately 200 students at the second semester of their freshman year.

METHODS: Data include OPI, background questions, attitudes toward education, college experiences, life-goals, political attitudes and interests, identity characteristics, major value concerns, occupational plans, family relationships, satisfaction with college, impact of college, academic experiences, relationships with faculty, peers, extracurricular activities, etc. Scales for conservatism, liberalism, attitudes toward civil liberties, civil rights, foreign affairs, interest in political action, etc. Three relevant studies are reported:

1. Activism during fall 1966 protest over university compliance with HUAC request for membership lists of student radical groups, opposition of some faculty members to grading if university cooperates with selective service system, and nonviolent sit-ins at the administration building. Four categories: no involvement, voted in referendum only, voted in referendum and attended 1 meeting only, high involvement.
2. Comparison of members of 2 campus political groups with random sample: "radical" group [SDS?] (highly militant, favored direct action, played leading role in 1966 protest, N = 38), "moderate" group (primarily involved in city politics, working for social change through established political parties, played a leading role in 1966 student coalition, N = 33), random sample (1962-63 cohort members in school in 1966 who did not belong to the 2 criterion groups, N = 745).
3. Analysis of Ss in study 2 who had strong antiadministration attitudes and high interest in student power, N = 151, divided into 3 groups: nonactivists (no protest involvement or referendum voting only, N = 41); moderates (attended teach-ins or rallies, N = 57); activists (engaged in direct action, N = 53).

Data presented largely in analyses of variance separately by sex.

RESULTS: Study 1. Activism is associated with support of residential college (men), identification with nonconformist (vs. vocational) subculture, rejection of narrow academic orientation, OPI complexity, aestheticism, thinking introversion, social maturity, religious liberalism, theoretical orientation (women); low emphasis on external rewards, rejection of professionalism (men), negative attitude toward fraternities and sororities (but no difference in membership), more group involvement and social activity, nontraditional self-concept, political leftism, high political interest, opposition to Vietnam war, political affiliation democratic or radical; identity-seeking definition of college goals, OPI impulse expression (for men, relationship is curvilinear). Male activism is unrelated to closeness to parents or readiness to turn to them for advice, but is related to value and ideological conflicts with fathers. Women activists report most emotional estrangement from families. Activism unrelated to satisfaction with college, related to self-perception of personal change (men), increased political interest and liberalism, change in religious-sexual values (women), freshman to senior increases in OPI complexity, aestheticism, thinking introversion, social maturity and (women only:) theoretical orientation, religious liberalism, and impulse expression; social sciences and humanities major. Unlike women activists, men activists (and uninvolved Ss) find courses dull, uninteresting, and unimportant. Activists attach greater significance to faculty than do other students, but do not have personalized relationships with faculty members. Activists' friendships and extracurricular involvements are not distinctive. Activism does not reflect problems in friendship; activists are not especially sensitive to impersonality of multiversity, but support S power and control.

Study 2. As freshmen, future radicals are farther to the left politically (especially men), more strongly approve of sit-ins, less concerned than moderates with "community citizenship." Male radicals are less career-oriented and have less desire to be "famous for my work"; female radicals especially value intellectual and creative things; both sexes rate selves less practical. Male radicals, female radicals and female moderates have families with a high proportion of parents who hold advanced or professional degrees. Radical women place special emphasis on intellectuality, are less confident, more anxious, typically solitary, but radical men do not show this pattern. Among males, radicals and moderates do not differ in conflict with parents, except that radicals report less disagreement with mothers about vocational plans. Female radicals report more disagreement over religious beliefs. But all radicals report feeling less close to parents than other groups before coming to college, and female radicals are very estranged from fathers. Author's summary emphasizes differences between male and female radicals, with females highly intellectual, less self-confident, more anxious, reporting more family conflict.

Study 3. With positive attitudes toward student power and anti-administration attitudes held constant, virtually all findings concerning activists in study 2 are replicated. Activists of both sexes are most likely to have disagreements with parents around value issues, report feeling less close to their fathers.

COMMENTS: Three invaluable studies built upon a very solid data base.

113. *Gurin, Patricia. 1967. "Civil Rights Protest and Ideological Change." Paper read at American Psychological Association, September 1967. 13 pp.

SETTING: 1964-65, black college in Deep South; major student movement developed in college in 1964-65.

SUBJECTS: Freshmen tested at beginning and end of first year. Divided into 3 groups: activists (members of protest group or took part in all major events), moderates (took part in 1-2 major events), inactives (nonpartici-pants in college and during high school). N in each group = 60-70.

METHODS: Background information, questions concerning broad political ideologies and specific race-related ideologies.

RESULTS: As incoming freshmen, activists most opposed to civil liberties and academic freedom, most often approved militant racial tactics; moder-ates most often approved liberal reform methods. No pre- or postchanges related to activism on most general political ideology issues, but activists decrease support for defense spending and increase disarmament support. Change in race-related attitudes directly related to activism: activists espe-cially decreased placing blame for black problems on blacks, activists (male) increase support for collective (vs. individual) modes of resolving discrimina-tion, increase support for militant strategies; moderates increased support for liberal reform groups. Author emphasizes that impact of protest on ide-ology is largely limited to race-related issues; contrasts general liberalism of white activists with race-related concerns of black activists.

COMMENTS: A thoughtful study of the impact of demonstrations on black freshmen in 1964-65; note specificity of attitude change to racial attitudes.

114. **Haan, Norma. 1972. "Activism as Moral Protest: Moral Judgement of Hypothetical Moral Dilemmas and an Actual Situation of Civil Disobedi-ence." In Kohlberg, L., and Turiel, E., eds. 1972. THE DEVELOPMENT OF MORAL JUDGEMENT AND ACTION. New York: Holt, Rinehart, and Winston. 37 pp. + App.

SETTING, SUBJECTS, AND METHODS: See Haan et al. 1968, Haan and Block 1969a, 1969b. 290 UCB Ss given moral dilemma based on FSM situation. Responses coded according to Kohlberg moral reasoning stages. Comparisons of each S's moral reasoning in FSM situation and as measured by Kohlberg standard test. Three types identified: stable (same level on both, 36%), gain (higher level on FSM, 42%), and loss (lower level on FSM, 22%).

RESULTS: Overall, moral reasoning about FSM is at higher level than general moral reasoning. Gains most notable among FSM arrestees (vs.

random sample, conservative Republicans and Democrats) and among women. With Ss' political conservatism-radicalism and stage of moral reasoning controlled, characteristics of stable, gain, and loss Ss were analyzed separately by sex. Compared to change Ss, stable Ss of both sexes define selves as less influenced by interpersonal situations, see parents as more clear, calm, detached, and resolute. Gain males define selves as more critical, guilty, report greater disagreement and conflict with mother, greater distance-coldness-disagreement with father; loss males describe selves as more genuine, free, tolerant, had close, warm, very dependent relationships with parents. Compared to loss females, gain females more influenced by close friends, more genuine and sensitive, mothers supportive and considerate, fathers demanding and authoritative.

Gains in men suggest developmental disequilibrium, malaise, and conflicted relationships with parents. Gains in women are associated with positive view of self and parents. Loss in males is associated with positive self-view, and with highly protective, involved relationships with parents. Loss in women associated with view of self as controlled and proud, view of mothers as determined, disciplining, and powerful.

Author argues that stable moral reasoning is associated with an equilibriated, settled view of self and parents; stresses different meanings of moral reasoning gains for men and women; sees loss in level of moral reasoning on FSM as occurring in Ss ill-prepared to cope with authority-challenging, confused, intense situation. Brilliant discussion of implications of results for general theory of development.

COMMENTS: An outstanding study of shifts in the level of moral reasoning around the FSM crisis, generally supporting the "conflict" or "disequilibrium" view of development.

115. *_____ , and Block, Jeanne H. 1969a. "Further Studies in the Relationship between Activism and Morality I: The Protest of Pure and Mixed Moral Stages." Unpublished paper, Institute of Human Development, Berkeley. 10 pp. + App.

SETTING, SUBJECTS, AND METHODS: See Block et al. Intro., Haan et al. 1968. Paper analyzes moral reasoning data for all 889 Ss who could be reliably scored on Kohlberg's Moral Judgment Test. Data analysis includes pure types (57%), transitional types (2 adjacent stages, 37%) and disjunctive types (2 nonadjacent stages, 5%). Random samples at UCB and SFSC show no difference in modal moral classification: e.g., 65% males and 75% females are conventional. Modal male stage is 4 (law and order); modal female stage 3 (personal concordance).

RESULTS: Inclusion of mixed types does not modify relationships described in Haan et al. 1968 between moral reasoning and activism. Activists least likely to be conventional, most likely to be principled. Premoral types, though infrequent in population, more likely to be activists. Fifty percent of activists in mixed stage vs. 35% of nonactivists. Females are generally at lower stages; predominantly principled female activists more often show some conventional moral reasoning. Authors conclude activists show greater moral growth and transition.

COMMENTS: Paper extends and confirms Haan et al. 1968. Note finding that women's moral development is likely to be more conventional than men's.

115. ** ____ . 1969b. "Further Studies in the Relationship between Activism and Morality II: Analysis of Case Deviant with Respect to the Morality-Activism Relationship." Unpublished paper, Institute of Human Development, Berkeley. 15 pp. + App.

SETTING, SUBJECTS, AND METHODS: See Block et al. Intro., Haan et al. 1968. Ss regrouped on the basis of 2 distinctions: conventional vs. principled moral reasoning; activists (termed activists and dissenters in other papers) vs. nonactivists (previously termed constructivists, conventionalists, and inactives). Four groups result: principled activists, N = 60, principled nonactivists, N = 34, conventional activists, N = 36, and conventional nonactivists, N = 236. Haan et al. 1968 showed strong association between activism and principled moral judgment, nonactivism and conventional moral judgment. This study examines "deviant cases" (conventional activists and principled nonactivists) to sharpen understanding of activism-moral development relationship.

RESULTS: Compared to conventional nonactivists, conventional activists are more often social science majors, have independent living arrangements, were influenced by organized groups, have dropped out, are not fraternity or sorority members, are not influenced by parents, male's parents better educated, female's parents more often divorced, mothers more often worked. In general these Ss have greater exposure to the youth culture and unusual family backgrounds. Compared to principled activists, principled nonactivists have attended more colleges, are more often Peace Corps volunteers or SFSC transfers from apolitical colleges; female Ss attribute greater importance to their parents.

Compared to principled activists, conventional activists come from similar social milieu; males less often intend to teach, vocational goals less prestigeful, ascribe greatest influence to persons and groups of higher status; females attribute more influence to mothers and men, less to siblings. Principled nonactivists characterized by close, involved, and possibly entangled relationships with families; describe themselves as personally sensitive and reserved. Conventional activists see parents as indulgent and overinvolved; describe themselves as personally aggressive, invested in interpersonal relationships and approval.

Some Haan et al. 1968 conclusions must be revised: infrequent church attendance, aggression, parental encouragement of self-expression, and mother's liberalism characterize activists, not principled Ss. S's definition of most influential others depends on moral level; conventional Ss ascribe influence to those of higher status, principled to those of equal status. Authors conclude that principled moral reasoning is highly related to activism, but not sufficient. In addition, activism requires (1) environment that permits recognition of social injustice and makes protest possible; (2) context that exposes S to information about social injustice; (3) personal aggressiveness; (4) willingness to be involved with groups.

COMMENTS: An extremely important paper, both conceptually and methodologically. Analysis of cases that deviate from the moral judgment-activism correlation demonstrates effects of contextual, environmental, and personality factors.

117. **Haan, Norma; Smith, M. Brewster; and Block, Jeanne H. 1968. "Moral Reasoning of Young Adults: Political-Social Behavior, Family Backgrounds, and Personality Correlates." JOURNAL OF PERSONALITY AND SOCIAL PSYCHOLOGY 10:183-201.

SETTING, SUBJECTS, METHODS: See Block et al. Intro. Analysis includes only Ss classified on the Kohlberg Moral Judgment test into "pure" types, N = 510. Separate analyses by sex by 5 types of moral reasoning for all other data. Presentation focuses on general groupings of moral types.

RESULTS: Principled Ss report more frequent interruptions of college, off-campus, and independent housing, liberals or radicals, supported FSM, agnostic or atheistic, background Jewish or nonreligious, parents liberal, mothers better educated, less parental influence, more peer influence, high sociopolitical activity, especially protests. Male Ss describe selves as idealistic, and value qualities like perceptive, empathic, altruistic, rebellious, and inconventional. Male Ss' mothers teased, had conflicted relationship, fathers encouraged sons to take chances. Female Ss describe selves dysphorically:

guilty, doubting, restless, impulsive, etc. Female Ss' mothers were disappointed in daughters, talked about their sacrifices, did not comfort them. In general, principled Ss have developed autonomous sense of self, stress interpersonal responsiveness and expressiveness, have arrived at ego-syntonic, nonconformist political position, feel self-made, describe parents as actively involved, often conflict-producing, insisting on own rights and respecting children's needs. Dysphoric self-descriptions of women point to special problems in developing principled morality for women.

Conventional Ss less often interrupt college careers, more often live in adult-approved housing, are politically conservative, agree politically with conservative parents, oppose FSM, Protestant or Catholic, church attenders, mothers less educated than fathers. Male and female Ss report family harmony, strong parental influence, greater influence from elders than from peers, describe selves as conventional, practical, orderly, but not rebellious, idealistic, or individualistic. Men's ideals: practical, competitive, conventional, sociable; women's ideals: orderly, logical, responsible, competitive yet self-denying. Parental child-rearing practices reported as unconflicted, trusting, relatively undemanding but with firm, clear rules. Overall, these Ss have harmonious relationships with traditional I's and authorities, are insulated from conflicting values and political pressures; their parents used clear rules, punishments and rewards in the context of family harmony, personal competence and political inactivity.

Premoral Ss have sociological characteristics like principled Ss, but more from Jewish backgrounds, mothers better educated and liberal, fathers less educated and more conservative. Men intensely involved in protests and politics, women join many organizations but not active in them. Both men and women see themselves as rebellious, but rebellion is not ego-syntonic. Men describe selves as reserved, nonresponsive, creative, aloof, stubborn, etc.; their ideals are playful, free, but not altruistic. Men's relationships with fathers involved great anger and conflict, paternal pressure to make good impression, mistrust of son, suppression of filial initiative; men's mothers were detached, laissez faire, indulgent. Women describe themselves as stubborn, aloof, unaltruistic and unimpulsive; their ideals are not self-denying, free or empathic, but practical, stubborn, idealistic, and sensitive. Women's mothers described as highly positive, comforting, permissive, perhaps overinvolved; father's described as uninvolved and permissive. Both sexes defined selves as rebellious but wish they were less so, neither endorses need to take role of others and both are concerned with personal fulfillment—women pragmatic, men expressive. Their families discouraged responsibility and autonomy. Both men and women were probably overindulged: for the mother's convenience in men, and to enhance child's dependency in women. Comparison of highly principled and premoral males shows many similarities, but greater "ego-effectiveness" for principled Ss.

For men, indices of conflict with both parents highest for premoral Ss, lowest for conventional Ss. For women, conflict with both parents highest for principled Ss, lowest for mothers of premoral Ss, lowest for fathers of conventional Ss.

Study of FSM arrestees shows extremely strong curvilinear relationship between arrests and level of moral development. Of total Berkeley sample, arrestees = 55% of 13 instrumental relativists, 13% of 54 personal concordance, 9% of 91 law and order, 44% of 41 social contract and 80% of 15 individual principle Ss.

COMMENTS: An extremely important study. Curvilinear relationship between level of moral reasoning and FSM arrest explains most of the variance in FSM arrests, and is probably the most striking single finding in the entire activism literature. Authors conclude that moderate and open family conflict promotes morally principled youth, but that excessive family conflict probably inhibits moral development and/or produces moral regression.

118. Hassenger, Robert. 1970. "Protest and the Catholic Colleges." In Foster, Julian, and long, Durward, eds. 1970. PROTEST! STUDENT ACTIVISM IN AMERICA. New York: William Morrow, pp. 483-96.

SETTING, INSTITUTIONS, AND METHODS: See Foster and long, Intro. 196 Catholic I's, mostly liberal arts colleges, in Northeast or Midwest.

RESULTS: 47% of the I's reported protests (largely verbal) in 1967-68, usually the first protests to occur on campus. In 4/5 of demonstrations no violations occurred, in 1/5 violations only of university rules. Size of protests small, with only 5% involving > 100 Ss. In 1% of I's, expulsion or suspension resulted. Eighty-eight percent of I's reported students on some, 14% on most or all, university committees. At 1/3 of I's neither students nor faculty were influential in setting policies, at more than 1/3 S government rarely made requests related to I policies prior to 1967-68. 1/4 of the I's had newspapers which made frequent critical remarks about policy (vs. 1/3 in Protestant colleges and public I's and 2/5 in private secular schools). Little direct supervision of student newspapers reported. Major focus of protests was on-campus issues. Twelve percent of I's reported protests in opposition to the war, the draft, armed services, or Dow Chemical recruiting (lower % than at private and public colleges). Only 5% of Catholic schools had "black power" protests (vs. 14% in public I's and 9% in private secular schools). Author concludes that protests at Catholic I's are increasing and becoming more like protests elsewhere.

COMMENTS: Results support other research on protests, although censorship is reported elsewhere to be more rigid at Catholic campuses.

119. Haug, Marie R., and Sussman, Marvin B. 1971. "Working Class Students and Images of Social Change." Paper read at American Sociological Association, September 1971, Denver, 13 pp. + App.

SETTING: 1970-71, junior college and midwestern state university.

SUBJECTS: Ss are largely children of blue collar or service workers, many inner city blacks, N = 812. 53% female, 27% black, 66% under 20, 54% fathers manual workers, blue collar or service.

METHODS: Dependent variable is question concerning groups that "will be most important in bringing about meaningful social change in U.S." (working people, blacks, students, political leaders, intellectuals, etc.). Measures of SES and mobility aspirations.

RESULTS: Whites more often mention students, blacks mention blacks as change agents. For whites only, identification of students as change agents related to higher anticipated SES, identification of workers and blacks related to anticipated lower or white collar SES. Identification of students as change agents highest for Ss who perceive parents' social class as middle (vs. lower, working, upper and upper-middle); of workers highest for Ss who perceive parents as upper and upper-middle; of blacks highest for Ss who perceive parents as lower and working. Ss' mobility patterns unrelated to perceived change agents. Authors stress that identification of students as change agents is unaffected by S's SES, but is related to youth, white race, high occupational expectations.

COMMENTS: One of the only studies that involves a large working class student sample.

120. Heath, G.L. 1969. "Berkeley Protest: A Mass Movement?" UNIVERSITY COLLEGE QUARTERLY 15 (November):3-9.

SETTING: Fall 1965, University of California at Berkeley.

SUBJECTS: Students in undergraduate sociology class conducted interviews with random sample of 349 Ss drawn from total university population.

METHODS: Questionnaire measures belief in democracy, number of friends, political apathy, etc.

RESULTS: Belief in democracy is unrelated to membership in political groups, but is associated with having more friends. Social isolation not related to willingness to protest disapproved federal law. Politically non-apathetic students would protest disapproved federal law more often, generally through legal channels. Membership in political groups is related to interest in national politics, involvement in campus and off-campus organizations, high GPA, liberal or independent politics, belief that breaking unjust laws is consistent with American political tradition; and is unrelated to congenial relationships with parents, class in college, and number of semesters at Berkeley. Militants show no special dissatisfaction with educational process. Protest involvement is associated to opposition to Vietnam war; war opposition is associated with frequent disagreement with government policy, support for civil disobedience, unfavorable image of South Vietnam government, disbelief in American government information, conviction of imperviousness of U.S. government officials.

COMMENTS: Lacking a clearer presentation of methods and results, study is difficult to evaluate.

121. *Heckman, D.M. 1970. "World Views and Students Who Take Risk for Ethical Conviction." Ph.D. dissertation, Graduate Technological Union, University of California at Berkeley. 149 pp.

SETTING: 1967-68, San Francisco area.

SUBJECTS: Male draft resisters and nonresisters at San Francisco Theological Seminary, N = 24, supplemented by interviews with other resisters largely from San Francisco area (total N = 40). Seminarians largely Presbyterian.

METHODS: Unstructured interviews, participant observation. Some interviews rated on religious beliefs, family relationships, previous religious and sociopolitical experiences, etc. N's not given, no significance tests.

RESULTS: Largely clinical account, focuses on question, Why do people take risks in the name of ethical convictions? Compared with nonresisters, resisters report more direct or "dialogic" relationship with parents, ministers or teachers, especially when the latter had sociopolitical concerns; more cultural contact with circumstances different from their own, more often initiated behavior to alleviate others' hardships, assume that ultimate Reality and Value are personal, are more uncertain about their personal futures. Mothers but not all fathers backed resisters, who felt no opposition to parents. Close male models (not necessarily parents) were crucial in adolescence, especially college. Resisters assume a personal-transactional relationship to "powers that be" rather than an impersonal, fated, manipulated relationship. Percentage experiencing "trans-cultural exposures" for resisters vs. nonresisters in precollege years, 38% vs. 4%; in college years, 85% vs. 29%; postcollege, 42% vs. 21%.

COMMENTS: Intellectually and conceptually interesting study of a rather undefined sample of religious war resisters, largely impressionistic and interpretive. Note resister's close contact with principled sociopolitically-oriented teachers; high incidence of cross-cultural exposure, and stress upon the "personal" nature of their relationships to the "powers that be."

122. Heist, Paul. 1965. "Intellect and Commitment: The Faces of Discontent." In Knorr, Owen A., and Minter, W. John, eds. 1965. ORDER AND FREEDOM ON THE CAMPUS. Boulder, Colorado: Western Interstate Commission for Higher Education, pp. 61-69.

SETTING: Feb. 1965, University of California at Berkeley.

SUBJECTS: Of 800 FSM arrestees, 33% responded; low response rate related to pending criminal charges and chain telephone call warning arrestees not to participate. Further samples include volunteers nominated by arrestee Ss, N = 58, arrested = 20; 1965 random UCB senior sample, N = 92 or 107; 1963 UCB seniors, N = 340; fall 1959 UCB freshmen, N = 2500.

METHODS: Data include psychosocial backgrounds, OPI. The several samples responses are cross-tabulated in presenting results; in some tables, arrestees and volunteer arrestees are grouped. Comparisons with Watts and Whittaker 1966a.

RESULTS: Arrestees overrepresented in social sciences and humanities, underrepresented in business and engineering. FSM volunteers and arrestees identical on most variables. Compared with 1965 Berkeley senior sample, arrestees and/or volunteers score > 6 points higher (standard scores) on OPI scales measuring thinking introversion, theoretical orientation, aestheticism, complexity (very large difference), autonomy, religious liberalism, and impulse expression; no differences on schizoid functioning, social introversion, lack of anxiety or response bias. On derived intellectual disposition measures, arrestees show broad, diverse interests with literary, aesthetic, symbolic or abstract perspectives. FSM trend toward higher cumulative GPA, significantly higher senior grades.

COMMENTS: The many samples used make this study difficult to interpret and evaluate. Its findings, however, are consistent with other FSM studies.

123. ____. 1966. "The Dynamics of Student Discontent and Protest." Paper read at American Psychological Association, September 1966, New York, 21 pp. + App.

SETTING: See Heist 1965. New data gathered in Bay Area in summer 1965, summer 1966, and in fall 1965 on Berkeley, Davis, Santa Barbara, and Los Angeles Campuses of University of California.

SUBJECTS: See Heist 1965. Samples of all incoming freshmen were tested at Davis, Santa Barbara, and LA Campuses of U of C. Of 39 nonrespondents in February 1965 FSM sample, 20 were interviewed in summer 1965. Seventy Ss interviewed in summer 1966, half from February 1965 sample of FSM arrestees respondents, half from nonarrested FSM participants.

METHODS: See Heist 1965. OPI scores used in analyzing data; sociopolitical and other activities studied in samples from summer 1965 and 1966.

RESULTS: See Heist 1965. Significant differences found on OPI scales measuring thinking introversion, theoretical orientation, complexity, autonomy, religious liberalism, impulse expression, and derived measures of intellectual disposition, with FSM arrestees highest, then FSM-supporting seniors, then 1965 senior sample, and 1959 freshmen lowest. OPI-derived ratings of emotional disturbance indicate that 39% of FSM senior arrestees and volunteers show minimal disturbance as compared to 30% of 1965 seniors. Freshmen at 3 non-Berkeley UC campuses who are "favorable and supportive" of FSM compared with freshmen who oppose FSM, show same OPI patterns as FSM arrestees and supporters. (See Mock and Heist 1969.)

Followups in summer 1965 and 1966 suggest increased sociopolitical activity for FSM Ss, who place strong emphasis on creative activities. Fifty-eight percent FSM arrestees (vs. 48% 1965 UCB seniors) indicate "strong attachment" to UCB.

COMMENTS: An amplification and extension of Heist 1965. Despite sampling problems, the study's results are consistent with other FSM studies.

Follow-up indicates increased political activity among FSM arrestees 1 1/2 years later.

124. Hodgkinson, H. 1970. "Student Protest—An Institutional and National Profile." THE RECORD 71 (Spring):537-55.

SETTING: 1968-69.

INSTITUTIONS: 1230 I's in Carnegie Commission study of Institutions in Transition.

METHODS: 355 I's report increases in protest. Comparisons involve location, I characteristics, size, selectivity, quality (% faculty Ph.Ds), type of control, highest degree awarded, student and faculty characteristics.

RESULTS: Greatest protest increases reported in Far West, MId-East, and Great Lakes (vs. Southwest, Southeast); higher population density in states reporting increases. Protest increases unrelated to public-private control or to age of I, related to highest degree awarded, size (relationship persists when public-private and region are controlled). No evidence of "critical mass" related to sudden jump in % reporting protest increase. Protest increases most common in I's that report recent changes toward greater student heterogeneity (in age, ethnicity, SES, out-of-state students and transfers), increased student involvement in policy decisions and volunteer programs, decreased authority of central campus administration, decreased control over students, increased underground films and publications, greater faculty involvement in research (vs. teaching), decreased faculty commitment to or increased opposition to I, increased faculty political involvement, and increased federal support. Excellent discussion of association between size and student protest.

COMMENTS: A study of I characteristics and protest, with very good interpretation of findings.

125. Hyman, Herbert H.; Wright, Charles R.; and Hopkins, Terrence K. 1962. APPLICATION OF METHODS OF EVALUATION: FOUR STUDIES OF THE ENCAMPMENT FOR CITIZENSHIP. Berkeley: University of California Press.

126. Jackson, John S. III. 1971a. "Alienation and Black Political Participation." Paper read at Midwest Political Science Association, April 1971, Chicago. 59 pp.

SETTING: Winter 1968-spring 1969.

SUBJECTS: Black college students at Fisk University, N = 150; Tennessee State University, N = 146; Arkansas Agricultural, Mechanical and Normal College, N = 151; black Nashville nonstudents, N = 54, Vanderbilt University students, blacks, N = 34 and whites, N = 122.

METHODS: Anomia, political efficacy, and political cynicism. Measures of protest activity and traditional political activity. Data analyzed in group comparisons.

RESULTS: Low anomia characterizes nonstudents and low-status college students, high anomia characterizes Fisk and both Vanderbilt groups. Protest activity is associated with low anomia, but traditional political activity is unrelated. Traditional activity positively related to political efficacy; protest activity shows positive trend. Political cynicism related to politicization: black Vanderbilt Ss and nonstudents highest, whites lowest. Political cynicism associated with protest activity, but not with traditional activity. Protest activity correlated with approval of black Muslims and Black Panthers.

COMMENTS: Recent study involving largely black student sample and control group. Study supports view that high anomia and low personal efficacy impede protest involvement; high political efficacy is associated with traditional activity.

127. ____ . 1971b. "The Political Behavior, Attitudes and Socialization of Selected Groups of Black Youths." Ph. D. dissertation, Vanderbilt University.

128. Jameson, J., and Hessler, R.M. 1970. "The Natives are Restless: The Ethos and Mythos of Student Power." HUMAN ORGANIZATION 29 (Summer): 81-94.

SETTING: Nov. 1968, University of Pittsburgh.

SUBJECTS: Random sample of undergraduates, N = 500 (71%).

METHODS: List of values, frustrations, etc. administered. Criterion of radicalism vs. conservatism: agreement with statement concerning need to "change the whole basic system" of education as opposed to working "through regular channels." Radicals, N = 24 and conservatives, N = 77, compared with total N. "Activists" defined as those who give "activists" as main reference group, N = 50. Ss 98% white, 38% Catholics.

RESULTS: Radicals are more often upperclassmen, social sciences and humanities, live alone, nonmembers of "established" religions, value intellectual companionship. Conservatives are more often freshmen or seniors, hard science or engineering majors, conventional religions. Most activists are not radicals, most radicals are not activists.

COMMENTS: Criteria of activism and radicalism are weak: radicalism = basic educational change. Note low relationship between activism and radicalism.

129. *Jansen, D.G. 1967. "Characteristics of Student Leaders." Ph.D. dissertation, Indiana University. 280 pp.

SETTING: Spring 1966, Indiana University.

SUBJECTS: 559 elected leaders of student organizations identified. Categorized as sociopolitical (85%), religious (90%), university residence hall (94%), activities (92%)—special interest, service, and program groups—fraternal (98%)—fraternities and sororities. One-third random sample taken of residence hall, activities and fraternal leaders to insure approximately the same number of Ss in each category. Overall response rates: male (90%), female (93%). Sociopolitical leaders classified as "liberal," N = 23 (85%), (ADA, NAACP, SDS, YPSL) and conservative, N = 23 (82%) (Conservative League, YAF, YR, YD). Final N = 235.

METHODS: Extensive discussion of validity, reliability, and correlates of 16PF, and CUES scales. Fifty-two analysis of variance used to test for differences among 5 student groups and male-female Ss. Comparisons of liberal and conservative sociopolitical leaders.

RESULTS: See Jansen and Winborn 1968, Jansen et al. 1968, Winborn and Jansen 1967, 1969, 1971. Author concludes that there is no evidence that student political leaders are more neurotic or unstable than other student leaders; expediency, independence and liberalism differentiated sociopolitical leaders from other leaders; a large amount of the difference between sociopolitical leaders and other leaders can be attributed to the liberal leaders; sociopolitical leaders see campus as low in emphasis on individual development, scholarship, and social cohesiveness; most of this difference can be attributed to liberals; liberal leaders score higher on SAT verbal than conservatives; sociopolitical leaders and particularly liberal sociopolitical leaders come from distinctive fields and particular socioeconomic backgrounds; sociopolitical leaders and especially liberal sociopolitical leaders seem significantly more altruistic than other leaders in terms of perceptions of group goals and chief satisfactions.

COMMENTS: Multivariate statistical analyses might have clarified the relationship between the many measures employed. Results are generally consistent with those of other research concerning left student leaders; study is unusual because comparison groups are other leadership groups.

130. _____ . and Winborn, B.B. 1968. "Perceptions of a University Environment by Social-Political Action Leaders." PERSONNEL AND GUIDANCE JOURNAL 47 (November):218-222.

SETTING, SUBJECTS, AND METHOD: See Jansen 1967. This report compares CUES scores of liberal and conservative sociopolitical leaders with CUES scores of other leaders.

RESULTS: Sociopolitical leaders score lowest of all leaders on CUES scales community, awareness, scholarship. Compared to conservatives, liberals are lower on community, awareness, higher on propriety.

COMMENT: Sociopolitical leaders, especially leftists, see the University of Indiana as less friendly, less cohesive, and less concerned with awareness than do other leaders.

131. _____ . and Martinson, W.D. 1968. "Characteristics Associated with Campus Sociopolitical Action Leadership." JOURNAL OF COUNSELING PSYCHOLOGY 15 (November):552-562.

SOURCE, SUBJECTS, AND METHODS: See Jansen 1967. Analysis of background characteristics, family variables, self-characterization, reasons for involvement, etc., for 5 leader groups.

RESULTS: Sociopolitical leaders have least leadership experience, most often emphasize personal interests or knowledge of group goals as leadership credentials, deemphasize leadership ability and personality. Compared to conservatives, liberal sociopolitical leaders are less influenced by parents, teachers, and classmates, awakened later to political interests, reject traditional political values, are more altruistic, agnostic, or irreligious. Liberal sociopolitical leaders report 9 out of 23 parents pleased at current leadership role, while 21 out of 23 conservatives' parents are pleased. Trend toward more parental participation in present-type group for liberals than conservatives. Authors critical of finding in other research that activists' orientations are consistent with families'.

COMMENTS: See Jansen 1967. Note that liberal activists report much greater parental displeasure or unconcern than do conservatives, but parents of leftists tend to be more involved in comparable leadership activities.

132. Johnson, David W. and Neale, Daniel C. 1968. "The Effects of Models, Reference Groups and Social Responsibility Norms upon Participation in Prosocial Action Activities." Paper read at American Educational Research Association, 1968. 14 pp. + App. Also in JOURNAL OF SOCIAL PSYCHOLOGY, 81, nos. 3-8 (June 1970):87-92.

SETTING, SUBJECTS, AND METHODS: See Neale and Johnson n.d. Ss asked about opinions of key others about social action, influence on Ss, attitudes toward Ss' participation in social action.

RESULTS: See Neale and Johnson n.d. Compared to nonvolunteers, volunteers indicate mothers, fathers, and sisters (but not brothers) more involved in social action, more favorable toward social action, mothers more influential on Ss' opinions about social action; mothers and sisters more approving of Ss' participant in social action. Comparable results for significant others, friends, members of positive normative reference group, with negative reference groups less favorable, less involved, less approving. Greatest approval and support (in order) from positive reference groups, significant others, mothers, friends, etc.

COMMENTS: Findings suggest that mothers play greater influence in prosocial action than fathers.

133. Jones, M.O. 1969. "Student Protest in the Junior College." JUNIOR COLLEGE STUDENT PERSONNEL SERVICES 2 (January):2.

134. Kahn, Roger M. 1968. "Class, Status Inconsistency, and Student Political Activism." Master's thesis, Department of Sociology-Anthropology, Northeastern University. 29 pp.

SETTING, SUBJECTS, AND METHODS: See Kahn and Bowers 1970. Activism cross-tabulated with family status variables and "achieved status" (mother's education, father's education, father's occupation, and family income).

RESULTS: Overall achieved status variables are associated with activism; Jews and blacks are more active than Catholics, Protestants, and whites. Control for religion shows that low-status Jews are less active than any other group. Author defines Jews as lowest ascribed status, interprets data to support status inconsistency theory of activism.

COMMENTS: Useful data from a large and representative sample. But author's theory should lead low-status Protestants to be activists, which they are not. Some cell sizes small.

135. _____. 1969. "The Rank and File Student Activist: A Contextual Test of Three Hypotheses." Paper read at American Sociological Association, September 1969, San Francisco. 13 pp. + App. See Kahn and Bowers 1970. This paper covers the same data, but does not report on field of concentration.

136. *_____, and Bowers, W.J. 1970. "The Social Context of the Rank and File Student Activists: A Test of Four Hypotheses." SOCIOLOGY OF EDUCA-TION 43 (Winter):38-55.

SETTING: 1966-67, I's.

SUBJECTS AND INSTITUTIONS: 946 Ss, mostly seniors (57% of located students who had constituted 60% response rate in 1962 freshmen study).

METHODS: Questionnaire includes activism index based on reports of participation in demonstrations, marches, or deliberate civil disobedience. 177 Ss (18.7%) termed "activists." Analysis examines relation between activism and other variables separately for 4 categories of I quality: "top ranking," "highly selective," "moderately selective," and "not very selective."

RESULTS: Overall association of activism with high parental SES holds only in highly selective schools. Overall connection of activism with grades and hours studying does not persist in "not very selective" colleges. Regardless of college quality, activists are more likely to be in social sciences and humanities than in physical sciences or preprofessional programs, and to report stronger intellectual orientations.

COMMENTS: A valuable study which suggests that institutional characteristics "mediate" relationship between social background and activism. Findings concerning low selectivity colleges anticipate those of studies conducted in later 1960s.

137. *Katz, Joseph. 1968. "The Activist Revolution of 1964." In Katz, Joseph, and associates. 1968. NO TIME FOR YOUTH: GROWTH AND CONSTRAINT IN COLLEGE STUDENTS. San Francisco: Jossey-Bass, pp. 386-414.

SETTING: 1962 and 1965, University of California at Berkeley.

SUBJECTS: 62 Berkeley seniors (35 males) arrested in FSM sit-in. Arrestees contrasted with 1026 males and 852 females. All Ss were part of longitudinal sample tested as freshmen in 1962 and in 1965.

METHOD: Data on SAT, GPA (from college records), OPI (1962 and 1965), and senior questionnaire from all Ss. Data analysis involves comparison of arrestees and remainder of longitudinal sample separately by sex, using freshmen and senior scores.

RESULTS: Freshman OPI scores show male arrestees higher on social maturity, aestheticism, developmental status, impulse expression, femininity-masculinity, lower on authoritarianism and ethnocentrism. Senior data shows male arrestees higher on same scales except femininity-masculinity. Freshman and senior data both show female arrestees higher on social maturity, developmental status, aestheticism, impulse expression, and lower on authoritarianism, ethnocentrism. SAT verbal scores higher for arrestees of both sexes; mathematical scores do not differentiate. Cumulative GPA higher for arrestees of both sexes.

Other findings: no differences in schizoid functioning scale; arrestees as freshmen resemble general college sample as seniors. Interviews indicate that arrestees have "history of involvement with relatively unorthodox ideas or actions," describe selves as having changed in college by becoming more expressive of feelings and more liberal, report greater conflict in deciding on major, more disagreement with fathers and between parents, and greater influence from ideas, intellectual content of courses, teachers, and close relations with adults and teachers. Arrestees have more permissive sexual attitudes, but only men report more sexual experience.

COMMENTS: A serendipitous study which, despite a small sample, indicates that FSM arrestees were even more differentiated from most Berkeley Ss as freshmen than as seniors. Availability of freshmen data makes this the most convincing of all FSM studies. Note general similarity between male and female arrestees.

138. Katz, Stuart, and Ashmall, Roy. 1968. "Survey of Graduate Students on the Selective Service." Institute for Social Research, University of Michigan. 19 pp. + App.

SETTING: Winter 1968, University of Michigan.

SUBJECTS: Graduate students polled at registration, N = 5619 (67.5%).

METHODS: Questionnaire on preferences concerning draft system. Data presented descriptively; cross-tabulated by sex, citizen/noncitizen, and pro- vs. antidraft positions.

RESULTS: 73% Ss favor abolishing draft system; if it is retained, 73% prefer retaining 2-S deferments for students making satisfactory progress towards a degree. Females and citizens more opposed to draft than males and noncitizens. CO's, 4-F's and theology students are most antidraft; students on active duty, in reserve, or veterans are least antidraft. Twenty-five percent of Ss advocate noncooperation with current draft laws.

COMMENTS: A descriptive study documenting widespread and strong draft opposition among graduate students in 1968.

139. Kelley, Jonathan, and Star, Shirley A. 1971. "Dress and Ideology: The Nonverbal Communication of Social and Political Attitudes." Paper read at American Sociological Association, September 1971, Denver. 20 pp.

SETTING: Spring 1967, University of California at Berkeley.

SUBJECTS: Undergraduates and graduate students at UCB, N = 410 (85%) sample representative.

METHODS: Interviews conducted by students. Ss' dress rated by interviewers, Ss asked to compare own dress with six drawings (for each sex) ranging from highly unconventional to highly conventional, asked to identify which dress types most likely to be in left wing politics, use drugs, etc. Questions on attitudes toward racial and foreign policy issues, lifestyle, drugs, SES, sociopolitical activities, definition of college goals, reactions to students of other political positions, etc.

RESULTS: 4 dress styles common: off-campus 9%, collegiate 61%, shaggy 23%, earthy 7%. Unconventional dress (shaggy-earthy) strongly related to liberal views on race, foreign policy, campus politics, lifestyle, political activism, marijuana use, slightly associated with high family SES. Ss correctly predict association of dress with political activism and drug uses, but underestimate association of conventional dress with tutoring deprived children and interest in Peace Corps, overestimate its association with collegiate culture and vocational orientation. Ss err by attributing to others behaviors or attitudes that are similar to their own and/or those of their friends. Choice of conventional dress styles is influenced by Ss' stress on conformity and, for marijuana users, by conventionality of friends' dress. Authors argue that reactions to dress express reactions to politics suggested by dress.

COMMENTS: An ingenious study that suggests association between students dress, politics and drug use, and the inaccuracy of stereotyping by dress on many issues.

140. *Keniston, Kenneth. 1968. YOUNG RADICALS. NOTES ON COMMITTED YOUTH. New York: Harcourt Brace and World. 368 pp.

SETTING: Summer 1967, national headquarters of Vietnam Summer (Cambridge, Mass.).

SUBJECTS: 11 "committed radicals" who had spent > 1 one year in organizing work, all leaders of national antiwar organizing project, 3 other Ss who met same criteria. N = 14, N women = 3.

METHODS: Intensive unstructured interviewing, averaging 4 hours; observation of group meetings and office work.

RESULTS: An essentially clinical and interpretative account of the personal nature of radicals' commitment, family relationships (stressing ambivalence toward father, principled parents, early conflict and sense of specialness), unusual early adolescent turmoil, late adolescent success followed by dissatisfaction and radicalization; aspects of the process of radicalization; special tensions of work in New Left; and continuation of change and development amongst Ss. Author stresses relationship of individual psychological development to sociohistorical changes and conflicts.

COMMENTS: An intensive clinical study of a small sample of radical leaders.

141. Kerpelman, Larry C. 1969. "Student Political Activism and Ideology: Comparative Characteristics of Activists and Nonactivists." JOURNAL OF COUNSELING PSYCHOLOGY 16 (January):8-13.

SETTING: 1968(?), "large Northeastern State University" (U. Mass.?).

SUBJECTS: 73 students classified into 6 groups: left activists (members of campus affiliate of national student left-oriented organization, N = 14); middle activists (campus student government organization, N = 10); right activists (loosely organized group of conservatives, N = 11); left nonactivists (chosen on the basis of Levinson Political Economic Conservatism Scale, N = 14); middle nonactivists (members of campus hiking club, N = 14); right activists (chosen by PEC scores in introductory psychology class, N = 14).

METHODS: All Ss given PEC, Kerpelman ACT-A and ACT-D (measures of actual and desired levels of activism, Borgatta and Corsini Quick-Word Test, Gordon Personal Profile Emotional Stability Scale, Gordon Survey of Interpersonal Values Recognition Scale, campus activities inventory. 2 X 3 analysis of variance.

RESULTS: Activism associated with intelligence; no differences on emotional stability, significant ideology effect on recognition scale, with right higher. No ideology by activism interactions. Discussion stresses activism and ideology distinction.

COMMENTS: A trial run for Kerpelman 1970; mainly important because of activism-ideology distinction and methods.

142. *_____ . 1970. "Student Activism and Ideology in Higher Education Institutions." Office of Education, Project No. 8-A-028, University of Massachusetts. 122 pp.

SETTING: Late 1968, early 1969, 3 coed colleges in Northeast: small private liberal arts, medium-size private university, large public university.

SUBJECTS AND METHODS: Study involved 3 X 3 X 2 analysis of variance design: 3 I's by 3 ideological levels (left, center, right) by 2 activity levels (activist, nonactivist). All Ss were active members of interest and hobby clubs, service organizations, professional clubs, etc. Ideology classification based on PEC, activism classification on Kerpelman's ACT-A and ACT-D Scales. Ss classified on PEC scores within each I, resulting in overlap on PEC scores between different ideological groups. Some cells N's are very small; highly significant correlation apparent between classification variables: ideology (left) and activism (high).

Other measures include Educational Testing Service Control Test AA (college-level academic aptitude), Gordon's Survey of Interpersonal Values, Gordon's Personal Profile, Borgatta and Corsini's Quick Word Test, Guilford-Zimmerman's Temperament Survey. Analysis of variance; group discriminant function analysis, with colleges combined.

RESULTS: No differences except institutional on intellectual ability. Activism not associated with emotional stability, ascendency and assertiveness, but with high sociability and low support. Rightists value leadership more than moderates or leftists; leftists value concern for others more than center, center more than rightists; no right-left differences in responsibility. Rightists more "thick-skinned" (less hypersensitive) than leftists. Leftists and rightists both higher on independence than center; rightists value conformity more than center or leftists; center highest on recognition, rightists next, left lowest.

Group discriminant analysis: 5 factors extracted; the first 2 account for 63.33% and 16.55% of the variance. Factor 1, labelled low "authoritarianism" (high benevolence, low conformity), discriminates leftists from rightists. Factor 2, labelled "autonomy" (high leadership and ascendency, low value on recognition and support) distinguishes activists from nonactivists.

Discussion emphasizes failure to find activism X ideology interactions, minimizes importance of "authoritarian" factor in group discriminant analysis, emphasizes importance of "autonomy" factor. Author is critical of characterization of left activists as high grades, emotionally stable, etc., and stresses importance of separating activism and ideology.

COMMENTS: Conceptually very valuable, but methodologically confusing. "Nonactivists" are active in nonpolitical groups, are not comparable with control groups used by most researchers; high correlation between activism and ideology, the classificatory variables, results in higher levels of activism among some "left nonactivists" than among "right activists"; some inferences are based on tiny cell sizes. The study clearly establishes the need to separate activism, ideology and I's.

143. Kimmel, Douglas C. 1967. "Sex-Differences and Personality Manifestations of the Subject/Object Orientation." Master's thesis, Committee on Human Development, University of Chicago. Abstract, 4 pp.

SETTING, SUBJECTS, AND METHODS: See Flacks and Neugarten Intro. Ss classified according to Sartre-De Beauvoir distinction between self as subject (dynamic, active, assertive force in world) and as object (dependent, reliant on others' standards, defines self through roles and status). Analysis includes relationship of subject/object orientation to political activism; partial correlations, controlling for political activism and for sex, of subject/orientation, personality traits, and family variables.

RESULTS: Political activists are more subject-oriented than nonactivists, regardless of sex.

COMMENTS: A further analysis of the Flacks-Neugarten data.

144. Kirkpatrick, Samuel A. 1969. "Attitudinal Consistency and Political Behavior." Ph.D. dissertation, Pennsylvania State University.

145. Kornberg, Alan, and Brehm, Mary L. 1971. "Ideology, Institutional Identification, and Campus Activism." SOCIAL FORCES 49 (March): 445-59.

SETTING: Feb. 1969, Duke University, after brief occupation of university office by 30 black students, police action resulting in 45 hospital-treated injuries.

SUBJECTS: Questionnaires mailed to 4,000+ undergraduates, 2,000+ graduate and professional students, 800+ faculty. Undergraduate, N = 3062 (71%). Sample judged representative.

METHODS: Data gathered on age, sex, religion, home town population, class in college, importance of grades, GPA, "institutional identification" (attachment vs. dislike of Duke), "ideological identification" (self-label from strongly conservative to radical), attitudes towards sit-in, administration and police. Reports of activities during sit-in form the basis for definition of 2 attitude groups (prosit-in, antipolice, antiadministration, N = 1118; antisit-in, proadministration, propolice, N = 874) and 2 activity groups (opposers, N = 163; passive and active supporters or participators, N = 630).

RESULTS: Multiple discriminant function analysis on attitude groups shows that ideological identification alone correctly groups 84.4% of Ss; adding I identification, age, sex, religion, and home town population increases % correctly predicted to 85.5%. Analysis of activity groups shows ideological identification alone correctly groups 82.6% of Ss; adding I identification, sex, age decreases % correctly grouped. For faculty, ideological identification is somewhat less predictive. Police action increased student support for sit-in from 22% to 40%, increased support for black students' demands from 25% to 30%. Authors emphasize S-faculty differences, underscore lack of relationship with background variables, and question political socialization hypothesis.

COMMENTS: Recent analysis of ideology and activity groups at a selective Southern university that indicates the critical role of ideological self-label in predicting protest attitudes and activity levels.

146. Kornhauser, William. 1967. "Alienation and Participation in the Mass University." Paper read at American Ortho-Psychiatric Association, 1967, Washington, D.C. Summary in AMERICAN JOURNAL OF ORTHO-PSYCHIATRY 37 (March): 196-97.

147. ____. 1971. "The Politics of Confrontation." In Aya, R., and Miller, N., eds. 1971. THE NEW AMERICAN REVOLUTION. New York: Free Press.

148. *Kraut, Robert. 1971. "Parental Conflict and Political Ideology." Unpublished paper, Department of Psychology, Yale University. 33 pp.

SETTING, SUBJECTS, AND METHODS: See Lewis and Kraut 1971. Resurvey of original sample in April of freshman year, N = 133 (81%). Questionnaire includes old scales and new items on parent-student conflict, past and present. Cross-lagged correlations used to examine causal relationships.

RESULTS: Virtually all direct measures of family conflict, especially political, are associated with left ideology. Leftism moderately related to reported mother-father conflict, and highly related to reports of specific high school conflicts with parents. Cross-lagged correlations show no temporal influences, except that political ideology at time 1 predicts reports of parental permissiveness at time 2. Author suggests that increased radicalism leads to reinterpretation of upbringing in accordance with popular stereotypes about "permissivist" parents.

COMMENTS: Excellent theoretical discussion of generational continuity vs. parental conflict controversy, and new data on the subject.

149. Krieger, David M. 1968. "Personality and Political Ideology." Ph.D. dissertation, University of Hawaii. 93 pp.

SETTING: Late 1960s, private university near Osaka, Japan.

SUBJECTS: 402 freshmen, 95% male, not representative.

METHODS: Ss given Cattell High School Personality questionnaire (derivative of 16PF) yielding 14 primary and secondary traits. Sixty-item attitude scale administered to all Ss to tap attitudes concerning tradition, militarism, international affairs, etc. Data analyzed by multiple regression and canonical regression of personality scale scores on ideology factor scores.

RESULTS: Factor analysis of attitude questionnaire (varimax rotation) produces 2 major factors—militarism and traditionalism. Multiple regression for entire sample of personality scores on ideology scores explains 12% of the variance of militarism, 7% of traditionalism. Canonical regression on traditionalism and militarism shows that personality measures predict 16% of variance of these 2 scores. Subdividing the sample according to S's party reference approximately doubles the % variance explained, regardless of regression method used. Author concludes that "personality" accounts for less than 10% of the variance of ideology, and that controlling for situational context (party preference) is necessary in studying the relation of personality and politics.

COMMENTS: Although Ss are Japanese, study methods are directly comparable to many American studies. Author's conclusion that "personality" is largely irrelevant to politics seems an overgeneralization from data, which show the irrelevance of Cattell's scales to the ideology measures used.

150. Lacy, Virginia P. 1971. "Political Knowledge of College Activist Groups: SDS, YAF, and YD." JOURNAL OF POLITICS 33 (August):840-45.

151. La Gaipa, J.J. 1969. "Student Power and Dogmatism." JOURNAL OF PSYCHOLOGY 73:201-207.

SETTING: Early 1969, Windsor, Ontario, after recent building occupation.

SUBJECTS: 140 upper-level high school students; 315 University of Windsor students.

METHODS: Demographic data, short-form D, 10 items measuring student power attitudes, support for occupation of university building, participation in student demonstration, and attitudes toward social and educational issues. Data analyzed factor analysis.

RESULTS: 3 factors interpreted as antipaternalism, antiintellectualism, and poor quality of instruction. D highly correlated ($r = + 0.61$) with prostudent power attitudes, related negatively to participation in student demonstrations ($r = - 0.26$), and positively to involvement in occupation in university building ($r = + 0.15$). No relationship found between protest activity and judgments of quality of instruction.

COMMENTS: A brief report from an unusual sample of high school and college students. Relationship of dogmatism with "student power" attitudes contradicts virtually all other research.

152. *Laue, James H. 1965. "Direct Action and Desegregation: A Study in Social Spontaneity and Institutionalization." Ph.D. dissertation, Harvard University. 395 pp.

SETTING: Feb. 1, 1960-Feb. 1, 1962, civil rights movement.

SUBJECTS: A participant-observation and sociological-historical study, which includes historical and evaluative data based on 45 interviews with 13 of 15 staff members of SNCC, 8 "adult leaders" (key leaders of civil rights organizations), and 24 indirect leaders and observers (secondary leaders or scholarly observers of civil rights movement).

METHODS: Intensive participant observation, including involvement in virtually all forms of civil rights activity, arrest, and imprisonment. Close familiarity with key civil rights student and adult leaders. Interviews with both "student leaders" and "adult leaders" were semistructured, only occasionally coded, and are used illustratively in the text.

RESULTS: A semiinsider's history of the development of the first 2 years of the civil rights movement, broken off at a point when that movement appeared to be becoming more "rationalized" through involvement with federal government, national foundations, and voter registration drives. Data placed in the context of Weberian-Parsonion theory of mass movements involving transition from spontaneous movement to rationalized organization.

COMMENTS: An outstanding account by a perceptive white observer of the early development and evaluation of the civil rights movement. Data on SNCC leaders emphasizes above all their roles and actions, rather than personality characteristics.

153. _____ . 1966. "Direct Action and Desegregation." In Cameron, William Bruce. 1966. MODERN SOCIAL MOVEMENTS. New York: Random House, pp. 11-120.

154. Laufer, R.S., McVey, Sheila. 1971. "Generational Conflict." In Altbach, Phillip; Laufer, R.S.; and McVey, Sheila. eds. 1971. ACADEMIC SUPER-MARKETS. San Francisco: Jossey-Bass, pp. 343-64.

SETTING: Spring 1970 (pre-Cambodia), University of Wisconsin at Madison.

SUBJECTS: 24 Ss enrolled in an experimental course; 2 Ss members of radical campus groups.

METHODS: 3-4 hour interviews conducted by Ss in graduate seminar. Largely descriptive-clinical report of Ss' attitudes, changes in political orientation.

RESULTS: Ss blame "the Establishment" but not their own parents for inability to act on convictions; are critical of American materialism and foreign policy based on imperialism; support "idiosyncratic individualism," noncompetitive interpersonal interdependence, a "community of tolerance," drug use in moderation; view America as corrupt but redeemable, are ambivalent to violence, generally reject "revolutionary" tactics. Cyclical pattern in Ss involves activism countered by social repression, withdrawal, and later reengagement in activism. "Radicalization" of 13 Ss was stimulated by opposition to the war, specifically spurred by contact with politicized atmosphere at UWM, experience of I betrayal, violence (especially witnessing or experiencing police violence), defeat of McCarthy in 1968, police action at Chicago Convention. Four Ss withdrew into extremely personalistic alienation, characterized by negative view of society, feeling of sociopolitical impotence, and rejection of radical left alternatives. Authors stress role of parents in shaping Ss' core values; radicalization as a response to specific political events of the late 1960s.

COMMENTS: A study valuable for its clinical depth, its emphasis on the relationship of experienced events to radicalization, and its distinction of 2 subtypes of oppositional students.

155. Levine, M., and Naisbitt, J. 1970. RIGHT ON. New York: Bantam Books. 256 pp. SETTING, INSTITUTIONS, METHODS, RESULTS: See Urban Research Corporation Intro. Data and results are mostly the same as those reported in Urban Research Corporation 1970f.

156. Levitt, M. 1967. "Negro Student Rebellion against Parent Political Beliefs." SOCIAL FORCES 45 (March):438-40.

SETTING: 1964(?), Howard University.

SUBJECTS: Students in the College of Liberal Arts, N = 396, N males = 169.

METHODS: Political self-label, father's and mother's political positions. Male vs. female comparisons.

RESULTS: Author notes a stronger tendency for Ss to move to the left of their parents than to the right.

COMMENTS: Brief descriptive study.

157. *Levy, Charles J. 1968. VOLUNTARY SERVITUDE: WHITES IN THE NEGRO MOVEMENT. New York: Appleton-Century-Crofts. 125 pp.

SETTING: 1963-67 author on faculty of predominantly black college in the deep South, active in Southern-based civil rights organization.

SUBJECTS: Whites who seek to become accepted by blacks, including civil rights workers, instructors, and students at black colleges.

METHODS: Unstructured participant observation of both whites and blacks. Strong emphasis on trust and mistrust; discussion organized around the stages through which whites in the movement passed as they moved toward a recognition of the mistrust directed at them.

RESULTS: An analytic account, with anecdotal illustrations, of the complex maneuvers involved as whites encounter blacks in the civil rights movement, as fellow students in predominantly black universities, or as faculty members in black colleges. Major issue is blacks' pervasive mistrust of whites; whites attempt to deny the existence of this mistrust, to exempt themselves from the category of mistrusted white, to abandon their whiteness, or to become "black." Six stages distinguished: (1) early contentment wherein the whites protect themselves (or are protected by blacks) from mistrust; soon gives way to (2) transient indignation. Once the extent of mistrust is perceived, whites (3) seek various forms of exemption by defining themselves as different from other whites who should be mistrusted. But exemption-seeking invariably collapses, since from the blacks' point of view there are no exemptions. Moreover, the white seeks intellectual exemptions, but the blacks' mistrust is emotional. (4) Dismay: whites seek to "convert" by becoming black. This process is constantly obstructed, both by whites and blacks. It leads to (5) role-reversal wherein the black assumes the role of superordinate, and the white accepts the role of "nigger." "Freedom organizations," for example, are a way of ensuring that white organizers will not manipulate or dominate the organized blacks. In the end, (6) "White Consciousness" increases, and "so does a disbelief in the mythology of a trust relationship with the Negro." There ensues a process of disengagement from blacks and a phasing out by the white from the civil rights movement. Paradoxically, then, the ability to "think black" leads the white civil rights worker to the conclusion that his efforts have been undermining the movement.

COMMENTS: Analysis along symbolic interactionist lines of the white-black confrontation in the movement. Process is seen as transactional, and the result—disengagement by the white—as inevitable. Analysis leaves no room for individual variation, the possibility of transcendence of the process, or interracial trust—barring a radical change in the nature of white-black relations on a national scale. Helps account for the withdrawal of most whites from the civil rights movement.

158. *Lewis, S.H., and Kraut, Robert E. 1971. "Correlates of Student Political Activism and Ideology." Unpublished paper, Department of Psychology, Yale University. 30 pp. + App.

SETTING: Oct. 1969, Yale College.

SUBJECTS: Freshman sample, N = 216 (55%, generally representative but females underrepresented). Data analysis based on white male Ss, N = 165.

METHOD: Questionnaire included Christie New Left Scale, items from Gould Manifest Alienation Measure, political alienation items, sociodemographic background items, conflict with parents, Christie Mach IV Scale, Marlowe-Crown Social Desirability Scale, ACL for self, ideal, and typical Yale freshman ideal. ACL factor-analyzed into 5 orthogonal scales: different-independent, practical-conventional, loving-humanistic, action oriented-impulsive, skeptical-moody. Ss classified by quartiles as radical, liberal, moderate, and conservative on the basis of scores on unidimensional left-right ideology scale derived from Christie New Left Scale. Ss split at median on self-reported high school sociopolitical activism. Left ideology and activism uncorrelated (r = +0.09). 4 X 2 analysis of variance (4 ideologies X 2 activism levels).

RESULTS: No effects or interactions on occupational status, education, religious preference, size of home town, birth order or number of siblings. Strong positive relationship between (left) ideology and both parents' (left) political position, political conflict with parents, disagreement with political opinions of parents, belief that father's generation has failed world, perceived dissimilarity between own and parents' political orientation, low influence by fathers on personal development and political beliefs. No ideology or activism effects related to conflict with friends, influence of friends on political beliefs and personal development, or permissive-democratic upbringing.

Values and personality measures associated with (left) ideology: low practical-conventional (both self and ideal), indefinite graduation plans, self perceived as different from Yale freshmen and average American, values different. Measures associated with (high) activism: "political and social issues interest me a lot," action-oriented-impulsive (self), "moral" (self), low Machiavellism, low self-ideal discrepancy, lower expectation of change in college, low desire to be like someone else. Activists' parents more involved and interested in social and political issues, which they more frequently discuss with their children. Variables associated with both (high) activism and (left) ideology: different-independent (self and ideal), loving-humanistic (self). No interactions between ideology and activism found.

COMMENTS: Authors conclude that political socialization theory holds up both for activism and for ideology, find more evidence of parental conflict among leftists. Activists less Machiavellian, more loving-humanistic, more "moral." Many characteristics attributed to left activists apply to activists in general.

159. *Liebert, Robert. 1971. RADICAL AND MILITANT YOUTH. A PSYCHO-ANALYTIC INQUIRY. New York: Praeger. 257 pp.

SETTING: May-Aug. 1968, Columbia University, following student occupation of 5 buildings and police actions.

SUBJECTS: Columbia College undergraduates and graduate students, Barnard College undergraduates. N blacks = 14, N females = 7, total N = 50. Twenty-eight Ss radical or militant; 2 Ss strongly antiradical or antimilitant; 14 Ss inactive. Analysis of term papers from 35 Ss, (5 radical, 7 active antiradical, 23 nonradical); by clinical summaries of 25 CU psychotherapy patients (3 radical, 1 antiradical, 21 nonactivists).

METHODS: Intensive, clinical, open-ended, 2-4 hour interviews with 50 main Ss.

RESULTS: Events and issues of Columbia demonstrations. Arrested white Ss predominantly upper middle class, not science-mathematics majors; arrested black Ss predominantly working class. Account emphasizes diverse experiences of students in communes (occupied buildings), contrast between experiences and fantasies of black and white students about building occupation and police, diversity of family background of activists, absence of parental sanctioning of Ss' militancy, relationships of students to faculty; distinguishes "idealistic" and "nihilistic" radicalism, each with distinct developmental origins; argues that "nihilistic" radicals were largely absent at Columbia. Concluding chapters emphasize social and political realities behind activism and psychohistorical context, especially fears of atomic annihilation during earlier childhood.

COMMENTS: A perceptive, sympathetic psychohistorical account of the varying motivations of activists and nonactivists in the 1968 Columbia demonstrations; valuable for its emphasis on the immensely complex origins of action and inaction. Useful distinction between "nihilistic" and "idealistic" poles of radicalism.

160. Lipset, Seymour Martin. 1953. "Opinion Formation in a Crisis Situation." PUBLIC OPINION QUARTERLY 17, no. 1 (Spring): 20-46. Also in Lipset, S.M., and Wolin, S.S., eds. 1965. THE BERKELEY STUDENT REVOLT: FACTS AND INTERPRETATIONS. New York: Doubleday Anchor, pp. 464-94.

SETTING: March 15-April 21, 1951, University of California at Berkeley, amid crisis over loyalty oath at UCB.

SUBJECTS: Representative cross-section of Berkeley campus, N = 480.

METHODS: Cross-tabulations based on anti- vs. pro-loyalty oath, approval vs. disapproval of Communist Party member teaching at university. Four classifications analyzed in terms of other variables. Six-item, liberal-conservatism scale (largely economic issues).

RESULTS: Antioath Ss who approve CP teacher and pro-oath Ss who disapprove CP teacher are generally at opposite extremes. Antioath, approve CP teacher Ss are most often liberal, Democrat, upperclassmen, nonreligious or Jewish (if nonreligious, then father's religion Jewish), father employed worker, proprietor, or business executive (not farmer or professional), have independent source of college financing, nonengineer job aspirations, do not live with family (but working-class Ss appear not to be influenced by residence, while middle- and upper-class Ss are). All groups see relevant others as disproportionately supportive of their views. Data interpreted to support cross-pressure theory of attitude formation.

COMMENTS: An early study, with many results comparable to later UCB research. In early 1950s, working-class background tended to produce liberal, not conservative, attitudes.

161. *Loken, Joel. 1971. "On Accounting for Student Activism in a Canadian Setting." Paper read at Conference for Canadian Professors in Education, June 1971, St. John's, New Foundland. 32 pp.

SETTING: 1970(?), University of Alberta.

SUBJECTS: Representative sample of registered students, N = 243 (85.5%). 14 Ss identified as "activists" for in-depth study.

METHODS: Tests included Kerpelman's ACT Scales (activism criterion), D, Christie's Mach V Scale, Succorance Scale from Personality Research Forms, Social Desirability Scale, PEC, theoretical orientation and cognitive complexity scales from OPI, measures of demographic background, political participation, and acceptance, control, communication from parents, peers, and teachers. Questionnaire data analyzed by correlations and stepwise multiple regression analysis, validated by dividing original sample into 2 independent groups.

RESULTS: Left activists higher than right activists on both ACT Scales. ACT-A associated with year in college, exposure to ideas, high father's income, high parents' education and high political participation, cognitive complexity (highest single correlation), theoretical orientation, leftism, low succorance and dogmatism, but unrelated to acceptance, control, or communication with any group.

Multiple regression performed on composite ACT-A and ACT-D with two subsamples of total N. Cross validation confirmed that cognitive complexity, political ideology, political participation, and (high) parents' education (in order) predict activism ($r' = 0.59$).

COMMENTS: Activism is here defined as general activism, not left activism, although the most active were left. Activists are concerned especially with Canadian issues. Author concludes that psychological variables are more important than sociological. Results similar to early American studies.

162. Long, Durward. 1970. "Black Protest." In Foster, Julian, and Long, Durward, eds. 1970. PROTEST! STUDENT ACTIVISM IN AMERICA. New York: William Morrow, pp. 459-82.

SETTING, SUBJECTS, AND METHODS: See Foster and Long Intro.

RESULTS: 10% of protests studied were over racial issues, but only 3 of 52 such protests occurred at black I's. Racial protests most frequent in universities, more disruptive and violent, drew less faculty support and more often involved nonstudents. Black I's had a higher % protests, higher % violent and obstructive protests, higher involvement of faculty members and more disciplining of protesters. Off-campus police, arrests, injuries, use of tear gas, force and other physical responses more frequent at black I's and in protests over racial issues. Racial protests involved highest % sit-ins and detention of officials. No trustees at black I's issued statements supporting protests while several did at white I's. Twenty-one percent of black administrations endorsed substance of protest (vs. 5% white I's). Higher % black than white I's adopted new rules to limit protest, broaden the right to protest, strengthen security forces and revised disciplinary procedures to guarantee due process. Eight-six percent of race-related protests occurred during April and May 1968, vs. 32% of other kinds of protest. (Martin Luther King killed in early April 1968.) Protests on black campuses were more often sudden and triggered by external events. Race-related protests focused on tangible gains: demands for black curriculum or black faculty most common.

COMMENTS: Study suggests changing nature of black student protest, with escalation of militancy, increasing violence, and increasing practicality of black (vs. white) protesters.

163. ____ , and Foster, Julian. 1970. "Levels of Protest." In Foster, Julian, and Long, Durward, eds. 1970. PROTEST! STUDENT ACTIVISM IN AMERICA. New York: William Morrow, pp. 81-88.

SETTING, INSTITUTIONS, METHODS: See Foster and Long Intro.

RESULTS: Incidence and severity of protests related to size of I. National issues stirred more violent protests than on-campus issues. Faculty most involved in protests involving censorship, Vietnam and the draft; least involved in race-related and *in loco parentis* protests; most involved at universities (vs. junior colleges), slightly more involved as leaders in protests which eventuated in violence.

COMMENTS: Familiar I correlates of protest; note higher faculty involvement in violent protests.

164. Longhi, Dario Enrico. 1969. "Higher Education and Student Politics: The Wisconsin Experience." Unpublished paper, University of Wisconsin.

165. Lyonns, Glen. 1965. "The Police Car Demonstration: A Survey of Participants." In Lipset, S.M., and Wolin, S.S. eds. 1965. THE BERKELEY STUDENT REVOLT: FACTS AND INTERPRETATIONS. New York: Doubleday Anchor, pp. 519-30.

SETTING: Late October 1964, University of California at Berkeley.

SUBJECTS: Participants in October 1-2 police car demonstration, N = 618. Comparisons with Somers 1965 sample. Questionnaire picked up in Bancroft-Telegraph strip where left activists tend to congregate: sample probably biased toward more activist demonstrators.

METHODS: Questionnaire filled out by respondents on the scene of demonstration and returned. Comparisons of all demonstrators with university sample, and internal comparison of first-time demonstrators (48%) vs. participants in one or more prior demonstrations.

RESULTS: Compared to Somers' sample, demonstrators more often live off-campus, have $> \$15,000$ parental income, are nonchurchgoers, liberal Democrats, Democratic Socialist, or Revolutionary Socialists; less often fraternity or sorority members, Republicans or Conservative Democrats. Seventeen percent of demonstrators have participated in > 7 previous demonstrations; 56% say they would risk arrest and expulsion if negotiations break down; 40% demonstrators (vs. 17% Somers' sample) expressed some dissatisfaction with "courses, exams, professors, etc."

Compared with first-time demonstrators, experienced demonstrators are older, more often live off-campus, are nonchurchgoers, have lower parental income, are more left-wing, parents more involved in politics between 1930-50, express greater dissatisfaction with courses, examinations, and professors, are more willing to risk arrest and expulsion. First-time demonstrators expect to become more politically active in other areas compared to experienced demonstrators (who already are very active). Sixty percent of Ss involved in > 7 demonstrations consider themselves "revolutionary socialists," most blame UCB administration for their own increased commitment.

COMMENTS: A methodologically unsophisticated study that gives some understanding of the early FSM participants and the differences between "veterans" and first-time recruits. Concordant with other early Berkeley research.

166. Maccoby, E.; Mathews, R.; and Morton, A. 1954. "Youth and Political Change." PUBLIC OPINION QUARTERLY 18 (Spring):23-29. Also in Eulau Heinz, et al., eds. 1956. POLITICAL BEHAVIOR. New York: Free Press.

SETTING: Nov. 1952, Cambridge, Massachusetts, just after 1952 presidential election.

SUBJECTS: 339 eligible voters, age 21-24, drawn from out-of-date voting list; sample not representative. Largely nonstudent sample.

METHODS: Data about own and parents' party choice, SES attitude items, party affiliation of friends and spouse, social mobility and education. Index of political change (high change = S differs from both parents on preferred candidate and party choice).

RESULTS: Strong overlap between parents' and children's political preferences. Greatest change found among Ss whose parents exerted strict control, in upper social classes, and among students. General agreement with spouse, most friends, and many co-workers on party choice. Political discussion with co-workers associated with agreement on politics, but political discussion with spouse is associated with disagreement. Friends exert greatest influence when S resents parental control. Upwardly mobile

Ss less often independent, more often pro-Eisenhower, but shifts to Eisenhower are not accompanied by ideological shifts to right. Increasing education is associated with party change away from parents, trend toward left, especially among college graduates. Among educated Ss only, party change is accompanied by ideological change.

COMMENTS: An early study of a largely noncollege population. Shows tendency among college-educated voters for general shift to the left in ideology and party preference. Generalizability from Cambridge, Mass. doubtless limited.

167. MacKinnon, Kitty. 1971. "Moral Development, Political Ideology and Attitudes toward Political Action in College Students, Spring 1970." Unpublished paper, Department of Political Science, Yale University. 33 pp. + App.

168. *Maidenberg, Michael, and Meyer, Philip. 1970a. "The Berkeley Rebels Five Years Later: Has Age Mellowed the Pioneer Radicals?" Seven-part series, DETROIT FREE PRESS (February 1-7, 1970).

SETTING: Restudy in July-Dec. 1969 of Sproul Hall arrestees of Dec. 1964.

SUBJECTS: Addresses located for 400 arrestees, N = 230 (57.5%).

METHODS: Ss rated selves on 9-point radical/conservative scale for pre-FSM, post-FSM and present. Sixteen-page mailed questionnaire supplemented by 13 random interviews. All data retrospective. No tests of significance.

RESULTS: FSM experience increased radicalization, which diminished only marginally in the 5 ensuing years (pre-FSM radicalism scores 6.3, post-FSM 7.5, current 7.4). FSM participation produced sharp rise in political activity: 35% more active than others before FSM, 55% more active after FSM. 54% now feel sit-in "appropriate and effective," 36% "appropriate but not effective," 9% "poor tactic." Seventy-four percent think FSM strengthened Reagan. Fifty-three percent think Berkeley freer today (59% in West, 39% in East). Women more skeptical of long-term effects (45% think Berkeley freer now).

Current situations and views: 88% metropolitan, 50% employed, 35% students, 7% housewives. Of employed, 27% teaching, 13% social work,

10% clerical work, etc. Sixty-four percent brought up West of Mississippi, 74% now live there. Median parental income $16,000. Ss' current average income between $2500 and $5000; at age 40 hope to make $13,000. Median parental education B.A., 40% of fathers "very interested in politics," 50% "mildly interested," 10% "uninterested." Thirty percent consider parents as radical as they. 1968 voting behavior: Humphrey 34%, Nixon 0%, Wallace 0%, others 38%, deliberate nonvote 22%, ineligible 4%. Ninety percent support recent campus disruptions at Harvard, Columbia, etc. Eighty-four percent "would do it all again." Five percent trust the government "just about always" or "most of the time" (vs. 69% national sample). Four percent feel "government is run for the benefit of all rather than a few big interests" (vs. 56% national sample). Eighty-nine percent feel there are "lots of ways other than voting to wield influence" (vs. 43% general public). Question on violence elicited 69 blank responses. Of respondents, 61% agree "more to lose from violence as a tactic than to gain" (43% men favored violence, 32% women).

Of all Ss, 29% did not gain in leftism post-FSM but virtually all of these were highly radical to begin with. Fifty percent gained in radicalism post-FSM and kept gain 5 years later. Twenty-one percent gained post-FSM but gains now erased.

Factors affecting persistence of radicalism: (1) strong traditional religious views make loss of radicalism 3 times more likely; (2) teachers and social workers (vs. business-oriented occupations) make retention of radicalism twice more likely; (3) loss of radicalism associated with disapproving parents (17% of parents severely disapproved, 25% disapproved mildly); (4) retention of radicalism associated with parents being radical; (5) social science majors most likely to retain radicalism, physical science and fine arts majors least likely; (6) women most likely to retain radicalism. Those now most radical in greatest trouble with the draft (33% would go to prison rather than be drafted), but evidence does not support view that change in draft pressures would increase activism.

COMMENTS: Despite lack of statistical tests, an invaluable study. The only long-term follow-up of activists, it demonstrates overall persistence of radicalism in virtually every area. The same factors that initially dispose towards radicalism also dispose towards its persistence. But authors note that "radical activity has slowed or stopped under the pressure of earning a living and raising a family." Interviews indicate many arrestees have moved into "cultural" or "new lifestyle" radicalism.

169._____ . 1970b. "The Berkeley Rebels: Five Years Later." Paper read at American Association for Public Opinion Research, May 1970, Lake

George, New York. 16 pp. Abstracted in PUBLIC OPINION QUARTERLY 34 (Fall):477-78. See Maidenberg and Meyer 1970a. Summarizes some of the results of the previous study.

170. **Mankoff, Milton. 1970. "The Political Socialization of Student Radicals and Militants in the Wisconsin Student Movement during the 1960s." Ph.D. dissertation, University of Wisconsin. 293 pp.

SETTING: May 1968, University of Wisconsin. Mid-October 1967 obstruction of Dow Chemical interviews; December 1967 Declaration of Responsibility signed by 2250 students accepting "responsibility" for obstruction.

SUBJECTS: 50% random sample of declaration signers (all foreign students eliminated; 350 Ss not located), N = 490 (68.4%). Control sample drawn at random from student directory, eliminating foreign students and declaration signers, N = 153 (63.4%). Samples pooled for data analysis.

METHODS: Data included 6 items on political beliefs, types of activism engaged in, political self-characterizations, demographic characteristics, educational experiences, parental political ideology and activities, parental discipline and estrangement from parents, field of study, number and type of political periodicals read. Students' political ideology dichotomized into radical/nonradical, using 9-point political self-characterization; paternal political ideology defined as liberal/conservative on the same basis. Student political militancy defined as participation in civil disobedience, violent or nonviolent; paternal militancy defined as involvement in any protest activity. Data analysis uses S's radicalism and militancy as dependent variables; and when 3 variables are involved, sometimes presents weighted effect parameters.

RESULTS: S's political ideology most affected by father's political ideology. Father's militancy, occupational status, and religion have independent effects on S's ideology, all of which disappear when father's political ideology is controlled. S's field of specialization (social sciences and humanities vs. others) affects S's ideology (radical), even when lower division, upper division, and graduate student status is controlled. Radicalism associated with self-reported GPA (only for Ss with conservative fathers), with parental permissiveness during adolescence and at present, and with rebellion from political authority during adolescence and at present. Control for father's political ideology eliminates association between ideology and adolescent permissiveness. Author interprets data to suggest distinction between "hereditary" and "rebellious" radicals.

Student militancy (activism) is associated with radicalism, paternal militancy, "veteran" status (3 or more years political activity), expectation of increased future political activity. For nonradical students only, militancy is associated with liberal paternal ideology, high father's education attainment, present rebellion from parents, humanities or social sciences major. All other variables are unrelated to militancy, including father's occupation, S's religious training, parental permissiveness in adolescence and now, adolescent rebellion from parents. Author notes that many militants never become radicalized and many radicals are not militant; "direct political indoctrination" in the form of paternal militancy is the best explanation of student militancy.

Ss report increasing radicalism and political activity in response to adverse societal reactions. Hostile societal reactions has greater impact on political ideology of high school nonradicals who later became militant or were radicalized. Author suggests that Ss not previous radical are particularly shocked and radicalized by societal repression.

Compared to nonveteran militants, "veterans" report more paternal liberalism and militancy, higher paternal occupational prestige and education, more often Jewish-atheistic-agnostic, parents more permissive during adolescence and now, come from larger cities, no greater rebellion, more often social science or humanities majors, higher GPA, more often read many and left-wing or liberal periodicals. Nonveterans are less radical and militant than veterans. S's ideology controlled, veterans have more liberal fathers; but with S's militancy controlled, father's militancy does not distinguish veterans. Author argues that newer recruits are less well equipped to deal with theoretical, strategic and tactical problems of increasingly revolutionary student movement.

COMMENTS: An outstanding study, valuable for its substantive findings and for clear distinction between ideology and action. Use of dichotomous variables limits study of interactions between variables and prevents the use of sophisticated statistical techniques. Veteran vs. nonveteran differences could be the consequence of the greater radicalism and militancy of veterans or of selective attrition among early student movement recruits. Hypothesis that the social base of the student movement is changing is a crucial hypothesis.

171. *____ , and Flacks, Richard E. 1971. "The Changing Social Base of the American Student Movement." ANNALS OF THE AMERICAN ACADEMY OF POLITICAL AND SOCIAL SCIENCES 395 (May):54-67.

SETTING, SUBJECTS, METHODS, AND RESULTS: See Mankoff 1970. Paper presents data comparing veteran activists, recruits, and cross-section on selected variables. Veterans most often from large cities, brought up as Jews or without religion, fathers have college or advanced degree, fathers liberal or radical, permissive child-rearing during adolescence. Nonveterans least likely to report parents approve present lifestyle, cross-section most likely. Veterans and nonveterans do not differ on self-reported GPA, importance attributed to career success, or % majoring in social sciences and humanities; but both activist groups differ from cross-section. Veterans strongly differentiated from nonveterans on informal political education measured by reading 9 or more (mostly left wing) political periodicals.

Authors argue that veteran/nonveteran differences show changing base of recruitment into the movement, point to increasingly generational base of movement and decreased relevance of pre-1968 findings about distinctive backgrounds and psychology of activists.

COMMENTS: See Mankoff 1970. A very important paper with a far-reaching discussion.

172. Matthews, Donald R., and Prothro, James W. 1966. "Negro Students and the Protest Movement." In Matthews, Donald R., and Prothro, James W. 1966. NEGROES AND THE NEW SOUTHERN POLITICS. New York: Harcourt, Brace and World, Inc., pp. 407-440.

SETTING: Jan. 1962, 30 "nonintegrated" black colleges in the South.

SUBJECTS: Random sample of 340 Ss drawn from colleges degree lists, N = 264 (84%).

METHODS: Questionnaire about involvement in protest activities, background, demographic information, attitudes toward racial issues, characteristics of college. Three levels of activism distinguished: participation (sat-in, picketed, took part in demonstrations or marches, involved in sit-ins, freedom rides, etc., or donated money, N = 65 (25%); membership (belonged to protest group but not active in protest), N = 38 (14%); inactive, N = 161, (71%). Data cross-tabulated with level of activism the key variable.

RESULTS: 84% of Ss support sit-ins and freedom rides. The most active Ss come from large cities and grew up in counties with 29-39% blacks, have high family income and white collar family head, rate current race relations in South as very bad, but express less racial hostility, pessimism and despair than moderately active or inactive Ss, believe relatively smaller % whites in South favor strict segregation, believe race relations in home community better than in South as a whole, better informed politically, read more newspapers and magazines, more often watch TV and radio and have more frequent contacts with whites.

College characteristics: % participating or members highest in high quality, private I's located in counties with low % blacks and in large cities. Quality of school and % blacks in county have independent effects on activism. In high quality schools with low % blacks in county, 65% of Ss participate, but in low quality schools with high % blacks in county, 14% participate. Control for family income does not wash out effects of college characteristics. College seniors, humanities, and physical science majors most active, freshmen, education, and business administration majors least active. Three differences persist when quality of college and % blacks in county are controlled for. Authors argue that the impact of education increases activism.

COMMENTS: A study of black students in the early civil rights movement. Multivariate statistics would have been useful in analyzing interactions in complex data. Most results concerning quality of I attended, SES, parental income, optimism, and field of study are similar to results obtained with early white activists, but some results are unique to black students: e.g., % blacks in college county. Most of activism can be explained by the variables studied here.

173. _____ . 1969. "Negro Students and the Protest Movement." In McEvoy, J., and Miller, A., eds. 1969. BLACK POWER AND STUDENT REBELLION. Belmont, California: Wadsworth, pp. 379-418. Essentially the same as Matthews and Prothro 1966.

174. *Maxmen, J.S. 1970. "Medical Student Activists." Residency thesis, Department of Psychiatry, Yale University School of Medicine. 251 pp.

SETTING: Fall 1968 to fall 1969, Yale Medical School, New Haven, Conn.

SUBJECTS: 13 medical students chosen for high participation in Student Health Organization (Yale Chapter) and degree of leftism. 9 males.

METHODS: Participant observation for 18 months in SHO. Individual interviews semistructured, lasted 2-5 hours. Data on political attitudes, development as physicians, personal background, and political behavior.

RESULTS: Average age 23; all but 1 single; 6 Jews, 5 Protestants, 2 nonaffiliated, no Catholics; all white; 8 upper-middle class, 2 middle class, 2 lower-middle class. All from predominantly liberal-Democratic homes: 3 fathers and 1 mother physicians; all but 1 of Ss have B.A., 4 in English, 3 history, 2 chemistry, 3 biology, 1 psychology; most from Ivy League Colleges; in 1968 election 5 voted for Humphrey, 2 Cleaver, 2 Gregory, 1 Socialists, and 3 no vote; prefer specialties of psychiatry and family practice. Five core values identified in Ss: humanitarianism, moral integrity, meaningful communication, groupism, activity. Parents described as warm, sensitive, intense, politically liberal, both parents close to children, tended to support and encourage Ss' medical careers and political activities. None of Ss were rebelling against their parents ideologically. Ss ambivalent about their intellectual accomplishments, attracted to medicine because they viewed it as a way to get things done, personally, for others, and politically. Stages in radicalization are (1) parental identification, (2) disillusionment, (3) the search for new alternatives, (4) activation, (5) role experimental, (6) the radicalizing influence of the medical school and ultimately, (7) integration. Most Ss experienced conflicts with faculty and within themselves. Many were active in the movement activities and oscillated from medical to political activities.

COMMENTS: An intensive study of a small sample of medical students activists, valuable for its descriptive and historical depth and breadth.

175. ____. 1971. "Medical Student Radicals: Conflict and Resolution. AMERICAN JOURNAL OF PSYCHIATRY 127, no. 9 (March):131-35.

SETTING, SUBJECTS, METHODS, AND RESULTS: See Maxmen 1970. Emphasizes apparent paradox of radicalism in traditionally conservative field of medicine. Three core values are distinctive in medical student radicals: humanitarianism, moral integrity, meaningful communication. SHO membership and medical student activism serves as means of self-validation, offers community, discharges the tensions of medical life through activity. Author notes personal conflict and "less common response of isolation and depression" in many medical students, emphasizes medical school as a "radicalizing" experience for some students because of humanitarian ethic, intimate clinical contact with results of injustice, poverty, racism and third-rate medical care, and realization that many "medical" problems are social and political in nature.

COMMENTS: Essentially a summary of parts of his lengthier thesis.

176. McDonnel, Thomas R. 1962. "Differences in Student Attitudes toward Civil Liberties." In Sutherland, R.L., ed. 1962. PERSONALITY FACTORS ON THE COLLEGE CAMPUS. Austin, Texas: University of Texas, pp. 29-42.

177. McDowell, S.F.; Lowe, G.A., Jr.; and Dockett, D.A. 1970. "Howard University's Student Protest Movement." PUBLIC OPINION QUARTERLY 34 (Fall):383-88.

SETTING: March 27, 1968, Howard University, the first day classes renewed after settlement of a 4 day sit-in.

SUBJECTS: 384 students in 10 classes, of whom 363 were enrolled in the College of Liberal Arts.

METHODS: Questionnaire with 18 statements about academic grievances, black identity issues, and student movement and tactical issues.

RESULTS: Majority agreement with all academic grievances, (especially those suggesting administrative tyranny), support for black awareness, overwhelming opposition to exclusion of white students and instructors, majority support for student take-over of administration building.

COMMENTS: Brief descriptive study that documents widespread support for Howard 1968 sit-in.

178. *Meyer, Marshall W. 1971a. "Harvard Students in the Midst of Crisis." SOCIOLOGY OF EDUCATION 44, No. 3 (Summer): 245-269.

SETTING: May 1969, Harvard University, 3 weeks after University Hall occupation and police bust.

SUBJECTS: Random 20% sample of Harvard and Radcliffe students, graduate students in arts and sciences, N = 937 (55%). Radical students underrepresented because of SDS opposition to questionnaire as "counterinsurgency research."

METHODS: Questionnaire mailed to all Ss, included self-rating on 9-point scale from far left to far right; scores on factor-analytic left-right scale on which self-rating is loaded + 0.80. Activism criterion: participation in antiwar demonstrations. Analysis focuses on changes in student attitudes as inferred from retrospective reports.

RESULTS: Unidimensionality of sociopolitical items suggests a high degree of ideological cohesion at Harvard prior to and concurrent with 1969 incident. No association of radicalism or activism with belief in value of Harvard education, amount of informal contact with faculty, estimation of concern of senior faculty with personal problems of students, concern of junior instructors with students, etc. Conversion rates on items measuring justification for building takeover and penalty for student occupiers vary with political self-ratings: right-wingers not converted, left-wingers show massive changes.

Activism associated with attitude change in the direction of justifying takeover and approving amnesty. Rightists show growing approval of calling police; leftists do not change re police. Ninety-one percent of those present saw police striking students. Leftism is not associated with perception of police violence but is highly related to whether students were perceived as offering "resistance." Leftists supported the strike primarily because of strike demands; centrists and rightists primarily because police had been called in. Centrist students (moderates and liberals) disapproved of building seizure but also disapproved of calling police and struck because of use of police force.

COMMENTS: An interesting and unusual paper in its emphasis on attitude *change*, rather than on the characteristics of protesters. Note high degree of prior ideologization followed by increased polarization after police action.

179. * ____. 1971b. "Harvard Students in the Midst of Crisis: A Note on the Sources of Leftism." Unpublished paper, Department of Sociology, Cornell University and New York State School of Industrial and Labor Relations. 30 pp. + App.

SETTING, SUBJECTS, AND METHODS: See Meyer 1971a. Dummy variable regression analysis with S's position on the left-right political spectrum as the dependent variable.

RESULTS: Father's education: $r' = 0.146$. Curvilinear relationship with leftism associated with both very little and very much education; rightism with father college educated. Religion: $r' = 0.197$, order from left is Jewish, none, Catholic, and Protestant. Father's occupation: sons of professors and blue-collar workers most left, professionals next, managers and proprietors least. Father's political position (as judged by son) correlates with son's position, $r = + 0.424$.

When participation in previous antiwar demonstrations is entered in regression equation first, author argues that "the effects of background variables all but disappear," but weights assigned to background variables do not substantially change. Previous political participation is a better predictor of leftism than any variable except father's political position. Correlation between father's political position (left) and antiwar demonstration involvement of son = 0.206. Father's political position and previous involvement in antiwar demonstrations are "separate sources of political belief of students."

COMMENTS: The dependent variable is weak, but the study indicates that father's perceived political position is the most powerful single predictor of students' position, followed closely by previous activism. Sociological factors not strongly related to political position at Harvard in 1969.

180. *Middleton, Russell, and Putney, Snell. 1963a. "Political Expression of Adolescent Rebellion." AMERICAN JOURNAL OF SOCIOLOGY 5 (March):27-35. Also in Sigel, Roberta, ed. 1970. LEARNING ABOUT POLITICS. New York: Random House, pp. 132-41.

SETTING: Late 1961, students in 16 I's; state university, state college, private university, and private liberal arts college in Far West, Midwest, Northeast, and South. Four I's church-affiliated.

SUBJECTS: 1440 Ss (Male N = 824) almost all between 17 and 22.

METHODS: Questionnaire includes political self-characterization on 5-point scale from socialist to highly conservative (also "no political beliefs") and perceptions of parents' political views. "Political rebellion" defined as student's political self-characterization different from parents. Measures of closeness to parents, strictness vs. permissiveness of parental discipline, "generalized rebellion" against parents (reports of defying parents in high school and doing things contrary to their wishes), estimates of parental interest in politics. Separate breakdowns by sex of student and parents.

RESULTS: About half of subjects exhibit "political rebellion." Trend toward association between "generalized rebellion" and "political rebellion." Both strict and permissive parental discipline associated with filial political rebellion (trend) and with less closeness to parents. Closeness to same-sex parents associated with lack of political rebellion, an association that increases when parents are interested in politics. Highly significant relationship between parental interest in politics and student-parent closeness.

COMMENTS: A widely-quoted paper that argues that "deviation from parental political viewpoint is associated with estrangement between parent and child—if the parent is interested in politics." Actually, the results are rather more complex, and the hypothesis holds for same-sex parent even if the parent is *not* interested in politics. "Political rebellion" is undifferentiated as regards deviation to the right and left from parents. Relevant especially to the parental conflict and filial politics thesis.

181. ____. 1963b. "Student Rebellion against Parental Political Beliefs." SOCIAL FORCES 41 (May):377-83.

SETTING, SUBJECTS, METHODS: See Middleton and Putney 1963a.

RESULTS: 33% of Ss moved left, 7.6% moved right, 42.6% agree with parents. Male Ss more likely to "rebel" to the left than females, who are more likely to remain "uncrystallized" (no political beliefs). Highly conservative students more likely to agree with parents than socialist or highly liberal students. The greater the interest of students in politics, the greater the likelihood of rebellion. "Political rebellion" is greatest when neither parent agrees with perceived conventional political position.

COMMENTS: Ss from conservative background seem more likely to remain conservative than Ss from liberal backgrounds are to remain liberal. Note trend in 1961 toward the left.

182. Miller, Paul R. 1969. "The Chicago Demonstration: A Study in Identity." BULLETIN OF THE ATOMIC SCIENTISTS 25, no. 4:3-6.

183. ____. 1970a. "Revolutionists among the Chicago Demonstrators." BULLETIN OF THE ATOMIC SCIENTISTS 26, no. 2 (February):16-21. Also in AMERICAN JOURNAL OF PSYCHIATRY 127 (1970):752-58.

SETTING, SUBJECTS, AND METHODS: See Miller 1970b. Paper compares 19 Ss (18%) sample who called selves "revolutionists" with 88 Ss who did not in arrested Chicago sample.

RESULTS: Compared to nonrevolutionists, revolutionists more often from outside Illinois, choose social activist career, received parental support for activism, supported SDS, anarchism, and communism, acknowledged that anarchists and communists took part in demonstrations, deny the demonstrations were taken over by "anarchists, terrorists, communists and assassins," believe capitalism a major social problem; less often support McCarthy, Kennedy, electoral activity, community action groups, educational efforts, and nonviolence. From anecdotal and illustrative material author argues that conversion of activist to revolutionist involves shift from concern with individual autonomy to concern with power.

COMMENTS: Small sample size limits generalizability, but data indicating greater parental support for revolutionists than for nonrevolutionists is of special interest.

184. ____. 1970b. "Social Activists and Social Change: The Chicago Demonstrators." AMERICAN JOURNAL OF PSYCHIATRY 126 (June):1752-59.

SETTING: Aug. 25-29, 1968, Chicago, Democratic National Convention.

SUBJECTS: Of 235 arrestees contacted after Convention demonstrations, 107 (45.5%) completed questionnaires. (16% of 668 arrested demonstrators.) Compared with all arrested demonstrators. Ss show no significant differences in age, sex, residence, occupation, or previous arrests, but tend to be younger, more out-of-state, and more often students.

METHODS: Questionnaire covering education, occupation, vocation, sympathy with various political movements, perception of those present at demonstration, previous arrests, attitudes to nonviolence, physical attack by police, mothers' and fathers' political attitudes and activities. Results presented descriptively.

RESULTS: Ss are 100% white, 90% male, 70% age 18-25, 65% midwestern residents, 41% students, 92% never arrested except for traffic violation or protest. Seventy-nine percent have attended college, modal social class is upper-middle with only 1% lower. Career choices are professional (60%), creative arts (9%), social activism (7%), business (5%), farming (2%), undecided (17%). Fifty-four percent fathers, 33% mothers have college or higher degrees; 73% fathers are executives, professionals, or medium-major proprietors; 48% mothers work outside the home (of them, 54% were executives or professionals). Most parents are liberal: 71% mothers, 65% fathers liberal Republicans, moderate-liberal Democrats, or radical liberals. Sixty-three percent mothers, 81% fathers politically active. A slight majority of mothers disapprove of S's protests, but 58% of Ss received approval from one or both parents. Seventeen percent previously arrested for civil disobedience, 74% never arrested except traffic violations. Forty-eight percent universally nonviolent, 23% situationally so. Fifty-four percent report they were attacked by police, 4% claim they resisted when arrested. Ss list major social problems facing American as racism, 76%; poverty, 39%;

Vietnam war, 33%; militarism, 27%; etc. Anticipated types of future activism are demonstrations, 55%, electoral activity, 41%, community actions, 28%, education, 26%, revolution, 18%, etc. Six percent self-labelled "drop-outs"; 18%, "revolutionists."

COMMENTS: A descriptive portrait of Chicago Convention arrestees which, although lacking any comparison group, is generally consistent with other portraits of activists.

185. Miller, Roy E. 1971. "Student Ideology at Southern Illinois University: An Empirical Test of Theory." Ph.D. dissertation, University of Illinois at Urbana-Champaign.

186. *_____ , and Everson, David H. 1970. "Personality and Ideology: The Case of Student Power." Paper read at Midwest Political Science Association, April-May 1970. 63 pp. + App.

SETTING: Winter quarter 1969, Southern Illinois University (Carbondale) including Vocational-Technical Institute.

SUBJECTS: Representative sample of 1000 of 21,000 students sent questionnaires. 394 nonrespondents, 107 partial respondents, N = 499 (49.9%). Final sample judged representative.

METHODS: Using factor analysis and cluster analysis, 3 attitude scales were developed: (1) militancy—readiness to take extreme or disruptive action to accomplish student power goals—(2) left-right political ideology— all items concerned with local campus issues—and (3) alienation—all university-related items that convey sense that university administration is indifferent to students, who are powerless. Militancy and leftism highly correlated. Three major subgroups distinguished: "militant radicals" (high militancy, high leftism, N = 29), "nonmilitant conservatives" (low militancy, high rightism, N = 84), and "moderates" (all others, N = 386). Militant radicals have most often demonstrated, rate selves more left, and believe university needs more change.
Ss given Rosenberg's Misanthropy Scale, McClosky and Schar's Anomy Scale, Paranoia, Personal Efficacy, short D, Christie Balanced F. Information on family background, religion, and parents' political preference gathered. Two composite measures developed: family political values (S's political characterizations of parent's views); family permissiveness index (S influenced family decisions, was rarely disciplined, and was disciplined by verbal means).

Data analysis involves comparisons of mean scores of 3 groups on personality scales and alienation measure, then several multivariate analyses, including multiple correlation and stepwise regression.

RESULTS: Radicals lowest on D, F, and personal efficacy; conservatives lowest on paranoia, alienation.

No significant results with regard to anomy and misanthropy.

Multivariate analyses: militancy and political ideology scales averaged as dependent variable. Independent variables divided into 3 sectors: (1) 2 family measures; (2) 6 personality measures; (3) "alienation" measure. Family measures not related to personality measures or alienation, but to ideology ($r'^2 = 0.15$) and ideology ($r'^2 = 0.44$). Stepwise solution shows the 2 best predictors of (radical) ideology are (low) F-scale and (high) alienation ($r'^2 = +0.48$). Family variables eliminated from causal consideration. Data do not permit clear decision between causal interpretations of findings. Authors conclude that "radicals" are not more healthy or more dogmatic than conservatives.

COMMENTS: Methodologically and statistically sophisticated study at a nonselective university. "Alienation," "militancy" and left "ideology" are all defined in terms of university-related issues, making the generalizability to other issues limited. Note elimination of family variables from causal analysis.

187. Mock, Kathleen, R. 1968. "The Potential Activist and His Perception of the University." Paper read at American Psychological Association, September 1968, San Francisco. 9 pp. + App. Also in JOURNAL OF APPLIED BEHAVIORAL SCIENCE (1970).

SETTING, SUBJECTS, METHODS, AND RESULTS: See Mock and Heist, 1969. UCB data used to substantiate some results. Pro-FSM freshmen more often favor student involvement in decisions about course content, course organization, and academic policy, favor greater involvement with off-campus politics rather than campus activities, oppose grade competition, choose self-expression over superior grades, more likely to transfer from original college and to plan academic careers. On some educational issues, however, all Ss agree in preferring large, public coed campus on the quarter system with no graduate school, little snob appeal and much attention to undergraduates.

COMMENTS: A somewhat more detailed analysis of data presented in Mock and Heist 1969.

188. ____ . 1970. "Some Psychological Differences in Highly Intellectual College Students between Those Opposed to and Those in Favor of a Political Protest Movement." Paper read at California State Psychological Association, January 1970, Monterey, 10 pp.

SETTING, SUBJECTS, METHODS, AND RESULTS: See Mock and Heist, 1969. Essentially a presentation of that part of Mock and Heist 1969 in which 40 pro-FSM and 25 anti-FSM students, all of whom shared high intellectual disposition scores on the OPI, were compared. One year follow-up of 10 high intellectual disposition anti-FSM students showed only 4 had remained strongly opposed to FSM. Persistence of anti-FSM attitudes related to limited growth of independence and continuing attachment to conservative backgrounds.

COMMENTS: See Mock and Heist 1969.

189. *____ , and Heist, Paul. 1969. "Potential Activists: The Characteristics and Backgrounds of a Capable and Challenging Minority." Center for Research and development in Higher Education, Berkeley. 32 pp. + App.

SETTING: 1966, University of California at Davis, Los Angeles, Santa Barbara and Berkeley; 1 year follow-up.

SUBJECTS: Freshmen on the first 3 campuses, supplemented by survey of freshmen at UC, Berkeley.

METHODS: Groups distinguished on the basis of Berkeley FSM attitudes: pro-FSM (extremely favorable, N = 79, 5% of total N), neutral (no opinion, N = 255, 18%), very opposed (N = 288, 20%). Freshmen with moderate opinions excluded. For some analyses, extremely pro-FSM and anti-FSM Berkeley freshmen used as comparison group. Non-Berkeley Ss given OPI, items about controversial issues, goals of higher education, description of college environment, political self-description, etc.

RESULTS: 1 year follow-up on non-Berkeley freshmen shows shift toward pro-FSM position, with strongly pro- up from 5% to 14%, and strongly anti-down from 18% to 10%. Pro-FSM group homogeneous politically (89% liberal or very liberal); anti-FSM group 45% conservative or very conservative, 34% moderate, 21% liberal or very liberal. Pro-FSM Ss anticipate involvement in or are sympathetic toward left-liberal campus protests. No overall differences in academic achievement between groups; but pro-FSM females at L.A. and Davis scored higher on academic aptitude tests than anti-FSM females. High intellectual disposition among all pro-FSM Ss; anti-FSM Ss below average. Pro-FSM Ss higher on OPI thinking introversion, theoretical orientation, aestheticism, complexity, autonomy, religious liberalism, impulse expression; no differences on other scales.

"High intellectual disposition" pro-FSM, N = 40, and anti-FSM, N = 25, Ss compared: applied, practical, analytic thinking characterizes anti-FSM Ss; complexity, tolerance of ambiguity, independence of judgment and aesthetic interests characterize pro-FSM group. Pro-FSM Ss have more aesthetic, feminine interests, resemble Ss with high potential for creativity in arts or humanities; anti-FSM males resemble Ss with high potential in physical sciences; anti-FSM females more attached to traditional familial and religious background.

Compared to anti-FSM Ss, pro-FSM Ss expect more professional education, define college less often as vocational preparation, more often as general education, prefer self-directed education, independent work, small seminars and group discussion, informal contact with faculty; emphasize importance of peers, literary artistic work, research, and interaction with classmates. Anti-FSM Ss prefer greater classroom structure, definite assignments and regular examinations, place more emphasis on parties, athletics, and student government. Pro-FSM Ss less certain about future way of life, but more often plan academic or creative life, major in fine arts and humanities, say they will seek challenging work, autonomy, and freedom to make decisions in future courses. Anti-FSM Ss often seek above-average income and job security.

No association of FSM attitudes with father's education, professional standing, or income. But pro-FSM mothers are better educated and have higher occupational standing, Ss more often from Jewish (vs. Protestant) backgrounds, 60% currently agnostic, atheistic, and nonreligious (vs. 19% anti-FSM). Largest shift away from parents' religion and politics found in pro-FSM Ss.

Two general patterns seen in families of potential activists: (1) liberal humanist family which passes intellectual orientations, scholastic values and liberal views on to children, (2) permissive family with nonauthoritarian child-rearing, democratic decision-making, nonorthodox religion and stress on thinking for oneself. Among Ss with high intellectual orientation, difference between pro- and anti-FSM Ss lies in the greater break with the cultural past on the part of the pro-FSM Ss.

COMMENTS: Study essentially replicates findings on FSM activists and supporters at Berkeley, but with samples of freshmen 1½ years later. Although attitudinal criteria were used, the results are remarkably similar to FSM studies in virtually all areas. Comparisons of highly intellectual pro-FSM and anti-FSM students especially interesting.

190. Moore, Lucy S. 1970. "Law and Order on Campus: A Study of the Disciplinary Action Following the 1969 Sit-In at the University of Chicago." Master's thesis, Committee on Human Development, University of Chicago. 119 pp.

SETTING: Late winter 1969-70, University of Chicago, following sit-in in administration building to protest nonrehiring of radical woman sociologist.

SUBJECTS: 165 students summoned to appear before 3 university disciplinary committees. Of these, 129 actually appeared, N = 86 (66.6%). Three distinct hearings involved: Ss identified as participating in the sit-in, N = 64, Ss who signed complicity statements, N = 11, Ss identified in demonstrations following sit-in, N = 11.

METHODS: Interviews conducted by volunteers; Ss remaining in Chicago cooperated except for some expelled radicals who refused on political grounds. Analysis examines relationship between punishment, evidence, political views, and cooperativeness before committees, especially for 64 noncomplicity Ss.

RESULTS: Males more often identified and summoned to committees, but politics and field of major were unrelated. Most students gave political defenses, but 1/4 gave no political statements in defense. Seventy-two percent of radicals received 4-quarter suspensions or expulsion, but 84% of apoliticals received no active suspension. Evidence of involvement in sit-in for more than one day is unrelated to severity of punishment, but delay of response is highly correlated to extreme punishment. With delay of response controlled, political views still determine severity of punishment. Number of days present in sit-in and regularity of participation in sit-in activities had no effect on punishment; radicals were more likely to be nonobsequious, disrespectful, and uncooperative to committees. Having counsel present diminished punishment. Investigating committees frequently inquired about political beliefs, especially of moderates; failure to offer an explanation for delay in response to committee or defiance in presentation contributed to punishment.

Author concludes that evidence had virtually no relationship to punishment, political views and delay of response are independently related to extent of punishment, delay of response to summons increased punishment only for radicals, political views were strongest single determinant of punishment.

COMMENTS: Study indicates that political criteria were used in disciplining students involved in the 1969 University of Chicago sit-in. Note possibility that an analysis which began from defiance, disrespect, and delay of response would show diminished effects of political radicalism on severity of punishment.

191. *Morgan, William R. 1970a. "Faculty Mediation in Campus Conflict." In Foster, Julian, Long, Durward, eds. 1970. PROTEST! STUDENT ACTIV- ISM IN AMERICA. New York: William Morrow, pp. 365-82.

SETTING, INSTITUTIONS, AND METHODS: See Morgan 1971. N non-protest I's = 52 in this paper.

RESULTS: See Morgan 1971. At I's with protests, N = 106, civil disobedi-ence occurred at 33, is associated with greatly increased campus disruption, large number of faculty participants, personal violence, administrative coercive control and disciplinary action, more faculty council resolutions on administrative control and recruiting policy, more student government resolutions on administrative controls and recruiting policy, likelihood of campus referendum on recruiting. Severity of administrative control meas-ures (ranging from demonstrators arrested by police to no confrontation) is highly associated with expansion of protest. Faculty mediation made possible by faculty sympathy with demonstrators' goals or moral commit-ment. When faculty council supported new restrictions on recruiting, administrative policy was most likely to conform. Author's discussion emphasizes that "student coercion has bred faculty and administration reasoning."

COMMENTS: Findings on severity of administrative response and subse-quent escalation of protest need replication with other factors controlled.

192. ____ . 1970b. "Student Protests and Racial Disorders: Formative Influence Relations." Ph.D. dissertation, University of Chicago.

193. ____ . 1971. "Campus Conflict as Formative Influence." In Short, James F., Jr. and Wolfgang, Marvin E., eds. 1971. COLLECTIVE VIOLENCE. Chicago: Aldine.

SETTING: 1967-68, I's with antirecruiting protests.

INSTITUTIONS: I's indentified by national, local, and student newspaper accounts. Protests I's matched with comparable I's that had no protests.

Questionnaires sent to 1 administrator, 1 faculty member and 2 students at each I. Some data available from 96% of I's. N protest I's = 106; N nonprotest = 26.

RESULTS: The more severe the protest, the more likely were new restrictions on on-campus recruiting and new regulations on demonstrations. When I's were matched on administrative liberalism, these same effects persist. The greater the prior discussion of issues on campus, the more likely were severe demonstrations. Author argues that demonstrations increased polarization, that civil disobedience was most likely to produce changes in recruitment policy and new restrictions on demonstrations increase inclusion of students in decision-making.

COMMENTS: A theoretically-informed analysis of on-campus recruiting protests, suggesting that severe protests produce more changes.

194. Mussen, Paul H., and Warren, Anne B. 1952. "Personality and Political Participation." HUMAN RELATIONS (February):65-82. Also in Sigel, Roberta, ed. 1970. LEARNING ABOUT POLITICS New York: Random House, pp. 277-92.

SETTING: 1948-49, University of Wisconsin, Madison.

SUBJECTS: Undergraduate volunteers from introductory psychology course and 8 student leaders of YR, YD, or Young Progressives, N = 156.

METHODS: 2 extreme groups defined on the basis of reported present and future political interests: actives, N = 45, apathetics, N = 37. Questionnaire included demographic variables, Anti-Semitism, Ethnocentrism, PEC and 10 projective questions. Comparisons of means of 2 extreme groups.

RESULTS: No significant relationships between attitude scales and level of political activity. Projective questions indicate that actives show more conscious conflict and guilt, less tendency to escape studies or quit school, more identification with socially-contributing rather than power- or success-oriented figures, greater inability to adjust to situations or face reality, less diffuse worry, less concern with social conventions and conformity, more concern with human betterment, less conventionalized and emotionally shallow thinking, more emphasis on intellectual, aesthetic, and scientific achievements, greater social consciousness, more stress on productive living, less emphasis on obedience, good morals, religious training, and "successful relations" with others, etc. Apathetics are less able to recognize personal responsibility or examine own emotions and feelings.

COMMENTS: An early study organized around concepts of THE AUTHORITARIAN PERSONALITY, interprets "actives'" reports of greater conflict in many areas as positive signs. Note absence of correlation between authoritarianism scales and activity.

195. Neale, Daniel C., and Johnson, David W. n.d. "College Student Participation in Social Action Project." Unpublished paper, University of Minnesota. 18 pp.

SETTING: 1967, University of Minnesota.

SUBJECTS: Student volunteers in work with culturally disadvantaged children, N = 84 (84%), random sample of UM undergraduates stratified by academic class, N = 418 (82%). Sixty-four volunteers female.

METHODS: Questionnaire concerning volunteer activities, campus activities, social responsibility scale, demographic data, etc.

RESULTS: Volunteers more active in and positive about social action projects, more often in college of liberal arts (vs. technology, agriculture, forestry, and home economics), in social sciences (vs. engineering, science, mathematics, agriculture, and business), higher GPA, not from large cities, more often live away from home and near campus, consider unselfish motives and rebellion more important in volunteer work, etc. No differences in social responsibility or knowledge of campus affairs. See also Johnson and Neale 1968.

COMMENTS: A study of student volunteers that finds them similar in some ways to activists as defined in other studies.

196. Nogee, Philip, and Levin, M.B. 1958. "Some Determinants of Political Attitudes among College Voters." PUBLIC OPINION QUARTERLY 22 (Winter):449-63.

SETTING: 1956-57, Boston University.

SUBJECTS: Students age 21-25, stratified by religion and college within university, N = 314 (87%).

METHODS: Questions concerning own and parents' presidential choice and party affiliation, attitudes toward workers vs. employers, government ownership of utilities, guaranteed government employment; permissiveness, restrictiveness or averageness of parental control. Data analyzed in tabular form with presidential preference, party preference, or ideology as dependent variables.

RESULTS: First-time college voters vote more often than general public; party preference strongly associated with ideological position of party; no evidence of marked generational revolt to right or left; no evidence that parental discipline is associated with departure from parental party choice. Schools of theology and education show most liberal change, business most conservative change, education and liberal arts change to more independents. Jews and Catholics more likely to be Democrats.

COMMENTS: Useful as background for major changes that occurred in 1960s. Mid-1950s data show virtually no parent-child political shift at BU at time of 1956 election. But note liberalization or greater independence in theology, education, and liberal arts college, conservatization in business school.

197. Nowicki, Stephen, Jr. 1969. "Conservatism and Liberalism in College Students." PSYCHOLOGICAL REPORTS 25, no. 1:252.

SETTING: Not stated.

SUBJECTS: 100 Ss in abnormal psychology class, 84 males.

METHODS: Ss given I-E Marlowe-Crown Social Desireability Scale, and questions concerning social, political attitudes. Ss classified as 50% liberal, 50% conservative.

RESULTS: Conservatives higher on Social Desirability, no differences on I-E. With Ss planning marriage and receiving financial support excluded, conservatives favor strict parental discipline, individual self-support in college; liberals favor racial integration, women having careers, social welfare, and ending arms race.

COMMENTS: A brief report.

198. Orbell, J. 1967. "Protest Participation among Southern Negro College Students." AMERICAN POLITICAL SCIENCE REVIEW 61 (June): 446-56.

SETTING, SUBJECTS, METHODS, AND RESULTS: See Matthews and Prothro 1966. Overall, activism is associated with low ANOMIA (but not in urban counties and private colleges), with dissatisfaction with position of black race (but not with frustration concerning racial treatment), and with less hostility toward whites. Author argues that when the context is unsupportive for protests, anomic Ss are less likely to be activists.

COMMENTS: See Matthews and Prothro 1966.

199. Orum, Anthony M. 1967. "Negro College Students and the Civil Rights Movement." Ph.D. dissertation, University of Chicago.

200. ____, and Orum, A.W. 1968. "The Class and Status Bases of Negro Student Protest." SOCIAL SCIENCE QUARTERLY 49 (December): 521-33.

SETTING: April-May 1964.

SUBJECTS AND INSTITUTIONS: Probability sample involving 50 predominantly black I's and approximately 7000 seniors, N = 3, 429 (49%). Sample somewhat biased toward women, Ss with high grades, physical sciences an; humanities majors. Seventy percent of Ss reported participation in economic boycotts; 32% claimed active participation in leadership. Percent participating in any role used as dependent variable.

RESULTS: Participation higher among students with high family incomes, and at I's with high mean student SES. With institutional SES controlled, individual SES effects disappear. Participation slightly associated with high occupational aspirations, especially if these are stable from freshman-senior year; not associated with perceptions of employment opportunities even among Ss with high aspirations. Authors argue that data refute theories of increasing impoverishment, rising expectations, and relative deprivation as sources of black civil rights activism.

COMMENTS: A study of the correlates of civil rights activism among black students that points to very high levels of participation in 1964 and contradicts much earlier research. See Matthews and Prothro 1966 for earlier data.

201. **Paulus, G. 1967. "A Multivariate Analysis Study of Student Activist Leaders, Student Government Leaders, and Nonactivists." Ph.D. dissertation, Michigan State University. 129 pp.

SETTING: Jan.-July 1966, Michigan State University.

SUBJECTS: 3 groups: (1) student activists (SA): members of SNCC, SDS, or MSU Committee for Student's Rights who spent > 1 hour/week and/or had demonstrated commitment to organization and/or had proselytized for organization; (2) student government leaders (SG): elected office-holders in the Associated Students of MSU; (3) control group (CG): matched with SA on sex, grade level, major, GPA, and verbal ability. N in each group = 25. Some lack of cooperation from activist group because of protests involving 50 arrests during study.

METHODS: 2 questionnaires: Educational Testing Service College Student Questionnaire including 5 scales measuring morale or satisfaction, 3 scales measuring sociocultural awareness, 3 scales measuring perceived independence; CUES. Multiple group discriminant analysis used.

RESULTS: Group comparisons: SA and CG more often in arts and letters compared to SG in social science. SA and CG have higher GPA and higher verbal ability. SA includes 17 scholarship winners (7 National Merit), CG 8 scholarships (4 National Merit), SG 7 scholarships (2 National Merit). Members of all groups came from top 10% of classes, were concerned about grades, high involvement in English, social science and science, and low athletic team participation. SA not close to high school teachers, SG report high rapport. SA report lowest peer relationships and dating, fewer high school extracurricular activities, greater dissatisfaction with secondary school. SA more often urban, irreligious, eldest children, parents Jewish or no religion and highly involved in cultural events. SA and SC come from highest high income families. SA parents evenly divided between conservative Republicans and liberal Democrats. SG parents overwhelmingly conservative Republicans, CG mostly Republicans. Twenty SA choose nonconformist philosophy; 24 SG choose extracurricular philosophy.

Multiple group discriminant analysis: 2 orthogonal functions distinguished: factor 1 = 82.7% of total group dispersion; factor 2 = 17.3%. First factor places SA high, CG intermediate, SG low. Factor pattern involves liberalism, family independence, cultural sophistication, and social conscience vs. extracurricular involvement, satisfaction with administration, and awareness on CUES. Second factor discriminates CG fron both SA and SG. Factor pattern involves low extracurricular involvement, high satisfaction with students and administration. Author concludes SA group most independent and socially aware; SG least; CG more satisfied with university than either other group. Ninety-two percent of total sample correctly classified by discriminant function scores.

In self-perception on Clark-Trow typology (vocational, nonconformist, academic, collegiate) 24 SA = nonconformist, 19 SG = academic. But 15 SG describe nonconformist type as their ideal.

138

COMMENTS: An important and sophisticated study that essentially replicates Berkeley FSM research, although matching of control group with activists washes out some differences. Note satisfaction with faculty and major does not discriminate activists, but family and peer independence does.

202. **Peterson, Richard E. Introduction.

SETTING: 1964-65, 1967-68, May-June 1970.

INSTITUTIONS: 1964-65: all 4-year accredited I's in U.S.; sample data from dean of students or other research agent, N = 849 (85%). 1967-68: same sample and informants, N = 859 (86%). 1970: questionnaire to presidents of all 2551 colleges in the country, N = 1856 (73%). Studies of nonrespondent I's indicate that all samples are reasonably representative.

METHODS: In 1964-65 and 1967-68, respondents given lists of protest issues; report yes-no on each issue. Protest issues factor analyzed (list somewhat different); roughly comparable factors in both studies; factor scores calculated. In 1970, questionnaire focuses on Cambodia/Kent/ Jackson incidents; questions concern events, incidents, and respones at each I. Descriptive summary of results; cross-tabulations and correlations of protest factors and specific types of protest with I characteristics. 1967-68 study examines shifts from 1964-65.

RESULTS: See Peterson 1966, 1968, 1970, Peterson and Bilorusky 1971, Peterson and Centra 1969, Sasajima et al. 1967.

COMMENT: An excellent series of studies focused upon incidence of protests and relationships with I characteristics. Good theoretical discussions and analyses of trends.

203. *Peterson, Richard E. 1966. "The Scope of Organized Student Protest in 1964-1965." Princeton, New Jersey: Educational Testing Service. 58 pp.

SETTING, INSTITUTIONS, METHODS: See Peterson Intro. Protest factors are described in Sasajima et al. 1967.

RESULTS: Civil rights protests most common nationally (38% of I's), followed by protests over food service, living regulations, off-campus civil rights, U.S. Vietnam policies, dress regulations, etc. Overall protests concerning on-campus issues, are most common; protests over instruction, faculty, freedom of expression are rare. Protests most common at large I's (> 10,000); protests over off-campus issues associated with I quality and presence of radical or civil rights groups on campus. Variation in types of protest most common at each of 8 types of I's (e.g., off-campus protests most common at independent universities). Percentage of Ss involved in protests (ranged from average of 8-9% in student regulations protests to 4% in academic freedom and faculty tenure protests). Off-campus issues typically involve less than 5% of student body.

COMMENTS: Good early study that shows high incidence of protest over on-campus issues in 1964-65, relationship between I characteristics and occurrence of protests. Good interpretation of data.

204. *____. 1968. "The Scope of Organized Student Protest in 1967-1968." Unpublished paper, Educational Testing Service, Princeton, New Jersey. 60 pp.

SETTING, INSTITUTIONS, AND METHODS: See Peterson Intro., Peterson 1966. Five new issues substituted for issues used in earlier study. Respondents indicated no protest, frequency of protest, % students involved, faculty involvement.

RESULTS: Most frequent protest issues were Vietnam policies, living group regulations, civil rights, student power, draft, on-campus military recruiting, and food service. Protests over instructional quality, faculty matters, and freedom of expression infrequent. Protests over off-campus issues (especially war-related) are related to indices of I size, quality and % of student body belonging to left-wing organizations; these relationships became stronger between 1964-65 and 1967-68. Student activists a small minority, with average of 9% involved in protests over dorm, dress and drinking regulations, and 4% on war-related issues. Percentage students involved in each of general types of protests unrelated to I characteristcs.

Comparisons with 1964-65 data show antiwar protests doubled; student power protests increased; civil rights protests declined among white students; black students increasingly demanded new educational experiences; % students active per I has not increased; % I's with left student groups almost doubled.

COMMENTS: Important study, especially interesting for examination of changes in student movement between 1964-65 and 1967-68.

205. *_____. 1970. "Cambodia, Kent, Jackson and the Campus Aftermath."
Report to Carnegie Commission on Higher Education, Berkeley, California.
8 pp.

SETTING, INSTITUTIONS, METHODS: See Peterson Intro. All statistics
computed separately for I's that reported impact from Cambodia/Kent/
Jackson events, N = 1064. Data from college presidents. Intensity of impact
indexed by four variables: student/staff strike greater than 1 day; student
efforts to communicate with local people; peaceful demonstrations; demonstrations involving property damage or injuries.

RESULTS: 57% of I's experienced "significant impact" from Cambodia/
Kent/Jackson. Most common responses were peaceful demonstrations
(44%), moderate leaders in command (43%), efforts to communicate with
local community (40%), seminars, etc. initiated (37%). Uncommon events
were radical leaders in command (3%), property damage or injury (4%),
outside police on campus (4%), faculty vote against war (2%), referendum
or convocation against war (2%). Modification of course contents at 28% of
I's, of exams and grading procedures by at least some faculty at 25%. At
most I's, less than 10% of faculty made such changes; junior faculty more
so than senior faculty. Departures from ordinary academic procedures most
common in social sciences and humanities (vs. education, business, engineering). Instructional activities interrupted for 1 day at 8% of I's, 2 days
7%, longer 6%. Eighteen percent of presidents believe spring events
damaged academic standards; 14% believe upheaval benefited I. Fourteen
percent report increased faculty polarization; 14% greater faculty unity.
Intensity of impact positively related to independent and public university
(vs. Protestant I or public junior college), high selectivity, large enrollment,
Northeast or Pacific (vs. Mountain or Southeast) location; high federal
grants to I (major research I).

COMMENTS: Important study describing widespread national impact of
Cambodia/Kent/Jackson events and demonstrating familiar correlates of
intensity of protest.

206. **_____, and Bilorusky, John A. 1971. MAY 1970: THE CAMPUS
AFTERMATH OF CAMBODIA AND KENT STATE. Berkeley, California:
Carnegie Commission on Higher Education. 175 pp.

SETTING, INSTITUTIONS, METHODS, AND RESULTS: See Peterson
1970. A more detailed, thorough, and thoughtful discussion. Violence only
slightly more common at highly selective I's, despite higher levels of
activism. Perceived reactions of off-campus constituencies in affected I's

were slightly favorable overall for trustees, alumni, parents, and local press, slightly unfavorable for local citizens and state legislatures. Presidents of small I's saw major benefit of Cambodia/Kent/Jackson as increased student concern about national and international problems; presidents of large I's saw benefit in increased concern about curricular change. Negative off-campus reactions most marked in mountain states; perceived detrimental effect on academic standards greatest in Northeastern states. Presidents at I's with the most disruption are most pessimistic about long-range prospects; presidents of large research universities almost entirely negative about impact of Cambodia/Kent/Jackson events on their I's. Authors stress lack of commitment to academic work among academically gifted students, inability of student movement to sustain itself in the absence of new issues and provocations, acceleration of educational reforms providing more student options, extension of student opposition to foreign and domestic policies, erosion of public support for the university, and possibilities of recurrence of comparable protests.

A detailed account and analysis (Bilorusky) of reactions on the University of California Berkeley campus to the Cambodia/Kent/Jackson events.

COMMENTS: The most comprehensive and thoughtful available analysis of responses to the Cambodia/Kent/Jackson events.

207. Peterson, Richard E., and Centra, J.A. 1969. "Organized Student Protest and Institutional Functioning." Princeton, New Jersey: Educational Testing Service.

208. Pierce, R.A. 1969. "Personality Styles of Student Activists." Unpublished paper, University Health Service, University of Rochester. Revised version 1971. 12 pp. + App.

SETTING: Late December 1967-February 1968, University of Rochester, after mid-December 1967 student strike over administration disciplining of graduate students for earlier Dow Chemical sit-in.

SUBJECTS: Initial group: random sample of 140 undergraduates. Brief questionnaire indicating involvement in strike, picketing, N = 126, (87%). February 1968: 140 Ss recontacted for 1-½ hour paid testing, N = 86 (59%). Second sample overrepresented strike supporters.

METHODS: 3 activism measures: strike support (4-point attitude scale), picketing (yes/no), and number hours picketing. OPI had been administered to 37 Ss in class of 1969 as freshmen; readministered to 24. Stern's Activity Index (AI) and College Characteristics Index (CCI) given to all remaining Ss. Jackson Personality Research Form (PRF)–20 Murray-type needs had been administered to Ss of classes of 1970 and 1971 as freshmen. N = 38. Correlational analysis; change scores for OPI, N = 24; separate analyses for men, women, and both. Only significant correlations reported. Small N's.

RESULTS: OPI results for males—strike support related to increased aestheticism, junior year autonomy, and social maturity. Picketing related to junior year aestheticism. For females, support related to freshman year impulse expression, low repression/suppression; picketing and hours picketing both related to high freshman developmental status; picketing related to decreased schizoid functioning, increased repression/suppression. Hours picketing related to freshman autonomy, freshman impulse expression, junior impulse expression, freshman low repression/suppression. Overall picture emphasizes increased aestheticism, persistent autonomy, generally high social maturity.

PRF scales: for males, support and picketing related to low deference. For females, support related to low affiliation, high autonomy, low nurturance; picketing and hours picketing related to high autonomy, low cognitive structure; picketing related to high change.

AI scales: for males, all activism measures related to impracticalness and low applied interests. For females, all dependent measures related to high change, low common response and low orderliness; strike support and hours picketing related to high ego achievement and low dependency needs; support and picketing related to low educability factor.

CCI scales: for males, picketing related to reflectiveness, hours picketing related to low order and reflectiveness. For females, picketing related to abasement, work vs. play, low intellectual climate; hours picketing related to abasement, work vs. play, low adaptability, low science.

Author concludes that politically active students generally welcome change and are uninterested in structure, accept ambiguity, question external authority, reject authoritarianism; intellectual interests of activists are aesthetic, not practical, conventional, or grade-oriented. Male activists compared to other males are more friendly, open, and undefensive; women activists compared to other women are impulsive, unconventional, rebellious, less friendly, nurturant or dependent. The college environment is congenial to activists, who nonetheless reject demands for abasement, arbitrariness of administration, and passivity of fellow students.

COMMENTS: Variables associated with strike support and prostrike behavior are different for men and women. Results for sexes combined do not reflect communality of groups, but rather the distinct characteristics of male and female activists.

209. Pinard, M.; Kirk, J.; and Von Eschen, D. 1969. "Processes of Recruitment in the Sit-in Movement. PUBLIC OPINION QUARTERLY 33 (Fall): 355-59.

SETTING: Dec. 16, 1961, Baltimore, Maryland, participants in "Route 40 Freedom Ride."

SUBJECTS: 386 Ss (60-80%), judged representative. Precise N's unclear, but about 240 black, 140 white, 120 nonstudents, about 50 of them black.

METHODS: Questionnaire, distributed at Baltimore terminal of ride, measuring occupational status, occupational mobility, status inconsistency (occupational vs. educational level), date of joining movement, length of participation in movement (1 year vs. less), level of activity (high = 3+ demonstrations). "Alienation" measured by "most politicians are corrupt," "little difference between parties," "letters are effective in influencing public policy" (disagree). "Ideologue" defined either as socialist or as left of mothers' political position. Cross-tabulations presented without test of statistical significance.

RESULTS: Ss are predominantly Democrats (56%), independents (19%), or socialists (18%); 89% are in or in training for upper-middleclass jobs. Low occupational status goes with high activity level for both races. For nonstudents, downward occupational mobility and status inconsistency are related to high activity. Left ideology is associated with high activity, and for those left of mother, low status goes with early joining. For those whose politics is like mothers, political alienation is associated with low status, but this is not true for those who are left of their mothers' political position. Taken together, low status, "ideology," and "rebellious aliena-tion" explain 56% of variance in activity level. Authors conclude that the most deprived are virtually absent among civil rights activists and are late joiners but that, once they are involved, they are the most active; most highly deprived individuals lack ideology.

COMMENTS: Generalizes broadly from data gathered on 1 freedom ride. Useful in describing upper-middleclass backgrounds of early civil rights activists. Definition of variables is at times misleading. No control for age in tables examining early joining, level of activity, or intensity of activity.

210. Pinkney, A. 1969. THE COMMITTED: WHITE ACTIVISTS IN THE CIVIL RIGHTS MOVEMENT. New Haven: College and University Press. 239 pp.

SETTING: December 1963-April 1964, names of civil rights activists obtained from CORE, SNCC, Northern Student Movement, individual suggestions and media in New York area.

SUBJECTS: 312 questionnaires mailed, 200 questionnaires returned. 24 Ss considered ineligible because of antinegro attitudes. All Ss white. Final N = 176 (56%). Interviews with 33 Ss in July and August 1964.

METHODS: Data on background, personality characteristics, extent of participation, social support for participation, motivation for participation, hardships encountered, and general attitudes about civil rights. Results presented in descriptive form.

RESULTS: 48% of respondents under 30 years, 93% attended and 64% completed college. Virtually no working class Ss. Forty-seven percent single, 32% "very religious," 36% nonreligious, 16% antireligious. Thirty-four percent socialists, 26% independents, 29% Democrats. Evidence of shift to left from fathers' political viewpoint. Fifty-six percent report no conflict with parents during childhood, 24 percent conflict with one or both parents or with parents and siblings. Ss who report childhood conflict have more concrete, less ideological motives for participation. Most Ss are optimistic about human nature, have been involved in CORE, SNCC, and SCLC, 55% have participated in demonstrations. Most-mentioned stimuli for involvement in civil rights movement are ideology, reading, family, and religious influences. Seventy-five percent first became interested in black-white relations under age 20. Parents characterized as very integrationist 19%, very segregationist 8%. About 40% say relations with parents very good as a result of civil rights activities, 20% fairly bad or bad. Most Ss supported by friends and spouses. Seventy-seven percent favor nonviolent resistance, 11% favor armed self-defense, most are positive about Malcolm X, desire complete assimilation of black into American life, see education, legislation, political action, and economic changes as about equally important.

COMMENTS: A descriptive study based on a nonrandom white sample. One of several studies that indicate positive, optimistic, integrationist, antiviolent attitudes of early white civil rights activists.

211. Pitts, J.R. 1970. "College Students and the Arab-Israeli Conflict." Unpublished paper, Oakland University, Oakland, Michigan. 9 pp. + App.

SETTING: Summer 1970, Michigan State University, Oakland University, Wayne State University, University of Michigan Summer School.

SUBJECTS: 984 Protestants and Catholics, 132 Jews, 64 blacks. Ss classified by religious or racial background, N = 1180.

METHODS: Guttman scales on attitudes toward Vietnam war, invasion of Cambodia, Arab-Israeli conflict, admired figures.

RESULTS: Protestants' and Catholics' attitudes are similar. Seventy-four percent of Establishment Protestants and Catholics, 88% Jews, and 83% blacks are Vietnam doves. About sixty-six percent of Protestants-Catholics, 86% Jews, and 97% blacks are unfavorable to administration on Cambodia. Seventy-six percent of Protestants-Catholics, 30% Jews, and 85% blacks are doves on Arab-Israel conflict.

   Ss classified as "revolutionary" on the basis of extreme answers and revolutionary heroes, as "radicals" on the basis of extreme answers and left political heroes. Sixteen white revolutionaries (8 Jewish), 33 white radicals. Thirteen percent of blacks classified revolutionaries or radicals vs. less than 5% of white sample. Discussion focuses on author's estimate that Jewish Arab-Israel doves will become hawks in case of a Middle-East crisis.

COMMENTS: A largely descriptive report with no data on representativeness of sample. Shows Jews and blacks more antiwar, more opposed to Cambodian invasion, blacks most likely to be Arab-Israel doves, Jews to be hawks.

212. Porter, Jack Nusan. 1971. "Student Protest, University Decision-making, and the Technocratic Society: The Case of ROTC." Ph.D. dissertation, Northwestern University. 278 pp.

SETTING: April 1970, spring 1971, Northwestern University during NROTC controversy and Cambodia/Kent/Jackson events.

SUBJECTS: Students classified by self-label as radical, N = 46, liberal, N = 145, and conservative, N = 55; total N = 236. Interviews with members of each group and extensive participant observation in 1970. All-campus polls conducted spring 1970 and spring 1971.

METHODS: Questionnaire covering NROTC attitudes, family background, parents' political party and religious preference, etc. Statistical findings are few; not interpreted; no significance tests.

RESULTS: Thesis is largely an analysis of NROTC controversy. Polls show radicals more often male, black, nonfraternity members, in college of arts and sciences (vs. technological institute). Linear relationship between low parental income and radicalism. Radicals' fathers more often teachers, professors, owners of business, skilled or unskilled workers; conservatives' fathers more often professionals or business managers-executives. Radicals politically more independent, parents more often Democrats or independents (especially mothers), and Jewish. Radical Ss are overwhelmingly irreligious, support immediate removal of NROTC from Northwestern. Interviews after Cambodia/Kent/Jackson showed no dramatic shift in attitudes, but "solidification" in the general direction of earlier beliefs. "Radicals became more radical; likewise for conservatives; and liberal students were even more inclined to work 'within the system' for peace candidates." 1971 data show no change in student attitudes toward NROTC, although controversy had subsided.

COMMENTS: Essentially a history of the student movement, with special focus on the NROTC controversy at Northwestern. Note finding that radicals come from families with *lower* income (influence of blacks?), self-employed business or teaching occupations, but not professional or managerial backgrounds.

213. Rosenhan, David L. 1968. "The Natural Socialization of Altruistic Autonomy." In Macauley, J., and Berkowitz, L., eds. 1968. ALTRUISM AND HELPING. New York: Academic Press, 30 pp.

SETTING: 1963-65 civil rights volunteers or financial contributors.

SUBJECTS: 8 black activists (2 female), 28 white activists (5 female), N = 36. Mean age 26-27. Seven black financial supporters, 25 white financial supporters, N = 34. Mean age 26-29. Ss obtained through cooperation of SNCC and CORE. 2 Ss refused to participate; 1 found research too distressing. Eighty percent of Ss came from urban or suburban centers of the Northeast or had spent significant time there.

METHODS: Semistructured interview about extent of involvement, personal history and perception of own and others' motivation for participation. "Partially committed" went on 1 or 2 freedom rides, N = 21, "fully committed" remained physically active in the South for a year or longer, N = 25. Interviews coded. Analysis of differences between fully and partially committed activists.

RESULTS: Partially committed's interviews are longer, because of lengthier self-description and perception of others. Nearly half of partially committed had psychotherapy vs. only 1 fully committed. Fully committed are more positive toward primary socializer; partially committed, negative or ambivalent. Much greater evidence of discrepancy between teaching and practice by a socializer among partially committed. Author infers that fully committed learn "autonomous altruism" through moral precepts and precepts of socializers, but partially committed are more conflicted, searching for values, attempting to define selves as "valuing people."

COMMENTS: A useful exploratory 1 study despite uncertain sample. Note continuity of perceived parental values with behavior in fully committed group, report of greater parental conflict and psychological disturbance in partially committed group.

214. *_____ . 1969. "Some Origins of Concern for Others." In Mussen, P.; Langer, J.; and Covington, M., eds. 1969. TRENDS AND ISSUES IN DEVELOPMENTAL PSYCHIATRY. New York: Holt, Rinehart and Winston. pp. 134-53.

SETTING, SUBJECTS, AND METHODS: See Rosenhan 1968. Adds a series of experimental studies, largely with children, to examine experimental effects of exemplification and rehearsal.

RESULTS: See Rosenhan 1968. Experimental findings interpreted to support theory that positively regarded altruistic model facilitates altruism; voluntary rehearsal of altruistic behavior with the model increases the likelihood of internalized altruism; but well-formed cognitive and affective structures are required for model's altruistic behavior to be incorporated and acted upon.

COMMENTS: Ingenious use of experimental work to confirm theory derived from naturalistic observations. Developmental level is important in determining effectiveness of rehearsal in inducing altruistic action.

215. Royer, Jeannie T. 1971. "Bombings and Bomb Threats in Colleges and Universities: 1970-71." Unpublished paper, American Council on Education, Washington, D.C. 13 pp.

SETTING, INSTITUTIONS, METHODS: See A. Astin et al. Intro., Bayer and Astin 1971. Analysis of I reports of bombings and bomb threats.

RESULTS: Of all I's, 41% experienced bomb threats, 2.3% bombings. Bombings most frequent at private universities (23%), public universities

(7.2%); absent at 2-year colleges and 4-year Catholic colleges. Bomb threats most common at public universities, private universities, 4-year public colleges; least common at 2-year private colleges, 4-year Protestant and Catholic colleges. Bombings correlated with bomb threats. Overall, bombings and bomb threats associated with large size, intermediate selectivity, Northeast, West, or Southwest location (but most common at low selectivity 2-year colleges, midwestern universities). Author suggests procedures for dealing with bomb threats.

COMMENTS: Note high incidence of bomb threats in 1970-71, general association with I factors that predict protest.

216. Sampson, Edward E.; Fisher, Larry; Angel, Arthur; Mulman, Alan; and Sullins, Connie. 1969. "Two Profiles: The Draft Resister and the ROTC Cadet." Unpublished paper, University of California at Berkeley. 87 pp.

SETTING: 1968, San Francisco Bay Area, University of California at Berkeley.

SUBJECTS: 11 indicted draft refusers; 20 contract ROTC UCB students nominated as outstanding, serious cadets.

METHODS: Intensive interviews with all Ss; TAT. Data presented clinically, organized around themes that differentiate typical resister and cadet.

RESULTS: Cadets have more sisters than brothers; families traditional, structured; dominant, strict, feared, and respected fathers, submissive housewife mothers. Resisters have more brothers than sisters; families looser, permissive; fathers soft-spoken, supportive; mothers more dominant and equal to fathers. Cadets prefer superior-subordinate contexts, but perceive dependency as weak except in structured masculine settings. Resisters oppose domination and subordination, seek freedom from restraint, accept dependency in close relationships, prefer unstructured, noninstitutionalized and unpredictable settings. Cadets planful and well-organized; draft resisters usually react to events.

Cadets value self-control, practicality, rationality, are not intellectual, find excitement in traditional extracurricular and masculine activities and reject abstract-theoretical careers, accept and embody Protestant ethic, have difficulty controlling temper, use denial, avoidance and rationalization, have fantasies of uncontrolled aggression, do not consistently apply universal standards to self. Resisters open to feeling and emotion, spontaneous, find excitement in intellectual matters (not school work), have literary, philosophical artistic tastes and tend toward introspective-sensitive careers, reject Protestant ethic, use hallucinogenic drugs to intensify experience, avoid physical aggression, are highly involved with people and feelings. Cadets are unconscious rebels who profess conformity but have fantasies of open hostility; resisters are both conscious and unconscious rebels.

Cadets appear closed and unchanging, have senior OPI scores like those of typical Berkeley freshmen, are resigned to fate, have negative view of human nature, and conventional-expedient value systems, are actively engaged with death as a game, pursue physical challenge but fear injury, have difficult, infrequent, exploitative relationships with women, are often explicitly self-centered. Resisters appear more adult and open to change, often underwent sudden awakening in college, view selves as responsible agents, hold principled value orientations, struggle against existing society in pursuit of selfhood, have complex, often troubled but more mature heterosexual relationships.

COMMENTS: An intensive clinical study of 2 extreme groups, both highly committed to action vis-à-vis war.

217. **Sasajima, M.; Davis, J.A.; and Peterson, Richard E. 1967. "Organized Student Protest and Institutional Climate." Princeton, New Jersey: Educational Testing Service. 19 pp. Also in AMERICAN EDUCATIONAL RESEARCH JOURNAL 5 (May 1968):291-304.

SETTING, INSTITUTIONS, METHODS: See Peterson Intro., Peterson 1966. 109 I's for which protest reports and recent, reliable CUES scores were available. Factor analysis of protest issues yields 6 rotated factors: (on campus) quality of instruction, faculty affairs, administration paternalism, politically extremist visitors; (off campus) civil rights, U.S. militarism. CUES used as measure of campus climate. Correlations and multiple correlations between protest scales and CUES scales; CUES scores for I's reporting (vs. not reporting) each of 6 types of protest.

RESULTS: R' of CUES scores with on-campus protest issues = > 0.26; civil rights = 0.63; U.S. militarism = 0.71. High awareness plus low propriety predicts civil rights protest; high awareness plus low community (correlated with large size) predicts antimilitarism protests. Practicality, community, and propriety are negatively related to all types of protests; awareness and scholarship are positively related to protests about off-campus issues. Authors suggest that I climate seems to attract certain kinds of students, who together make for a more protest-prone atmosphere.

COMMENTS: An excellent early institutional study, despite the limited number of measures employed. Outstanding discussion of the problem of attributing causal significance to correlational results.

218. Schedler, P. 1966. "Parental Attitudes and Political Activism of College Students." Master's thesis, Committee on Human Development, University of Chicago. Abstract, 3 pp.

SETTING, SUBJECTS, AND METHODS: See Flacks and Neugarten Intro. Ss divided at the midpoint on activism scale, yielding 51 activists and 49 nonactivists. "Tolerance": defined as approval of child working in slum area, having affair, and dropping out of school. "Permissiveness" defined as (a) allowing child to decide for himself whether to participate in above activities and (b) composite score based on factor analysis of ratings made by parents and Ss of child-rearing practices when S was growing up. Activists and nonactivists are similar in SES.

RESULTS: Activists' mothers and fathers are more tolerant and permissive about working in slums and having an affair, but do not differ from nonactivists' parents with regard to dropping out of school. Mothers, but not fathers, of nonactivists scored higher on strictness measure.

COMMENTS: Important for finding that "permissiveness" (b) does not characterize fathers of activists, but does distinguish mothers. Other results on permissiveness and tolerance can be interpreted as reflecting liberalism of activist parents.

219. **Schiff, Lawrence F. 1964a. "The Conservative Movement on American College Campuses." Ph.D. dissertation, Harvard University. 166 pp.

SETTING: 1963(?), conservative groups at Boston College, Boston University, Holy Cross College, Harvard College, Northeastern, Ohio State, Tufts, University of Connecticut, and Yale College.

SUBJECTS: Student conservatives who included virtually the entire core memberships of all groups studied. YAF chapters at University of New Hampshire and Dartmouth refused cooperation. OSU chapter permitted interview only with chairman. All Ss male, N = 47.

METHODS: Interview gradually standardized as research progressed, covered political beliefs and behaviors, nuclear and extended family relationships, childhood, adolescent, and college adjustment. Attitude scales given to all Ss and to "comparison group" of 10 members of "liberal organization": manifest anxiety vs. ego control, extrovertive vs. introvertive emotionality, manifest vs. controlled aggression, authoritarian vs. non-authoritarian conformity, suppression vs. subjective experience of anger, repression vs. overt experience of anxiety. Results focus on patterns of "conversion" to right-wing position, use clinical psychoanalytic interpretations, emphasize psychodynamic functions of conservatism.

RESULTS: Conservatives distinguished from liberal Ss by higher scores on authoritarian conformity, ego control, and repression. Three main patterns of entry into conservatism: continuity without abrupt shift with parental beliefs, postadolescent or "obedient rebellion" conversion, and adolescent conversion. Converts show great instability (more parental death and divorce, interruptions of school, and explicit reports of personal instability) in adolescence or later.

"Obedient rebels" had more "totalistic" conversions, rapid and dramatic ideological changes moralistic reactions in the context of an intense challenge to preexisting identity components. Backgrounds of such Ss involved unusually strong, clear and intense prescriptions from family, emphasis on morality and innerdirected paths to success, which fell with particular weight on these Ss, all but one of whom are eldest or only sons. Personal crisis led to identity foreclosure and the repudiation of rebellion against parents. Particularly important were confrontations with alien points of view during college; all Ss "converted" during their college years, and at a point when they had begun to veer away from the "plan" laid down by family morality and expectations. Conservatism appealed to Ss because of its high prestige value, basic congruence with parents' values, espousal of deference to authority and traditional morality, emphasis on risk-taking and romanticization of achievement-oriented behavior, allowance of expression of otherwise inexpressible hostility.

For "adolescent rebels," important roles were played by adolescent heroes: older men who were personally attractive and "knew the ropes," gave interpersonal support and were useful in providing self-definition. Personality development continued after conversion. Background involved pervasive closeness and intense relationships with parents, strong adolescent parent-child ties. Author concludes that adolescent conservative conversions served essentially positive developmental ends, and their overall effect was emancipative.

COMMENTS: A perceptive, psychodynamically-oriented discussion of the processes of entry into conservative student action groups. Emphasizes different avenues for entering conservative activism, varying psychological

functions and meanings of conservatism, and psychodynamic meaningful-
ness of conservative "conversions." No control group. The only in-depth
study of conservative activists.

220. ____ . 1964b. "The Obedient Rebels: A study of College Conversions to
Conservatism." JOURNAL OF SOCIAL ISSUES 20 (October):74-95.

SETTING, SUBJECTS, AND METHODS: See Schiff 1964a.

RESULTS: Converts closest to "core participants" in conservative movement, most committed. Conservatism evolves in reaction to shock at
confrontation with "liberal indoctrination" in college, disappearance of
previous external social controls, need to reject perceived amorality of
liberals. Family background of conservatives characterized by achievement
pressures on children. Incipient rebellion against "parental blueprint" dealt
with by rebellion to conservatism, often after failure to comply with
parental hopes. High parent-child congruence in moral values, occasional
complaint that parents were not strict enough. Author interprets conservative rebellion as identity foreclosure, stresses congruence between character
structure, personal background, and developmental conflicts of conservatives, sees conservatives as a group as nontotalitarian and democratic.

COMMENTS: See Schiff 1964a.

221. ____ . 1966. "Dynamic Young Fogeys: Rebels on the Right." TRANS-
ACTION (November):30-36.

SETTING, SUBJECTS, METHOD, RESULTS, COMMENTS: See Schiff
1964a. A popular summary that stresses the anticommunism of conservatives.

222. *Schneider, Patricia. 1966. "A Study of Members of SDS and YD at
Harvard." Bachelor's thesis, Wellesley College. 150 pp.

SETTING: 1965-66, Harvard College.

SUBJECTS: Comparison of 8 "leading members" of Harvard YD (700
members) with 8 "leaders" of SDS (175 members).

METHODS: Intensive interviews, 2-5 hours, organized loosely around 32
open-ended questions concerning political development, political orientation, current social behavior, personal history, family structure, etc.

RESULTS: Distinguishes between early indoctrination, evolution, and conversion as pathways to political involvement. Conversion found in 3 SDS members, no YD. Early indoctrination is characterized by high degree of political interest in family, warm and encouraging relationships between parents and son, high correspondence between parental and filial politics. Evolution is characterized by slow move toward greater political involvement and leftism in context of good parent-son relationship but with more evidence of conflict. Conversion is characterized by relatively strong move away from parents, greater parent-son estrangement; catalytic experiences involving direct encounter with social injustice.

Author contrasts various orientations to professional or career: professional, political, social, and existential types called "self-oriented"; ideological, political, and moral types called "other-oriented"; YD members all are self-oriented "instrumental believers"; all SDS members all other-oriented (ideological-political or moral), exhibit belief-centered behavior, lack manifest personal ambition, and focus moral concern on "injustice." Moral concerns apparently antedated ideological concerns, which in some cases developed after joining SDS. SDS members more committed to SDS goals; YD members more involved in career-testing.

Parents of all Ss in both groups were political liberal. All YD's eldest sons; 5 SDS eldest sons. 6 SDS from large cities, 6 YD from suburbs. 6 YD's planning to enter law; 7 SDS unsure of career plans, tend toward academic professions and writing. Six YD fathers business, no SDS fathers business. SDS members characterized by greater feeling of personal responsibility to induce change. Author sees YD as "instrumental and pragmatic" in personality style; SDS as "expressive and ideational." Religion did not differentiate groups.

COMMENTS: An outstanding undergraduate thesis. Stylistic and motivational variables distinguishes YD from SDS: crucial difference is instrumental-pragmatic-legal-career-testing orientation of YD; moral-political-ideological-expressive-exploratory style of SDS. Useful distinction between indoctrination, evolution, and conversion.

223. Scott, J.W., and El-Assal, M. 1969. "Multiversity, University Size, University Quality and Student Protest: An Empirical Study." AMERICAN SOCIOLOGICAL REVIEW 34 (October):702-09.

224. Searles, Ruth, and Williams, J.A. 1962. "Negro College Students' Participation in Sit-ins." SOCIAL FORCES 40 (March):215-220.

SETTING: May, 1960, 3 black colleges in Greensboro and Raleigh, N.C.

SUBJECTS: Black students; questionnaires administered in classes, N = 827.

METHODS: Data gathered on background, image of peers, black and white adults, motivation for protest, readiness to move from South, optimism, and participation in protest. Ninety percent protesters. Three groups: high participators (sit-down demonstrators and picketers, leaflet distributors, committee members, etc. 24%), low participators (no involvement or mass meeting and boycotts only, 44%), intermediate participators (31%). No tabulations or tests of significance.

RESULTS: High participators from higher social status, most optimistic about black and white protest support, least likely to believe whites cheat blacks or to hold whites in general responsible for blacks conditions, participate most in extracurricular activities.

COMMENTS: An early descriptive study that interprets black protest as indicating identification with or positive reference to white middle class.

225. Selvin, H.C., and Hagstrom, W.O. 1960. "Determinants of Support for Civil Liberties." BRITISH JOURNAL OF SOCIOLOGY 11, no. 1:51-73. Also in Lipset, S.M., and Wolin, S.S., eds. 1965. THE BERKELEY STUDENT REVOLT: FACTS AND INTERPRETATIONS. New York: Doubleday Anchor, pp. 494-518.

SETTING: Dec. 1957, University of California at Berkeley.

SUBJECTS: 894 students in stratified sample to represent place of residence and major field.

METHODS: 15-item "libertarian" scale organized mostly around opposition to restriction on Communists, but also including some general procivil-liberties items. Subjects classified into slightly libertarian (20%), moderately libertarian (46%), and highly libertarian (34%). Seventy-one percent of sample favored Eisenhower in 1956.

RESULTS: UCB students more libertarian than national cross-section, national community leaders, and national sample of social science teachers. Libertarianism associated with upper classmen and graduate student, father blue-collar worker, free or salaried professionals (vs. clerical and public service workers), interest in national and world affairs, Jewish or irreligious, independent and Democrats, no church attendance, high reported GPA (especially in upper division), social sciences and humanities (vs. engineering, education, and business administration), off-campus, independent residence (vs. fraternity-sorority) large number of elected leadership positions and high elected leadership position. Homogenizing effect of college apparent in increasingly libertarian attitudes during last 2 years of college.

COMMENTS: Prefigures later studies about FSM support and activism at Berkeley, but note high proportion of blue-collar libertarians.

226. **Simon, William, and Gagnon, John H. 1970. "The Politics of Working Class Youth." Paper given at World Congress of Sociology, September 1970, Varna, Bulgaria. 19 pp.

SETTING: Late 1960s working class ethnic regions in midwestern city; midwestern and northeastern states.

SUBJECTS: Major data from survey of 500 Ss in midwestern city.

METHODS: Ss given 6-item modified index of authoritarianism; 1-item measure of economic liberalism (government should see that everyone has a decent standard of living), index of individualism.

RESULTS: About 1/3 of Ss high on authoritarianism, which declines with youth. Authoritarianism related to respect for and frequent interraction with parents, (especially among males), low educational aspirations, low mobility aspirations, conservatism on sexual attitudes and intolerance of deviance. Group divided about 50-50 on economic liberalism item. Group cross-classified on economic liberalism and authoritarianism. Liberal non-authoritarians least supportive of George Wallace; liberal authoritarians in general most conservative. Indices of individualism unrelated to authoritarianism, but liberal authoritarians most individualistic. Authors interpret data to indicate considerable generational continuity in working class youth, accompanied by a continuation of commitment to authoritarianism among the young. Attenuation of authoritarianism is associated with upward mobility and possible departure from the working class.

Ethnographic studies suggest 4 major types. Greasers resemble working class "street corner boys" of earlier studies, antiacademic, about 50% males will drop out of high school, concerned with cars and motorcycles, mechanical skills, physical prowess, sexual success, inattentive to political issues except race and housing integration. Collegiates have high mobility aspirations, academic involvement, middleclass orientation, low economic liberalism, high social liberalism, probable movement into middle class.

Hippies are largely disconnected, form middleclass hip community, derive "hip" image from media, involved with drug use, nonpolitical, nonracist, highly privatized, alienated from family. Family-oriented youth are largely nonmobile, probable core of future respectable working class, authoritarian, and economically liberal. All groups are remote from politics. Greasers most mobilizable for violence along racial, ethnic, or political lines. Compared to men, women remain more family-oriented, have goals more similar to middleclass goals, are more influenced by mass socializing media, most oriented toward wife-mother role, most likely to be dissatisfied by adult working class life because of middleclass aspirations.

COMMENTS: Virtually the only study of working class youth and politics; contains a wealth of hypotheses, observations, typologies and speculations. An outstanding paper.

227. *Simon, William; Carns, Donald E.; and Gagnon, John. 1971. "Student Politics: Continuities in Political Socialization." Unpublished paper, Stonybrook: New York, State University of New York. 16 pp. + App.

SETTING: Spring 1967, 12 colleges and universities, overrepresentation of "quality" I's.

SUBJECTS: Approximately 100 Ss at each college. Fifty percent male, 50% female, approximately 300 freshmen, sophomore, juniors, and seniors each. Total N = 1149.

METHODS: Political characterization of self and parents on 4-point scale from very liberal to very conservative. Ss classified into 4 groups: stable liberals (S and father liberal, 38%); conservative apostates (father conservative, S liberal, 31.5%); liberal apostates (father liberal, S conservative, 6%); and stable conservatives (S and father conservative, 24.5%). S's responses to questions concerning perceived parental SES, father's education, self-rating as to whether S more liberal, same, or more conservative than parent, degree mother/father understand S, degree S can talk freely with mother/father, degree mother/father are aware of things S does and feels, degree S would turn to parents for advice on personal problems, political evaluation of friends, score on liberal political attitude scale, and self-comparison in terms of more liberal, same or more conservative than other students and with professors.

RESULTS: Analysis of political self-characterization by college class shows no differences by class, is interpreted by authors to demonstrate lack of effect of college education on political views. Over 60% of all college classes, both male and female, consider selves more liberal than parents. Conservative apostates 5 times more numerous than liberal apostates. Stable liberals and stable conservatives both tend to consider selves more liberal than parents, conservative apostates, greatly more liberal, liberal apostates more conservative. Stability associated with high parental SES, father had some college education or more. Trend for liberal apostates to report greatest closeness with same-sex parents, most likely to turn to parents for advice, conservative apostates uniformly report lowest closeness with both parents, least likely to turn to parents for advice. Authors argue that political apathy continues to characterize most American students, generation gap is greatly overrated, and college has no effect on politcal attitudes.

COMMENTS: An interesting study that uses limited statistical methods. One of the authors' main points, the noneffect of college on political attitudes, must be judged not proven because the same Ss were not studied longitudinally.

228. *Smith, M. Brewster; Haan, Norma; and Block, Jeanne. 1970. "Social-Psychological Aspects of Student Activism." YOUTH AND SOCIETY 1 (March):261-88.

SETTING, SUBJECTS, AND METHODS: See Block et al., Intro. Comparison of 5 basic groups, males and females, emphasizing demographic variables, self and ideal Q sorts, parental role practices, and parental influence and conflict.

RESULTS: Activists and dissenters are disproportionately from Jewish families, parents and Ss both more liberal, Ss more often plan volunteer service after college. Conventionalists generally opposite in these respects. Activists have most educated parents (especially fathers), activists and dissenters have most professional fathers.

On Q sort, inactive males describe selves as conventional and foresighted; females as proud. Conventionalist males are ambitious, masculine, and optimistic; females, conventional, practical, self-controlled, etc. Constructivist males responsible, practical, tolerant; females helpful. Activist males rebellious, restless, informed, assertive; females rebellious, restless, receptive, worrying, and uncompromising. Dissenter males idealistic, perceptive, individualistic, curious, critical and self-centered; females individualistic, informed, open, and frank. Ideal descriptions show conventionalists and inactives very similar, valuing Protestant ethic characteristics.

Constructivists have a blurred ideal, emphasizing male empathy and helpfulness, female optimism and argumentativeness. Activist males value qualities much like those they allege they possess; females value similar qualities: rebellious, orderly, sensitive, restless, creative, curious. Dissenters (male and female) value freedom, absence of hang-ups, openness, frankness, and idealism.

Inactives present as undifferentiated picture of parents that suggests maternal control and intrusion for males. Conventionalists' parents (especially mothers) relate to children in conventional sex-appropriate way. Constructivists' fathers set firm, well-established rules for both sexes, have generally warm relationships; mothers somewhat restrictive. Activists' fathers appear child-centered, child-respecting, encouraging of subjectivity, close to sons. Constructivist women see fathers as affectionate, respecting, permissive, and moderate conflict; warm and respecting. Dissenters of both sexes describe parents as disappointed in them; women describe warm, child-centered father, nonconflicted relationship with mother, but daughter feels herself a disappointment, males report demonstrative affection and conflict with fathers, intrusiveness, conflict and nagging with mothers. Overall, conventionalists show greatest agreement with an influence from both parents on most issues. For women, in particular, activists and dissenters report highest disagreement with and lowest influence from parents.

Discussion emphasizes that inactives and conventionalists are "rearguard of the Protestant ethic, nurtured in relatively restrictive, repressive and punitive family settings." Protesting types (activists and dissenters) value spontaneity, openness, creativity, and sincerity, come from humanistic families that seem more open to impulse and individuality. Activist and dissenter families give evidence of conflict that was openly expressed, negotiated, and discussed in the family.

COMMENTS: An important study, but often papers in the series permit better distinctions between social and psychological variables.

229. Smith, Robert B. 1969. "Campus Protests and the Vietnam War." Paper read at the American Sociological Association, September 1969, San Francisco. Also in Short, James F., and Wolfgang, Marvin E., eds. 1971. COLLECTIVE VIOLENCE. Chicago: Aldine.

230. *____ . 1971. "The Vietnam War and Student Militancy." SOCIAL SCIENCE QUARTERLY 52 (June):133-56.

SETTING: 1968-1970, University of California at Santa Barbara; extensive student demonstrations, bank-burning, killing of student and 900 arrests in March 1970.

SUBJECTS: December 1968: systematic sample of 655 Ss, N = 348 (53%). March 1970: Ss polled in classes 2 weeks after bank-burning, N = 497 (66%).

METHODS: "Disaffection" = choice of "dove" self-label = 74% in 1968-69. "Militancy" = willingness to engage in confrontation, including civil disobedience, when existing channels prove inadequate = 68% in 1968-69. Data concerning attitudes about black power, war opposition, complaints about university, SES, drug use, GPA, ethnicity, etc. Analysis includes use of Coleman's stochastic model for multivariate analysis.

RESULTS: 1968-69 data. Disaffection (dove) associated with non-Protestant or no religion, minority ethnicity, disagreement with controversial government policies, disrespect for existing laws and I's, personal loneliness, worry, drug use, letters and sciences major (correlations low); unrelated to sex, GPA, year in college and father's SES. Multivariate analysis (with disaffection as dependent variable, war opposition and black power support and intervening variables) shows that religion and ethnicity affect disaffection indirectly, academic major affects disaffection directly and indirectly via effect on war opposition. Militants more often support leniency for nonviolent protesters, only 8% label selves radical, support Black Student Union protest at UCSB in October '68, and Berkeley People's Park protesters.

1970 data: militants more often radical or liberal, believe America imperialist, oppose capitalism, Vietnam war, and UCSB administration firing of controversial professor, support civil rights, black power, chicano power, and ecological action, believe nonviolence ineffective, are tolerant of violent dissent, use drugs (marijuana use very high), approve premarital sex, interested in "new consciousness"; few differences in personal problems; no differences in GPA, academic conscientiousness, or graduate school plans. Control for disaffection (dove) does not alter these relationships.

Analysis of UCSB polls from 1967 to 1970 shows marked increase in war opposition and marijuana use; analysis of student newspaper reports from 1967 to 1970 shows fewer antiwar protests, more violent-forceful protests, firebomb threats, broken windows, and police punitive actions. Multivariate analysis of 1968-69 data indicates that war opposition and demand for social justice with new domestic priorities account for more than half of the variance with new domestic priorities account for more than half of the variance of student militancy; 1970 data indicates that war opposition is the major determinant of militancy. Author concludes that Vietnam War, University unresponsiveness, police harrassment on marijuana, desire for social justice with new domestic priorities explain militants' shift to more violent tactics.

COMMENTS: Recent study of campus with highly publicized demonstrations supports thesis that opposition to Vietnam war plays a central role in growing student militancy and change to more violent tactics.

231. Solomon, Frederic, and Fishman, Jacob R. 1963. "Perspectives on the Student Sit-in Movement. AMERICAN JOURNAL OF ORTHOPSYCHIATRY 33:872-74.

232. _____ . 1964a. "The Psychosocial Meaning of Nonviolence in Student Civil Rights Activities." PSYCHIATRY 27, no. 2 (May):91-99.

SETTING, SUBJECTS, AND METHODS: See Fishman and Solomon 1963. Nineteen experienced black civil rights workers, 16 males, 11 interviewed once, 8 interviewed repeatedly. Fifteen out of nineteen Ss are or were students in the "upper South" or Washington, D.C. Paper analyses psychological meaning of nonviolence.

RESULTS: Ss considered, nonviolence secondary to achieving civil rights, a "good strategy," a way of "not hurting the movement." Trend for activists from Deep South to adopt nonviolence less pragmatically, more as a part of a Ghandian outlook. Psychologically, nonviolence asserts aggression while minimizing provocation. Maintaining nonviolent stance in the face of provocation and without displaying fear is psychologically difficult but essential; so, too, is the need to display friendliness toward opponents (despite inner feelings of hostility, contempt and fear) in order to overcome stereotype of violent or cowardly black. Ss have a high awareness of favorable publicity attained by nonviolence, and a sense of inevitability of desegregation. Authors emphasize that for most of Ss, nonviolence is a pragmatic tactic, and ask how long the commitment to nonviolence will persist.

COMMENTS: A clinical paper that anticipates the later disappearance of the commitment among militant blacks to nonviolence.

233. *____. 1964b. "Youth and Peace: a Psycho-Social Study of Student Peace Demonstrators in Washington, D.C. JOURNAL OF SOCIAL ISSUES 20 (October):54-73.

SETTING: Feb. 16-17, 1962. Washington, D.C., peace demonstration sponsored by Turn Toward Peace involving about 4000 students who were confronted by 200 counterpicketers from conservative groups.

SUBJECTS: 218 demonstrators completed short-answer questionnaire, 29 completed interviews, 128 Ss (58%) gave "optional" name and address, 45 of these returned follow-up questionnaire sent 18 months later (35% of follow-up). Ten interviews with counterdemonstrators.

METHODS: Questionnaire about background, goals of demonstrators, family attitudes, and past affiliations.

RESULTS: Description of peace protesters: mean age 18½, underclassmen overrepresented, 95% white, 3/5 male, 3/4 urban, 19% from New York area. Excluding only children, 75% are eldest child of sex in family, 2/3 humanities or social sciences majors (vs. natural sciences or preprofessional), career plans indefinite, centered in teaching, social service, and research, 51% nonreligious, 14% Unitarian or Quaker, 20% Jewish, only 1 Roman Catholic.

Goals of demonstrators were to express concern, heighten public awareness of issues, and strengthen peace movement. Personal motivations included efforts to reduce isolation of peace-concerned students, combat feelings of helplessness vis-à-vis arms race and personal uncertainty about future, and also desires to act, to alleviate guilt over inaction, and to strive for purity of humanitarian principles. Half of participants felt participating in demonstration involved risk of peer or government ostracism.

Close to 50% saw parents as supportive, 22% report overt opposition. Twenty-three percent reported parents behaved "inconsistently" toward student's activities, supporting principles but not action. Of interviewed Ss, 16 came from "liberal" homes, 9 from "conservative" homes; 7 out of 16 liberal parents and 2 out of 9 conservatives were politically active. Disagreement with fathers twice as common as with mothers. Of 72% reporting previous activism, "about half" had civil rights experience. Older participants (22+) showed more evidence of family pathology and prolonged searching. Authors distinguish 2 types: general rebellion against politically conservative parents (20-30%); combination of overt rebellion and underlying identification with liberal parents (70-80%). Rank and file Ss discuss issues more moralistically, leaders discuss them using "hard-nosed" government language.

Counterdemonstrators are largely local Washington students recruited by Young Americans for Freedom, white, predominantly Catholic, preparing for careers in business, law, or foreign service, express intense distrust of Soviet Union, emphasize maintaining American strength, see nuclear war in terms of conventional warfare, stress action, potency, and aggression.

Of follow-up Ss, 89% are still actively engaged in sociopolitical action, usually civil rights. Of 10 first-time 1962 demonstrators, 8 had continued activism. Reasons for discontinuation varied from sense of earlier naiveté to return to graduate studies. Trend toward becoming conscientious objectors evident in follow-up sample.

COMMENTS: The first study of white peace activists. Despite inevitable methodological problems, its essential findings have been replicated in many studies since. Authors' distinction between "types" of activists has generally been neglected.

234. *_____ . 1964c. "Youth and Social Action II: Action and Identity Formation in the First Student Sit-in Demonstration." JOURNAL OF SOCIAL ISSUES 20, no. 2 (April):36-45.

SETTING, SUBJECTS, AND METHODS: See Fishman and Soloman 1963. Sept. 1963 reinterview of principal Ss, extensive interviews with 1 of students who "started" sit-in movement in Greensboro, North Carolina in 1960, supplemented by intensive nondirective clinical interviewing of other "veterans" of the civil rights movement, studied for 3 or more years.

RESULTS: Report concretizes issues discussed in Fishman and Solomon 1963, by giving an account of 1 black student and his 3 friends, all on scholarship at A & T College in Greensboro, who saw sitting-in as a way of translating "bull sessions" into action. Stresses interpenetration of conscious and unconscious motivations; sitting-in as part of "healthy" adolescent development; spontaneous, impulsive, and risk-taking nature of first sit-in. 3½ year follow-up with prime S showed increased anxiety during 3 years of civil rights work combined with full-time preprofessional academic work; illness and personal crisis over whether to resume studies or devote full time to civil rights. (S chose full-time studies.) Other "veterans" of civil rights movement experience similar crises, which authors relate to defeats and frustrations, noninvolvement of other black youths, and financial problems in activists' families.

COMMENTS: A moving account of one of the 4 first civil rights demonstrators, stressing unplanned, spontaneous action, discouragement, frustration and despair produced by continuing civil rights activity.

235. Solomon, Frederic; Walker, W.L.; O'Connor, G.; and Fishman, Jacob R. 1965. "Civil Rights Activity and Reduction in Crime among Negroes." ARCHIVES OF GENERAL PSYCHIATRY 2 (March):227-36.

236. *Somers, Robert H. 1965. "The Mainsprings of the Rebellion: A Survey of Berkeley Students in November 1964." In Lipset, S.M., and Wolin, S.S., eds. 1965. THE BERKELEY STUDENT REVOLT: FACTS AND INTER-PRETATIONS. New York: Doubleday Anchor, pp. 530-57.

SETTING: Late Oct., early Nov., 1964, University of California at Berkeley, after October 2 police car sit-in.

SUBJECTS: Stratified sample of UCB population, with graduate students slightly underrepresented, N = 285.

METHODS: Interviews of student sample by undergraduates: covering general sociopolitical attitudes, family political backgrounds, etc. Ss divided into 3 groups: militants (agree with both purposes and tactics of police car demonstration, 30%), moderates (support goals but not tactics, 30%), conservatives (oppose both goals and tactics, 22%), others omitted.

RESULTS: Educational dissatisfaction not strongly related to FSM support, and overall dissatisfaction with the university very low. Militants are strongly libertarian: support civil rights of right-wing extremists more than conservatives do, have more "idealistic" image of the university with regard to free speech. Forty-five percent of those reporting B+ or better average are militants, 10% are conservatives. Militancy related to social science and humanities major (vs. business administration, engineering, agriculture, or architecture). Militants more likely to live off-campus (vs. fraternities or sororities), have liberal-left political preferences, report mother's and, to a lesser extent, father's political preferences are liberal or left. No relationship between family income and militancy. Militancy slightly related to professional and semiprofessional parental occupations, mother's college or more education, and suburban residence. Eight percent of sample expressed strong disagreement with parents on intellectual issues, future goals, or religion. Of these, a disproportionate number likely to be militant. Six percent of sample disagree strongly with parents' political beliefs; of these 2/3 are militants. But greater militancy also found among those who strongly agree with parents' political beliefs. Half of militants have no religious preference, as compared with 10% of conservative. Jews most likely to be militant, Protestants to be conservative. Same relationships, lower significance for parents' religion. Mistrust of UCB administration somewhat associated with militancy.

Trend toward polarization about the adequacy of UCB administration's consideration to the rights and needs of students. Comparative data (1960 and 1961 with 1964) show net movement of 14% to more extreme categories, mostly disagreement. High optimism among militants as to the likelihood of success for their efforts.

COMMENTS: The first, much-cited FSM study. Dependent variable is attitudes toward tactics and goals of FSM, but results overlap with studies of later arrestees. Note "libertarian" pro-civil-rights position of FSM supporters, relation between Ss' and parents' political attitudes, and no relationship of militancy to parental income.

237. ____. 1969. "The Berkeley Campus in the Twilight of the Free Speech Movement: Hope or Futility?" In McEvoy, J., and Miller, A., eds. 1969. BLACK POWER AND STUDENT REBELLION. Belmont, California: Wadsworth, pp. 419-40.

SETTING: Feb.-March, 1968. University of California at Berkeley, controversy over suspension of students.

SUBJECTS: Random sample of students, N = 492.

METHODS: Questionnaire administered through interviews, many items comparable to Somers 1965 and Gales 1966. Guttman item used to classify Ss into 4 groups: radicals (American society unjust, revolutionary changes needed, 14%), reformers (American society unjust, changes within system needed, 11%), moderates (American society just, important changes needed, 39%), conservatives (American society just, no changes needed, 1%). Thirty-five percent refused all statements. Separate analyses on some variables of Ss who were at UCB during the FSM episode. Report emphasizes comparisons between 1968 and 1964 or early 1965. No tabulations or tests of significance.

RESULTS: Decline from 1964-5 to 1968 in faith in college administration, increase in desire for more control over educational policy, increase in % supporting FSM, decline in % who thought FSM partly successful. Satisfaction with courses, examinations, and professors declined from 82% in 1964 to 69% in 1968. But author argues that "students' conception of the university as a factory is not in itself sufficient cause for rebellion; their conception of the university as a conservative force inhibiting and distorting their political vision does seem to be." High consensus in 1968 opposing Johnson Vietnam policy, believing blacks do not have sufficient rights; 3/5 believe university "too closely tied to the Establishment." Students are more liberal than their fathers: 2/3 have moved at least one step to left, only 6% more conservative than fathers, but despite shifts correlation between father-son beliefs remains high.

COMMENTS: Note declining faith in administration, lack of association between radicalism and specifically educational dissatisfaction.

238. Spreitzer, Elmer; Perry, Joseph B., Jr.; and Pugh, M.D. 1971. "Participation in Anti-War Demonstrations: A Test of the Parental Continuity Hypotheses." Paper read at American Sociological Association, September 1971, Denver. 9 pp. + App.

SETTING: May 1970, Bowling Green State University, antiwar demonstrations, class moratorium, teach-ins and sit-in at president's office.

SUBJECTS: Questionnaire available at on-campus locations, mailed to commuters and off-campus students, N = 716. Protesters or activists defined as involved in antiwar protest at state capital or Washington, D.C., or in president's office sit-in.

METHODS: Party identification of Ss and parents, 5-point political self-label for parents and Ss, estimates of generation gap with each parent, Christie New Left Scale.

RESULTS: Protest involvement associated with S's party to the left of parents, S more liberal than parents, strong perceived generation gap with parents (only for Ss with moderate political ideology). Authors argue that family socialization hypothesis is inadequate to explain data, find no evidence that Ss whose ideology and actions are "consistent" are closer to fathers.

COMMENTS: Further evidence for the dispersion of student protest to new groups in the late 1960s.

239. ____, and Snyder, Eldon. 1971. Rank and File Student Activism at a Non-Elite University. "Unpublished Paper, Department of Sociology, Bowling Green State University. 15 pp. + App.

SETTING, SUBJECTS, METHODS: See Spreitzer et al. 1971. Data analysis compares subsample of leftists, N = 140 and rightists, N = 175, defined by Christie New Left Scale. "Consistent" Ss are leftist protesters and rightist nonprotesters; inconsistent Ss = others. All tabulations separate left and right Ss.

RESULTS: Activism associated with high status family and high GPA regardless of S's ideology; all consistent Ss are more likely to be from Republican families (but overall, leftism is associated with parents Democrats, rightism with parents Republicans). Leftists more liberal than parents, most likely to demonstrate; rightists same as parents, least likely to demonstrate. Overall, activism associated with "rebellion to the left." Left activists report largest generation gap with both parents (vs. right nonactivists, smallest), are most dissatisfied with course offerings, degree requirements, and instruction. No association between dissatisfaction and activism among rightists. Data interpreted to refute theory that determinants of activism differ from those of ideology.

COMMENT: Recent study at nonselective university supports early findings concerning relationship of activism to parental SES and student GPA, but finds activism associated with educational dissatisfaction (leftists only), with "rebellion to the left," and with perceived generation gap.

240. Stein, Morris I. 1966. VOLUNTEERS FOR PEACE. New York: Wiley and Sons. An intensive study of 62 Peace Corps volunteers (1961) who worked in a community development project in Columbia, studied during training, at 6 months, 1 year, and departure from Columbia, 6 months and 1 year follow-up. Follow-up data indicate volunteers not especially radicalized, but become more politically active, show heightened interest in national problems, become slightly more liberal, more interested in international affairs, and somewhat more critical of American life and values, have become "more expressive of impulse-related needs—aggression, sentience, sex and exhibition—and less concerned with more socially oriented needs, such as . . . affiliation, . . . deference and . . . blamavoidance." Useful as an early contrast with Gottlieb et al.; (1971) study of Vista volunteers.

241. Stern, George G. 1969. "Campus Environments and Student Unrest." In Smith, G. Kerry, ed. 1969. AGONY AND PROMISE. San Francisco: Jossey-Bass, pp. 123-35. An excellent summary of Stern's research on college characteristics, student characteristics, and perceptions of campus problems, but no data on actual protests, demonstrations, or politicization.

242. Stillion, G. 1968. "Values, Perceptions, and Characteristics of Student Leaders Compared with General Student Population at Florida State University." Ph.D. dissertation, Florida State University. 68 pp. + App.

SETTING: Fall quarter 1967, Florida State University.

SUBJECTS: Student government leaders elected or appointed by the president of the student body, compared with random sample of students.

METHODS: Ss given AVL, CUES, and ACESIF.

RESULTS: Student government leaders are less theoretical, less intellectual, more social, less economically oriented and more politically motivated than students. Leaders are more supportive of student freedoms, oppose administrative control of student activities, but are motivated by a stronger need for social acceptance. Author concludes that in many respects student leaders are "foreign" to the average student.

COMMENTS: Study indirectly relevant because it suggests the contrast between traditional student government leaders and student activists as studied in other research.

243. Stout, Robert J. 1970. "A Study of Alienation on Three Diverse Ohio College Campuses." Ph.D. dissertation, Bowling Green State University. 207 pp.

SETTING: 1968 or 1969, 3 Ohio colleges, 1 highly selective and "liberal"; the other 2 moderately selective, 1 state-supported "moderate," the third "conservative."

SUBJECTS AND METHODS: Alienation and other scales given Ss at each I, included Shostrom's Personal Orientation Inventory. All comparisons between 3 I's.

RESULTS: Students at "liberal" I are more alienated and self-actualizing than at other 2, also more likely to protest. Posttest finds that students at all 3 colleges showed increased willingness to commit themselves by direct involvement or active support to college protests.

COMMENTS: An inter-I comparison that provides data that could have been analyzed to explore individual variations.

244. Strickland, B.R. 1965. "The Prediction of Social Action from a Dimension of Internal-External Control." JOURNAL OF SOCIAL PSYCHOLOGY 66:353-58.

SETTING: Feb.-March, 1963, Southern states.

SUBJECTS: 2 groups, all blacks: (1) SNCC members active in civil rights movement, N = 53, males = 34, mean number of arrests per person = 5; (2) students at 3 black colleges tested in 3 different required classes, N = 115, N males = 72. Group 2 largely inactive in civil rights movement.

METHODS: All Ss given I-E, Marlowe-Crowne Social Desirability, and questionnaire about civil rights activities, number of arrests, and threats of violence.

RESULTS: Active Ss more likely to be internal on I-E, trend toward higher social desirability, are older, have completed more grades.

COMMENTS: Results suggest that black SNCC activists more influenced than nonactivists by internal controls.

245. Surace, Samuel J., and Seeman, M. 1967. "Some Correlates of Civil Rights Activism." SOCIAL FORCES 46:197-207.

SETTING: Region and date not given, probably West Coast.

SUBJECTS: 2 groups: 208 college students enrolled in evening extension courses, 142 civil service personnel in a county agency, N = 350. Only data from white college students' N = 170 and blacks, N = 129, analyzed.

METHODS: Data concerning interracial contact, experiences and attitudes, civil rights actions, attitudes, powerlessness (vis-à-vis social movements), status concern, McClosky Liberalism-Conservatism scale, priority to civil rights goals.

RESULTS: Trend for high contact whites and low contact blacks to favor stronger civil rights action. Interracial contact experiences unrelated to civil rights attitudes and activities for whites or blacks, but prointerracial contact attitudes related to both civil rights attitude and activity. No overall correlations among either whites or blacks between civil rights activities and attitudes and generalized powerlessness, civil rights powerlessness, liberalism-conservatism, or status concern. For whites only, positive contact attitude is correlated with civil rights activity and attitudes when powerlessness and status concern are low. Authors conclude that ideology and contact have very little to do with activism among blacks, favorable attitudes about contact are related to pro-civil-rights attitudes among whites.

COMMENTS: Most important result is the difference between correlations observed in white and black samples. But note that almost half of the blacks are female civil servants. Study points to the need for separate analyses of data from blacks and whites.

246. Surgeon, George P. 1969. "Political Attitudes at Wesleyan." Unpublished paper, Wesleyan University, Connecticut. 78 pp. + App.

SETTING: April 1969, Wesleyan University (Conn.), after sit-in by black student group.

SUBJECTS: Second semester freshmen, N = 219 (68%).

METHODS: Political self-characterization on 7-point scale (collapsed into 3 categories: conservative, liberal, leftist), background data, current behavior and affiliations, attitudes and outlooks. Analysis focused on political self-label. Sample skewed toward underrepresentation of blacks, overrepresentation of conservative fraternity men.

RESULTS: Leftism associated with opposition to Vietnam war, left-wing presidential preference, mistrust of police behavior, tolerance for student disruption, support for black student sit-in and approval of marijuana, Jewish background (vs. Protestant), public high school (vs. day prep school). No relationship between leftism and any measure of SES. With SES controlled, most important determinant of S's political self-label is father's political position. Large city origin and liberal fathers interact dependently to produce leftism. Leftists are more influenced by friends or by no one, conservatives more influenced by parents.

Vocational definition of college associated with conservatives, academic definition with liberals and leftists self-discovery with leftists. Leftists have highest GPA, conservatives next, liberals lowest, especially for Ss with "academic" college philosophy. Leftists list future occupation as artist, actor, writer, or unknown; conservatives as business or government. Fraternity affiliation and participation in Wesleyan sports associated with conservatism.

COMMENTS: A recent study as a selective liberal arts college that finds no relationship between parental SES and leftism.

247. Teger, A. 1970. "The Effects of a Building Occupation on Attitudes and Images of Conflict." Unpublished paper, University of Pennsylvania. 25 pp.

SETTING: Spring 1969, Princeton University, after demand that Princeton sell stocks in companies dealing with South Africa, class boycott by Association of Black Collegians (ABC); ABC occupation of South Administration Building, court injunction and departure of students the same day.

SUBJECTS: 2 surveys: (1) preoccupation: 393/640 replies from random sample; (2) postoccupation: a different group, 518/640 random sample.

METHOD: Ss questioned in dining hall and at meals about acquaintance with issues, agreement with radical students' demands, approval of building occupation, attitudes toward participants and occupation.

RESULTS: Analysis of data focuses on pre-post comparisons. High level of acquaintance with issues both times. Support for radicals demands drops from 41% to 30%, but approval of building occupation increases from 14% to 27%. At both times, administration rates more powerful, more rational in methods, and more realistic in goals than protesters; protesters rated as having stronger moral commitment. Occupation resulted in more positive image for administration, no change in image of radicals. Ss are consistently positive or negative toward administration or protesters at both times; administration and radical group are generally perceived as opposite, although less so in second survey. Perception of administration and protesters as opposite was absent among Ss who recommended compromise solutions. Author emphasizes decreased approval of radical goals and increased acceptance of tactics despite absence of police bust. Also notes that "mirror image" view of protestors vs. administration applies only to those who hold polarized positions on issues.

COMMENTS: An interesting study of attitude formation and change in a confrontation situation. Evidence for absence of mirror-image among moderate group somewhat less strong than the discussion suggests. One of the few studies of an actual confrontation in process.

248. Tessler, M.A., and Hedlund, R.D. 1970a. "Students Aren't Crazies." THE NEW REPUBLIC (September 12):17-18. Essentially a popular summary of data reported more thoroughly in Tessler and Hedlund 1970b.

249. ____ . 1970b. "Student-Faculty Attitudes Toward the November Vietnam Moratorium." Paper read at Midwest Political Science Association, 1970, Chicago, 33 pp.

SETTING: Nov. 1969, University of Wisconsin at Milwaukee and another major Midwestern university.

SUBJECTS: Stratified samples defined for each I, quotas filled by asking faculty members to distribute questionnaires to classes. 924 Ss at university A and 722 Ss at University B. Faculty samples at both universities. All samples representative.

METHODS: Questions about U.S. Vietnam policy and November Moratorium. Measure of activism: attending classes on November Moratorium Day. Attitude items intercorrelate $> + 0.30$ and are loaded on a single factor. But no attitude item correlates $> + 0.18$ with classes attended for students. Results emphasize variables associated with moratorium and war attitudes.

RESULTS: Opposition to war is associated with Jewish or other religion and low importance given to religion. Correlations between student attitudes and perceived parental attitudes on 6 items, calculated separately for each university, range from $+ 0.43$ to $+ 0.69$. Students living off campus (not at home) and veterans are most prowar, antimoratorium. No relation between SES and attitudes, but blacks are most antiwar, promoratorium. War opposition and moratorium support associated with social science, humanities, fine arts major (vs. business administration, engineering, or education), previous level of political involvement, perceived attitudinal similarity of friends. Faculty results also reported.

COMMENTS: In late 1969 sample, variables like SES, off-campus residence, and ethnicity are unrelated to leftism. Study supports thesis that S protest is becoming more dispersed, but finds relations with perceived parental leftism, major, nonreligiosity, and previous involvement in protests.

250. *Thomas, L. Eugene 1968. "Family Congruence on Political Orientations in Politically Active Parents and Their College-Age Children." Ph.D. dissertation, University of Chicago. 135 pp.

SETTING: Sept.-July 1969, Chicago North Shore including 6 prosperous suburban communities.

SUBJECTS: 2 groups of families: liberals (active members of antiwar, open housing, and other liberal groups, N = 30, 91%), conservatives (identified active members of conservative groups, active involvement against open occupancy, etc., N = 30, 63%). One parent (about 50-50 mother-father) and 1 college-age child interviewed in each family. Only families that scored in top 10% of national sample on Woodward-Roper Political Activity Index (PAI) included. Parents modally 46-55, fathers' education postgraduate, mothers' education college or college graduate, income $20-35,000, 25/30 conservatives Protestant, 14/30 liberals Jewish, fathers' occupation managerial, in top 1-2% on PAI. Children undergraduates, mostly age 18-21, attending 41 colleges and universities.

METHODS: Structured interviews include 3 levels of political attitudes: "political community," "regime," "partisan issues." Six reliable ratings made of family variables: parental dedication to causes, parental political tutoring, parental permissiveness, warmth, family conflict and family interaction. Students given 6-item Flacks 1966 "radicalism" (sociopolitical activism) scale. Correlations between parents' and students' ratings of same family variables range from + 0.45 to + 0.60. Data analysis includes multiple regression for entire sample on family congruence measures of attitudes, S's activism, S's political activity.

RESULTS: High similarity and congruence between both liberal and conservative parent-child dyads on all political issues. Parents tend to be more polarized than children. Higher parental cause dedication, political tutoring, and family permissiveness in liberal than conservative families. Compared to nonactivist children of liberal families, activist children, N = 16, are more left-wing, have more radical parents, and show no tendency to diverge from parental political position. Liberals' children are much more activist than conservatives' children. For liberal families, parent's "dedication to causes" correlates + 0.64 with student activism, for conservative families + 0.22. Intrafamily congruence highest for liberal families with activist children, lowest for conservative families.

Multiple regression on student activism shows activism related almost exclusively to parental cause dedication (r = + 0.547), with political tutoring next (r = + 0.276). Family political variables explain 30% of variance; family structural variables (permissiveness, conflict, warmth, interaction) add only 2% more.

Multiple regression on PAI scores shows family political tutoring most important (r = + 0.392), cause dedication next (r = + 0.256). Family political variables explain 15.5% of variance: adding family structural variables increases % variance by 6%.

COMMENTS: An ingenious, sophisticated study that starts from highly politicized parents to examine the relative impact of family political climate and structure on filial activism and conventional political activities. Generalizability is very limited because of unusual sample. Note irrelevance of permissiveness in multiple regression.

251. *____. 1971a. "Family Correlates of Student Political Activism." DEVELOPMENTAL PSYCHOLOGY 4, no. 2 (March):206-214.

SETTING, SUBJECTS, METHODS: See Thomas 1968. This paper includes new regression analyses on student activism and conventional political activity for subsamples defined by parents' politics and Ss' sex.

RESULTS: See Thomas 1968. Conservative families more permissive to males than to females. In liberal families parental dedication to causes is the decisive predictive variable for males ($r' = 0.75$), while parental cause dedication and family permissiveness predict activism for females ($r' = 0.75$). In conservative families, low family interaction and low family warmth predict activism for males ($r' = 0.55$); parental cause dedication and family warmth predict activism for females ($r' = 0.55$). Multiple regression washes out impact of permissiveness for all groups except liberal females.

COMMENTS: Study points to the importance of distinguishing males and females, conservatives and liberals, and suggests that the antecedents of activism are different for males and females and for the children of politically active conservative and liberal children.

252. ____. 1971b. "Political Generation Gap: A Study of Liberal and Conservative Activists and Non-Activist Students and Their Parents." Unpublished paper, Department of Child Development and Family Relations, University of Connecticut. 20 pp. Also in JOURNAL OF SOCIAL PSYCHOLOGY, 84, no. 71 (1971):313-14.

SETTING, SUBJECTS, METHODS: See Thomas 1968. Analysis of intragenerational and intergenerational agreement and congruence data.

RESULTS: In these highly politicized and consensual families, parents are more polarized than their children, activist students, liberal or conservative, are closer to parents' political attitudes than nonactivist students. Author finds no evidence of generation gap, for children of activist parents are especially close politically to parents' views.

COMMENTS: See Thomas 1968. Study cannot be generalized to activists of right or left who do not come from high status activist families.

253. **Thorne, Barrie. 1971. "Resisting the Draft: An Ethnography of the Draft Resistance Movement." Ph.D. dissertation, Brandeis University. 394 pp.

SETTING: 1967-69, Boston.

SUBJECTS: Draft resistance movement in the Boston area.

METHODS: Highly involved participant observation.

RESULTS: Study explicitly rejects a focus on personalities of resisters to examine the history, dynamics, activities, and issues involved in the 2 major Boston draft resistance groups. Emphasizes the conflicting ideologies of the resistance groups, the dynamics of risk-taking, the resistance's experience of time, strategies of confrontation (in particular, the use of dramatic and theatrical encounters), the uses of expert knowledge through draft counseling, techniques of gaining attention and establishing persuasion. Notes the gradual disconfirmation of the "charter myths" of the 2 resistance groups and the decay of the resistance. Employs a symbolic interactionist framework to understand the relationships between the resistance, the government, potential draftees, and the public. Author provides an excellent discussion of the problems of participant observation.

COMMENTS: An outstanding study which, precisely because of its refusal to examine personality characteristics and motives, counteracts the excessively individual-oriented emphasis of most activism research and illumines the dynamics and life history of movement organizations. Many of the author's conclusions would apply equally well to other movement groups.

254. *Troll, Lillian E. 1967. "Personality Similarities between College Students and Their Parents." Ph.D. dissertation, University of Chicago. 148 pp.

SETTING, SUBJECTS, AND METHODS: See Flacks and Neugarten Intro. This study examines the correlates of personality similarities between mother and father and between each parent and child. Stepdown regression analysis was conducted utilizing all families with complete parent-parent and parent-child dyads, N = 78, with student activism used as a control variable. Appendix lists correlations between family variables and student activism scores. Family variables include 7 general value orientations, 13 personality characteristics for both parents and child.

RESULTS: (Relevant to student activism.) For mothers, filial activism is correlated with all value orientations (dedication to causes, intellectualism, low moralism, self-realization, aestheticism, humanitarianism, and low materialism) and with low same-sex identification, cognitive complexity, low passivity-dependency, high achievement need and intraception.

For fathers, all value orientations are associated with filial activism, but conventional moralism is most predictive ($r = -0.60$). Paternal personality characteristics associated with filial activism are introception, sensitivity, and cognitive complexity.

For students, all value orientations are related to activism, especially dedication to causes ($r = +0.82$), humanitarianism, self-realization, intellectualism, low materialism, and low moralism. Highest personality correlations for students are low passivity-dependency ($r = -0.77$), gregariousness, cognitive complexity, achievement needs, intraception, etc.

Author does not discuss activism findings. Results suggest that a cause-dedicated, achievement-oriented, nondependent mother and a highly unmoralistic, intraceptive, and sensitive father disposes toward filial activism; that the parental personality characteristics that predict filial activism are not the same as the filial characteristics (except for cognitive complexity and intraception); and that a high % of the variance of filial activism can be explained from parental values and personality traits.

COMMENTS: Extremely valuable (incidental) report of relation of parental values and personality characteristics with student activism.

255. ____ ; Neugarten, B.L.; and Kraines, R.J. 1969. "Similarities in Values and Other Personality Characteristics in College Students and Their Parents." MERRILL-PALMER QUARTERLY 15 (October):323-36.

SETTING, SUBJECTS, AND METHODS: See Flacks and Neugarten Intro. Revised list of family values and personality traits used. Stepwise regression analysis in which student activism, sex of child, and 8 family characteristics were first controlled, and correlations between mother-father, mother-child, and father-child dyads on 9 values and 11 personality traits were tabulated both before and after partialling out of activism, sex, and family characteristics.

RESULTS: Control for student activism, sex, and family characteristics reduces intrafamilial value correlations in most cases, but does not altogether destroy them; intrafamilial value resemblances persist to a greater degree than do personality resemblances.

COMMENTS: Student activism used as a "control" variable in this report which permits no conclusions about the direct relationship between activism and family climate.

256. Trow, Martin. 1971. "Preliminary Findings of the Carnegie Commission Survey of Students and Faculty." Carnegie Commission for Higher Education, Berkeley. 28 pp.

SETTING: 1969, 300 I's, representative of the 2500 colleges and universities in the country.

SUBJECTS: 65,000+ college and university teachers; 30,000+ graduate students; 70,000+ undergraduates.

METHODS: Questionnaire covering a large variety of attitudes concerning education, politics and society, political orientation, etc., distributed and administered by ACE.

RESULTS: Preliminary description of some findings. Thirteen percent undergraduates very dissatisfied with educations; 63% very satisfied or satisfied; 23% on the fence. Students are most satisfied at the most selective I. Most students are satisfied with friendships with other students, faculty-student relations, quality of classroom instruction, intellectual environment, administration, and course variety. Seventy-five percent undergraduates agree "rules governing student behavior sensible," 8% disagree. Most students (and to a lesser extent, faculty) desire more relevance to contemporary life, more attention to emotional growth of students, requirement to spend a year in community service or abroad. Students (but not faculty) desire faculty-student governance, abolition of grades, making courses elective. Thirty-three percent of faculty and graduate students, 50% undergraduates agree "meaningful social change cannot be achieved through traditional American politics." Seventy-one percent of teachers and undergraduates agree there is no justification for using "violence to achieve political goals," but 30% do not agree. Among faculty, 3/4 under-30 in leading universities are left/liberal vs. 1/2 of general faculty sample, youth-related patterns are found concerning use of violence, support of campus disruptions, nonexpulsion of disrupting students, and legitimacy of faculty strike. Age gap sharpest in social sciences. Differences reported between faculty, graduates, and undergraduates on a variety of student power issues.

COMMENTS: A descriptive, preliminary report of data that will undoubtedly receive much further analysis. Note low incidence of global dissatisfaction with college.

257. Tygart, C.E., and Holt, N. 1971. "A Research Note on Student Leftist Political Activism and Family Socio-Economic Status." PACIFIC SOCIOLOGICAL REVIEW 14 (January):121-28.

SETTING: 1966, University of California at Los Angeles.

SUBJECTS: Every eighth undergraduate mailed questionnaire, N = 1029 (65%).

METHODS: Index of protest sympathy-participation combines measures of sympathy, giving money to and participating in demonstrations about civil rights, free speech, and antiwar. Seven-point scale constructed.

RESULTS: No relationships found between left activism and father's or mother's education, parents' income (trend toward Ss with mothers with graduate work or degree to be more active).

COMMENTS: Adequacy of index of sympathy-participation measure questionable; results contradict much early research.

258. Urban Institute, The. 1970. "Survey of Campus Incidents as Interpreted by College Presidents, Faculty Chairmen and Student Body Presidents." Washington, D.C. 62 pp.

SETTING: Summer 1970.

INSTITUTIONS: Of 2789 accredited I's, responses received from college president or chairman of faculty senate or president of student government in 68% of cases.

METHODS: Informants asked to indicate number and characteristics of incidents that resulted in disruption of normal functioning during 1967-68, 1968-69, 1969-April 30, 1970, and after May 1, 1970. Data presented descriptively, cross-tabulated with college characteristics, region, arrests, etc.

RESULTS: Retrospective reports suggest great increase in the number of protests over 3 years, e.g., only 6% of I's report protests in 1967-68, but 32.4% after May 1, 1970. Substantial decrease over 3 years in % protests involving National Guard, or off-campus police, or arrests, that are related to incidents involving personal violence or property damage. Number incidents and % serious incidents related to I size, presence of ROTC, liberal arts emphasis, and high spending per student. Female colleges report more incidents; co-ed colleges report more serious incidents; I's with low acceptance standards greater % serious incidents. Seventy-nine percent administrators do not anticipate further disruptive or violent demonstrations. Administrators and faculty rank Indochina war first cause of campus unrest, students rank it second (lack of communication first). About half of students, faculty, and administrators attribute campus unrest to on-campus causes, especially at selective, high expenditure per student, liberal arts, black, female, and religious I's.

COMMENTS: A preliminary analysis. The correlates of protest and of violent protest are familiar, but retrospective reports of protest incidence in earlier years are clearly inaccurate.

259. *Urban Research Corporation. Introduction.

SETTING: January 1, 1969 to July 1970.

INSTITUTIONS: In 1969, 232 I's monitored. In 1970, N I's surveyed is not clear.

METHODS: Data gathered from national and student press, supplemented by other primary source materials, telephone contacts and direct on-campus interviews. Written chronologies verified by school administrators, school government leaders, faculty members and/or student organizations. Methods often not clear in reports. Analyses include descriptive chronologies of protests, tabulations of protest issues, cross-tabulations of protests with variables like size, selectivity, data concerning protests per week in 1970.

RESULTS: See Levine and Naisbitt 1970, Urban Research Corp. 1970a, 1970b, 1970c, 1970d, 1970e, and 1970f.

COMMENTS: Absence of information on methodology, sample representativeness, etc., makes these studies less conclusive than those of A. Astin et al. and Peterson, although general findings are similar.

260. Urban Research Corporation. 1970a. "Code Book for the Urban Research Corporation Student Protest." Unpublished paper, Chicago. 43 pp.

SETTING, INSTITUTIONS, METHODS, AND RESULTS: See Urban Research Corporation Intro. Detailed discussion of codes used in URC student protest research from Jan. 1-June 30, 1969. 154 variables, including date, target, disciplinary actions, apparent causes, issues, tactics, procedures, demands, consequences, numbers involved, and institutional characteristics (enrollment, sex, region, highest degree, median SAT, etc.). Data for 249 I's, 292 protests.

COMMENTS: These data are available to researchers for further analyses. URC publications have not, in general, thoroughly analyzed data.

261. ____ . 1970b. "Continuing Revolt on Campus." URBAN CRISIS MONITOR 3, no. 13 (March 27): 16-43.

SETTING, INSTITUTIONS, AND METHODS: See Urban Research Corporation Intro. Jan. 15-March 8, 1970. 65 I's.

RESULTS: Brief descriptions of each protest. Contrary to mass media and administrations, student protests are continuing, with no discernible lessening in scope or intensity.

COMMENTS: See Urban Research Corporation 1970e, 1970f.

262. ____ . 1970c. "Legislative Response to Student Protest." Unpublished paper, Chicago. 10 pp.

A descriptive account of past and pending bills in early 1970 before state and federal legislatures concerning campus protests. Sources of information not given. Most bills are directed at publicly controlled I's (unlikely to be effective with private colleges and universities), deal with federal-state aid to disruptive students, general state aid to colleges and universities, mandatory expulsion of students or firing of faculty, control of public address system and public speakers, charges for trespassing, preventing free use of property, carrying firearms, authorization for calling state militia, development of policies for handling campus disorders. Most frequently passed bills involved bringing new charges for preventing free use of property (8 states), for trespassing (8 states), and for carrying firearms (6 states).

263. _____ . 1970d. "On Strike . . . Shut It Down!" Unpublished paper, Chicago, 133 pp.

SETTING, INSTITUTIONS, AND METHODS: See Urban Research Corporation Intro. April 30-May 15, 1970; 760 I's that had protests.

RESULTS: Violence occurred at fewer than 5% of I's in May 1970, whereas in 1968-69 23% of protests led to violence. War in Indochina was central issue (in 1968-69 it was central in 22% of protests). After Kent State killings, strike activity increased at the rate of 100+ new campuses each day for four days. After the Jackson State killings, rate of student protests continued to decline. Protests most frequent in Northeast and Midatlantic (vs. South). Compared to 1969, involvement of community colleges lower, of theological seminaries and professional schools higher; I's with enrollments > 10,000 had highest % protests; number of moderate student participants increased; faculty participated more. Twenty-five percent of I's had strikes with class boycotts or suspensions. Duration of most protests one day, but 18% lasted one week, 10% closed for rest of year. Ten percent of protests focused on buildings, with occupations of ROTC or administration building most common. Destruction of property infrequent. Police and/or National Guard involved in < 7% of protests; 1800 demonstrators arrested from May 1-15; 315 students suspended; confrontations occurred in 3% of protests, curfews on 7 campuses; 100 demonstrators, 28 police and 2 National Guardsmen reported injured. On some of campuses, counterstrikes organized or support for Nixon expressed.

COMMENTS: Variable descriptions and histories of protests, but almost no analysis or explanation of trends and events. See Urban Research Corporation 1970d, 1970f; Peterson 1970, Astin 1970b.

264. _____ . 1970e. "Special Issue on Student Protests." URBAN CRISIS MONITOR 3, no. 3 (June 5):2-54.

SETTING, INSTITUTIONS, METHODS: See Urban Research Corporation Intro. March 8-April 30, 1970, 89 colleges in 26 states. Descriptions only.

RESULTS: Each I had at least 1 major protest, several had 3 or 4. Minority recognition top issue 28%, war-related 24%, student power 18%, quality of student life 16%, ecology 7%, other 4%. What occurred after Cambodia invasion was not merely a reaction to that event, but continuing protest.

COMMENTS: See Urban Research Corporation 1970d, 1970e.

265. *____ . 1970f. "Student Protests 1969: Summary." Unpublished paper, Chicago. 39 pp.

SETTING, INSTITUTIONS, METHODS: See Urban Research Corporation, Intro. January-June, 1969; 292 protests in 232 I's. Coded data on each protest (see Urban Research Corporation 1970c) incompletely analyzed in this largely descriptive report.

RESULTS: Most important protest issues are black recognition 49%, student power 44%, quality of student life 28%, war-related 22%, university and community 18%, etc. Most specific demands involve race-related issues. Only 4% of protests sought full student control; less than 1% sought draft changes. Protests most frequent at state universities, large universities, private I's, urban I's, 4-year liberal arts colleges, I's with high admission standards; less common in technical, denominational, 2-year, small, rural I's. Blacks involved in 51% of protests, 16% racially mixed, 49% led by whites. SDS and other radical groups active in less than 50% of white protests, less than 28% of all protests. Major black students issues are black recognition, student power, quality of student life. Major new left issues: war and student power. Fifty percent of protests involve "forceable" tactics including strike, building seizure or disruption. Forceable tactics most often related to university, community and war-related protests, to involvement of new left groups, and to black protests at black schools. Injuries in 7% of protests, bombing or fire damage in 19%. Police used force most often in protests involving racially mixed groups. Seventy-seven percent of protests involve no violence from any source. Disciplinary or police action taken in 39% of protests, with students (more often blacks) arrested in 17%. Black demands most often granted; blacks' success associated with strikes, disruptions, and building seizure; white success negatively related to use of forceable tactics. Students most likely to be disciplined are black students at black schools and new left students. Protest duration association with success.

COMMENTS: Descriptive and I study that only scratches the surface of extremely rich data that deserve further analysis.

266. *Useem, Michael. 1970. "Involvement in a Radical Political Movement and Patterns of Friendship: The Draft Resistance Community." Ph.D. dissertation, Harvard University. 262 pp.

SETTING: Spring 1969, Boston area.

SUBJECTS: Draft resisters who had taken illegal action in defiance of Selective Service System, N = 97. An estimated 1,000 resisters in Boston, of whom Ss constituted about 10%.

METHODS: Ss contacted through use of snowball technique, starting with 9 Ss, carried through at least 5 stages; 10 refusals, 11 Ss who could not be reached. Each S interviewed 1-4 hours (average 2), with special reference to changes in ideology pre/post joining resistance. Internal analysis of data from resisters.

Resisters are active politically, full-time political workers, and less often "straight," religious, or students. Resisters are 60% students (graduate or undergraduate), predominantly in humanities (20% social sciences), upper-middleclass childhood milieu, 1/2 fathers, 1/3 mothers college graduates, 16% father's high status occupation), homes in large cities, 1/4 Jewish background, 1/3 Protestant, 1/8 Catholic; 70% currently nonreligious, 15+% Unitarian, Quaker, Buddhist, or other. Prior to resisting, almost 75% had secure deferments.

Only a minority of resisters had clear radical positions before resisting. Two unrelated motives for resisting: to bear witness and to develop mass political movement. Those with second motive were most radical-revolutionary and involved in action organizations before resisting. Decision to resist was painful and emotionally meaningful, occurred after long period of rumination for 80% of Ss. Resistance was accompanied by radicalization (those calling selves "radical" or "revolutionary" increased from 44% to 92%), more political activity in left organizations, more exposure to political writings, growing ideologization, break with earlier assumptions about U.S. social structure, sense of "finding political self," victimization and delegitimization of U.S. society, increased questioning of competitive, achievment values, growing interest in "communal" living, waning interest in academic career, increased salience of political concerns, growing interest in the development of alternative cultures. Resisters tended to move on to other political activities when resistance collapsed.

Resisters report increased estrangement from earlier friends and commitments, new identification with resisters "community," movement into other activities ranging from highly political SDS work to communal living arrangements. Initially, resisters often felt moral superiority, estrangement from previous friends and nonresisters, generally followed by greater tolerance. Parents usually changed from opposition or ambivalence to support when they discovered that resisters' convictions were sincere and strongly held.

Resisting marks sharp disjunction in friendships, with political perspective, social awareness and lifestyle becoming more crucial. New friendship networks involve other resisters, politically active persons, radicals, others with similar social awareness, and with "hip" lifestyle. Carry-over friends change in the same direction as resisters (but not as far), while dropped friends do not change. Compared to new friends, carry-over friends are less like resisters. Retrospective pre- vs. postresistance comparisons show increasing congruence of resister and friends. Despite turnover of friends, resisters formed new relationships with friends whose nonpolitical characteristics were like those of their former friends, but whose political characteristics diverged.

COMMENTS: Valuable analysis of changing interpersonal relationships and characteristics of friends of draft resisters contributes to understanding the interpersonal process and consequences of radicalization.

267. Venable, Alan. 1966. "Generational Aspects of Liberal Activism." Bachelor's thesis, Department of Social Relations, Harvard University.

268. Volkwein, James F. 1968. "Relationship of College Student Protest and Participation in Policy-making to Institutional Characteristics." Ph.D. dissertation, Cornell University.

269. Vollmer, Barbara M. 1971. "Students in the Woman's Liberation Group at the University of Denver." Unpublished paper, Department of Education, University of Denver. 54 pp.

SETTING: 1970-71, University of Denver.

SUBJECTS: The "5 core members" of local Women's Liberation group.

METHODS: Intensive interviews.

RESULTS: History of University of Denver WL group, clinical summary of Ss. Author argues that WL members studied include both alienated and activist types. Activist women express more concern with helping other people; alienated were in WL for own benefit.

COMMENTS: Results not generalizable, but interesting clinical analysis of 2 types in sample of 5 women. Compare with Cherniss 1977.

270. Von Eschen, Donald; Kirk, Jerome; and Pinard, Maurice. 1969a. "The Conditions of Direct Action in a Democratic Society." WESTERN POLITICAL QUARTERLY 22 (June):309-25.

SETTING, SUBJECTS, METHODS, AND RESULTS: See Pinard et al. 1969. The most deprived Ss are the most active. Extent of previous activism is related to occupational aspirations higher than expectations and to low occupational status. Compared to general Maryland white and black populations, Freedom Riders over 25 years have higher educational levels. Ss whose occupational expectations exceed their aspirations and low status Ss who are left of mothers are more likely to have joined before 1961. Least alienated black Ss and most alienated white Ss joined earliest. White participants are more ideological than blacks. Socialist participants ("ideologues") have been most actively involved previously, especially if they are white. Authors stress different backgrounds of black and white participants—whites are radical and politically alienated, blacks less so. Disunity in the movement was rooted in its social structure. Joining movement led to increased optimism concerning desegregation for blacks and, to a lesser extent, whites.

COMMENTS: See Pinard, et al. 1969. Broad generalizations about social movements based on a single sample.

271. ____. 1969b. "The Disintegration of the Negro Non-Violent Movement." JOURNAL OF PEACE RESEARCH 3 (Fall):215-34.

SETTING, SUBJECTS, METHODS, AND RESULTS: See Pinard et al 1969, Von Eschen et al 1969. In addition to data reported earlier, conclusions are based on studies of civil rights movement in Nashville, Tennessee and of biracial committees in Florida. Authors argue that sustained activism in civil rights movement required the contradictory characteristics of high deprivation and high sense of efficacy: the result was low participation. The movement succeeded because it created disorder, which mobilized friends and punished opponents, could be created by small numbers, and underlined preexisting conflicts between racism and American egalitarianism. Commitment to nonviolence disappeared because violence seemed to work, which in turn destroyed pessimism about success as an inhibition to participation and increased recruitment of working class members.

COMMENTS: Interpretive reanalysis of data also presented elsewhere.

272. Wainerman, C.H. 1967. "Intellect and Dissent: A Survey of Cornell Students." CORNELL JOURNAL OF SOCIAL RELATIONS 2 (Spring): 101-122.

SETTING: April 1967, Cornell University.

SUBJECTS: 351 undergraduates, of whom 276 randomly selected, 75 members of "Students For Education" (SFE), a student educational reform group.

METHODS: Dependent variable is "disenchantment" scale (5 items) finding "Moral decay and hypocrisy" in American society. Data on GPA, field of major, satisfaction with various aspects of education, generalized alienation (distrust), etc.

RESULTS: SFE membership associated with disenchantment, high GPA, but not with distrust. Disenchantment associated with liberal arts college (vs. agricultural), dissatisfaction with administration, desire for more personal education and better educational atmosphere, desire to participate in curriculum decisions and sense of obligation to alleviate social injustice; unrelated to satisfaction with education.

COMMENTS: "Activist" group is primarily concerned with educational reform. Note absence of dissatisfaction with education.

273. *Watts, William Arthur; Lynch, Steve; and Whittaker, David. 1969. "Alienation and Activism in Today's College-Age Youth: Socialization Patterns and Current Family Relationships." JOURNAL OF COUNSELING PSYCHOLOGY 16 (January):1-7.

SETTING, SUBJECTS, AND METHODS: See Whittaker and Watts Intro. Data analysis compares pooled cross-section groups, activists and nonstudents on Anomia, Thorndike Verbal Intelligence Test, SES, interest in national politics, relationships with parents.

RESULTS: Activists highest on Thorndike Vocabulary test; activists and nonstudents higher on Anomia. Activists' fathers have highest occupational status, both parents are most educated. Activists most often Jewish, activists and nonstudents most often no religion. Religious affiliations of activists' parents differ from cross-section parents in the same direction as children's religious affiliation. No religious differences between cross-section and nonstudents' parents. Ninety-one percent activists "very interested" in politics; 41% cross-section; 44% nonstudents. But 27% nonstudents, 12% cross-section, 0% activists report "no interest" in politics. Activists' parents also highly interested in politics (61% activists' fathers, 32% cross-section fathers, 31% nonstudent fathers.) Activists most often discuss intellectual ideas and politics with parents, most often agree strongly on intellectual ideas and politics with parents, but activists report greater % strong agreement and greater % strong disagreement with parents on politics than cross section. Nonstudents least often discuss intellectual ideas and future goals with parents, most often strongly disagree with parents on religion, future goals, and political ideas. Compared to cross section, activists report greater disagreement with parents on future goals.

Data interpreted to support socialization theory for activists, rebellion, alienation, and estrangement among nonstudents.

COMMENTS: A unique study that compares both activists and nonstudents with random student control groups. Data shows high parental interest in and and discussion on politics among activists, along with high agreement for some activists on political issues with parents.

274. *Watts, William Arthur, and Whittaker, David. 1966a. "Free Speech Advocates at Berkeley." JOURNAL OF APPLIED BEHAVIORAL SCIENCE 2, no. 1 (January-March):41-62.

SETTING: December 2, 1964, University of California at Berkeley. Data on FSM participants gathered inside Sproul Hall during building occupation between 2:00 and 5:00 P.M., before building was evacuated by police the following morning.

SUBJECTS: 172 FSM sit-ins sampled during sit-in: virtually no refusals. Compared with random sample of Berkeley students, including graduate students, N = 146, (80%). Random sample of 181 FSM arrestees compared with 174 random students on GPA from official UCB records.

METHODS: Questionnaire included demographic and religious attitudes, items from CPI Flexibility scale and Rehfisch Rigidity Scale.

RESULTS: Random sample reports slight shift between October and December toward more pro-FSM support. Compared to random Ss, FSM Ss younger, more homogeneous in age, more often female, (but not arrestees), social sciences, creative or fine arts, and humanities majors (vs. engineering and business), both parents have more education, especially large % parents with post-B.A. degree, Ss less Protestant, more Jewish, and much more nonreligious, mothers less Catholic, more Jewish, more nonreligious, similar trend for fathers, Ss more often never attend church, report little or no religious influence on life or on attitudes toward minority groups, much lower on Rigidity/Flexibility. No connection between mixed religious parental marriages and FSM participation.

Cumulative GPA for FSM undergraduate arrestees slightly but not significantly higher, FSM graduate arrestees slightly but not significantly lower than random samples. Both FSM groups showed increasing GPA between fall and spring 1964.

COMMENTS: Data gathered in the midst of building occupation, not from arrestees, which may explain minor differences in results from studies of actual FSM arrestees. Mother's religion more important than father's in distinguishing FSM Ss, who are highly flexible. A much-cited early study.

275. ____. 1966b. "Some Socio-Psychological Differences between Highly Committed Members of the Free Speech Movement and the Student Population at Berkeley." Unpublished paper, University of California at Berkeley. 34 pp. + App.

276. ____. 1967. "Socio-Psychological Characteristics of Intellectually Oriented, Alienated Youth: A Study of the Berkeley Nonstudent." Unpublished paper, University of California at Berkeley. 34 pp. + App.

SETTING, SUBJECTS, AND METHODS: See Whittaker and Watts Intro. Comparison of nonstudents and student control group.

RESULTS: See Watts and Whittaker 1968, Whittaker and Watts 1969. Compared to students, nonstudents value off-campus political activities more highly, describe selves as more "liberal" with regard to heterosexual behavior, more often support legalization of consenting adult homosexuality, would less often reject fiancé if he/she had had homosexual/heterosexual relationship; males are less often married, females more often married or divorced. 27/151 nonstudents (vs. 1/56 students) spontaneously mention drug usage.

COMMENTS: Overlaps with other published papers on nonstudents; new data concern marriage, sexual attitudes, and drugs.

277. _____ . 1968. "Profile of a Non-Conformist Youth Culture: A Study of the Berkeley Non-Students." SOCIOLOGY OF EDUCATION 41 (Spring): 179-200.

SETTING, SUBJECTS, AND METHODS: See Whittaker and Watts Intro., Whittaker 1967, Whittaker and Watts 1969. Special attention to family contact, areas of family discord, evaluation and purposes of education, political affiliation, organizational membership, and protest activities. Comparison of nonstudents with student cross section.

RESULTS: See Whittaker and Watts 1969. Nonstudents very high on Anomia, UCB Ss average. Low nonstudent scores on OPI personal integration scale interpreted as evidence of greater nonstudent alienation. Nonstudents report less contact with parents in all areas (personal contact, receive letters, write letters), less often discuss politics, future goals, intellectual ideas and personal problems with parents, report greater disagreement with parents on intellectual ideas, religion, goals, and politics. No differences in discussion of religious beliefs with parents. Intelligence levels of all groups high, but male students highest. Nonstudents dropped out because of boredom, meaninglessness of higher education, constriction of formal education; indicate far higher dissatisfaction with formal education than do students, rate vocational training less important purpose of college education, developing ethical standards and learning to get along with people more important. Eighty-eight percent nonstudents report no religion or exotic religion. Highly significant with students, but religious affiliation of parents of 2 groups is not as distinct. Slight overrepresentation of Jewish parents among nonstudents. Nonstudents much less Republican, more often "other" than students.

Parents of nonstudents slightly more left-wing, but not as markedly so as their children. Nonstudents frequently attend meetings of SNCC, CORE, Young Socialist Alliance, YPSL, Du Bois Club and Independent Socialist Club but tend not to be members; are more involved in picketing, community organization, protests, and civil disobedience on both civil rights and the Vietnam war. Authors conclude that nonstudents are alienated from both family and society, oriented toward creative fields, uninterested in careers, not conventionally political yet involved in protest activities.

COMMENTS: Supplements earlier picture of "nonstudent" with emphasis on high parental conflict, tendency for parents to be slightly more nonconformist, but children to be greatly more nonconformist than UCB cross section. Despite rejection of conventional politics and high anomia, nonstudents are highly involved in protest activities.

278. Wehr, Paul C. n.d. "The Sit-Down Strikes: A Study of the Passive Resistance Movement in North Carolina." Master's thesis, University of North Carolina.

279. *Weissberg, C. 1968. "Students against the Rank." Master's thesis, Department of Sociology, University of Chicago. 34 pp + App.

SETTING, SUBJECTS, AND METHODS: See Flacks 1966, Study 2. Data from randomly selected students, N = 63, sitting-in on the third day of building occupation. Comparison group of dormitory nonparticipants, N = 34. Sit-in Ss divided into 3 groups on the basis of 4-item scale measuring leafleting and canvasing, rallies and protest, picketing and marching, civil disobedience: high activism, N = 21, medium, N = 18, low, N = 24. Ss interviewed about sit-in attitudes, political memberships and activities, values and family, demographic variables. Data analysis concentrates on internal comparisons between activist groups. Because of small N's, trends reported as results.

RESULTS: Compared to nonparticipants, sit-in Ss less religious, more humanistic-existential, less career-oriented, more liberal; parents more highly educated, higher income, more professional, more Jewish or irreligious, and more liberal.

High activist Ss most radical-humanitarian, SDS members, most organizational affiliations, strongly intellectual, but did not have high grades; parents had highest incomes, most education, least religious commitment, most liberal, most approved of children's social action; most working mothers, fathers in intellectual-artistic-humanitarian professions. Medium activist group most romantic and "alienated," uncertain about future, apathetic, pessimistic, concerned with self-exploration; parental data suggest identification with dominant humanitarian-professional mothers, rebellion against conventional values of parents. Low activist Ss highest GPA, least organizational involvement, most committed to academic careers, most supportive of liberalism and pacifism, parents less educated, prosperous and liberal, fewer working mothers, less parental support for activism. Author emphasizes that differences within activist group preclude a unitary explanation of activism.

COMMENTS: A useful exploratory study that both confirms and qualifies previous generalizations about activists, suggest important distinctions between Ss involved in building occupation.

280. Westby, David L., and Braungart, Richard G. 1966. "Class and Politics in the Family Backgrounds of Student Political Activists. AMERICAN SOCIOLOGICAL REVIEW 31 (October): 690-92.

SETTING: Spring, 1965, University of Pennsylvania (?).

SUBJECTS: Membership bodies of 2 campus activist organizations, Students for Peace, N = 29, and Young Americans for Freedom, N = 19.

METHODS: Questionnaire includes attitude items on Vietnam war; family income, SES, political opinions of parents.

RESULTS: Compared to YAF, Students for Peace have higher family income and SES, are more often Democratic or socialist. Data taken to confirm that "right activists" come from status-threatened groups.

COMMENTS: Perhaps the first study comparing right- and left-wing activists. Superseded by later studies by Braungart that demonstrate that parental political belief is the strongest determinant of student beliefs.

281. _____. 1970a. "Activists and the History of the Future." In Foster, Julian, and Long, Durward, eds. 1970. PROTEST! STUDENT ACTIVISM IN AMERICA. New York: William Morrow, pp. 158-83.

SETTING, SUBJECTS AND METHODS: See Braungart 1969a. SDS, YD, YR, and YAF members wrote "the history of the United States from the present to the year 2000." Essays coded for major themes. Five utopian conceptions identified: Progressive utopia (steady improvement), revolutionary utopia (otherthrow of existing structure), conversionist utopia (downward drift followed by "rapid awakening"), linear decline dystropia (steady decline), eschatological utopia (sudden cataclysm).

RESULTS: SDS emphasizes revolution, guerilla warfare, totalitarianism, American colonialism, and imperialism. YD and YR emphasize social justice, civil rights, humanitarianism, technology, elections, decline in world tensions because of U.S. actions. YAF emphasizes state socialism, conservatism and conservative ideals, Communist takeover, U.S. crusade for world freedom. SDS highest on revolutionary and eschatological utopian types. YD and YR highest on progressive, YAF highest on conversionist.

Authors suggest the conception of utopia is related to process of politicization in each group, conclude that neither class theory nor mass theory fits their data, and that other factors are involved, like "achievement pressure, status concern, emphasis on principle, maternal dominance, and psychological processes."

COMMENTS: An ingenious analysis with a speculative discussion.

282. ____ . 1970b. "The Alienation of Generations and Status Politics: Alternative Explanations of Student Political Activism." In Sigel, Roberta, ed. 1970. LEARNING ABOUT POLITICS. New York: Random House, pp. 476-89.

SETTING, SUBJECTS, AND METHOD: See Braungart 1969a. Comparison of SDS and YAF groups.

RESULTS: Leftward shift away from parents and parental indifference or disapproval in SDS, slight rightward shift and greater parental approval of student political activity in YAF. Higher alienation from parents, from authority figures in high school, from religious figures and fewer religious practices among SDS than YAF. SDS members have higher parental occupational status and higher father's education (64% SDS upper-middle-class vs. 32% YAF), family incomes somewhat higher, 53% SDS have partial East European ethnic background (vs. 21% YAF); 45% SDS exclusively North European (vs. 78% YAF). Author concludes that SDS members have high social status and low ethnic status; YAF, low social status and high ethnic status.

COMMENTS: A reworking of data largely reported elsewhere. Note problem in defining "low ethnic status" as "Eastern European background."

283. *Whittaker, David. 1967. "Psychological Characteristics of Alienated, Nonconformist College-Age Youth." Ph.D. dissertation, University of California at Berkeley. 180 pp. + App.

SETTING, SUBJECTS, AND METHODS: See Whittaker and Watts Intro. Detailed report of comparisons between nonstudents and control group. AVL, OPI, ACL, SVIB data analyzed separately for males and females, comparing nonstudents and student control group.

RESULTS: Virtually all of the thesis results have been presented in other Whittaker et al. publications. Complete results presented for psychosocial characteristics, AVL scales, OPI scales, ACL scales, SVIB scales. Discussion stresses nonstudents' alienation and anomie, psychological maladjustment, nonconformity, intellectuality and creative potential, but lack of discipline and achievement potential. Nonstudents are seen as in the midst of a prolonged and stressful identity crisis.

COMMENTS: An outstanding Ph.D. thesis with a thorough presentation of methods, and a cautious, well-documented but far-ranging interpretation of the data.

284. *____ . n.d. "Masculinity-Femininity and Non-Conformist Youth." Paper read at American Psychological Association, August 1969, Washington, D.C. 7 pp.

SETTING, SUBJECTS, AND METHODS: See Whittaker 1967. Compares nonstudents and cross-section on selected scores from OPI, ACL, AVL, SVIB.

RESULTS: Similarities found between nonstudent males and females, and greater sex-differentiation in the student control group. Variables that differentiate nonstudent males from control group males on personality tests tend also to be those that differentiate nonstudent females from control group females. Compared with same-sex student control group, male and female nonstudents score higher on OPI measures of aestheticism, complexity, autonomy, and lower on masculinity-feminimity, higher on ACL, measures of autonomy, change, succorance, exhibitionism, and heterosexuality; low on dominance, achievement, order, and endurance. On AVL, nonstudent males and females rank values in the same order (from aesthetic to economic) but cross section shows sex differences. On SVIB, all nonstudents score high on artistic, creative occupations, and reject pragmatic, routinized occupations. Nonstudent males are less "masculine" compared to cross-section males and non-student females less "feminine" compared to cross-section females. Author questions whether this result indicates maladjustment or creativity.

COMMENTS: An interesting analysis of data around masculinity-femininity issues. When "femininity" is defined as aesthetic interests, sensitivity, emotionality, and admission of feelings, nonstudents score higher regardless of sex. Findings suggest that culturally-defined "feminine" traits are more valued in nonconformist, nonstudent subculture.

285. ____ . 1968a. "Alienated Youth and Their Psychological Propensity." Research resume, STATE CONFERENCE OF THE CALIFORNIA ADVISORY COUNCIL ON EDUCATIONAL RESEARCH 38: 97-99.

A brief report of findings which have been reported at greater length in other papers by Whittaker and Watts.

286. ____. 1968b. "Vocational Dispositions of the Nonconformity, Collegiate Dropout." PROCEEDINGS OF THE ASSOCIATION FOR INSTITUTIONAL RESEARCH. May 1968, San Francisco, 16 pp.

SETTING, SUBJECTS, AND METHODS: See Whittaker 1967. This paper analyzes academic major, tentative vocational decision, ideal vocational choices, avocational creative needs, SVIB results for nonstudents and student control group.

RESULTS: See Whittaker and Watts 1969. Nonstudents more often mention creative arts as tentative vocational choices; males less often choose theoretical and applied sciences, law or business; females less often choose teaching. Ideal vocational choice on open-ended question categorized by researchers into 6 types. Male and female nonstudents choose individualistic person, creative artist, and versatile person; female students, educator, versatile person, social servant; male students, governmental-political, individualistic person, and social servant. Nonstudents rate creative expression outside of vocation more important than do students.

SVIB (men): nonstudents emphasize independent intellectual and creative careers; oppose occupations involving business detail and administrative responsibility. No differences between students and nonstudents on willingness to specialize or choice of high-status occupations. Students score higher on interest maturity, nonstudents lower on masculinity and higher on occupations reflecting "intellectual disposition," lower on "applied professional." SVIB (women): nonstudents higher on author, artist, and music performer; lower on home economics teacher, dietician, high school physical education teacher, nurse, etc. Overall pattern for nonstudent women similar to that for men.

COMMENTS: Further confirmation of the antipractical, "creative" outlooks of the nonstudents in this study. Note similarities between male and female nonstudents.

287. Whittaker, David, and Tallman, J. 1968. "Heroes and Values of Berkeley Youth." CALIFORNIA EDUCATIONAL RESEARCH SUMMARY (June): 94-99.

SETTING, SUBJECTS, AND METHODS: See Whittaker and Watts Intro. Analysis of open-ended questions: "What famous men and women, living or dead, past or present, real or fictitious, do you admire?" "Why?" Ss responded with average of 4 names; 4 judges examined data independently and agreed on coding. No analysis of sex differences. Comparison of nonstudents with student control group.

RESULTS: Rank order of types of heroes (with % for nonstudents and students): religous heroes 17%, 4%; literary heroes, 16%, 6%; political-conventional heroes, 15%, 42%; fine arts, 11%, 5%; philosophical, 9%, 8%; political-unconventional, 8%, 4%; scientist-mathematician, 2%, 8%. Most cited figures by nonstudents: Christ, Buddha, John F. Kennedy, and Ghandi; by students: John F. Kennedy, Einstein, Churchill, and Stephenson. Reasons for admiring heroes were (in order) for nonstudents: courageous idealist, humanist, enlightened and free man; for students: courageous idealist, square, intellectual, and humanist. In general, values of sociability more stressed by students; mystical and idealistic qualities, iconoclasm and innovation more stressed by nonstudents. Nonstudents listed more esoteric people and qualities.

COMMENTS: A brief article summarizing another aspect of the nonstudent study.

288. **Whittaker, David, and Watts, William Arthur. Introduction.

SETTING: Late summer-early fall 1965, winter 1966-1967, Berkeley, California. In December 1966, students cited by UCB administration for alleged violations of campus rules in connection with picketing of Navy recruiting table.

SUBJECTS: 4 groups. Nonstudents (Aug. 1965). Using a snowball method, 151 "nonstudents" living in Telegraph Avenue area were involved in 3-4 hours of testing, paid $5.00 each. Cross-section I. (late summer-early fall 1965). Random sample of 56 UCB students (77%) given same tests. Student activists (winter 1966-67). Of 77 students cited by university administration for violation of rules in connection with picketing Navy recruiting table, 33 (43%) participated in research. Cross-section II. Random sample of 154 UCB students (74%). Although data were gathered at different times, responses of 2 cross sections were sufficiently similar as to justify combining them for some analyses. All samples were similar in terms of age and sex.

METHODS: Demographic and background questionnaire, Anomia, Thorndike Multiple Choice Vocabulary Test, questions about frequency of discussion with parents in several areas and extent of agreement in each area, extent of family contact, OPI, ACL, scored into 15 need scales, AUL, open-ended list of admired figures and heroes, SVIB, open-ended questions concerning vocational goals and commitments. Data analyses usually involve F-tests, distinguishing male and female subjects, for activists and/or nonstudents vs. control groups, with differences between 2 specific groups tested using Marascuilo's test for chi-square in data involving multiple comparisons.

RESULTS: See Watts et al. 1969, Watts and Whittaker 1967, 1968, Whittaker 1967, n.d., 1968a, 1968b, Whittaker and Tallman 1968, Whittaker and Watts 1966, 1967, 1969, 1971.

COMMENTS: Especially valuable series of studies because contrast of activists with both nonactivist students and alienated nonstudents permits study of two types of dissent and nonconformity.

289. Whittaker, David, and Watts, William Arthur. 1966. "Personality and value attitudes of intellectually disposed, alienated youth. Paper read at American Psychological Association, September 1966, New York. 10 pp.

A preliminary report of nonstudent vs. control group comparisons, which have been reported in other papers by Whittaker and Watts.

290. _____. 1967. Psychological needs and nonconformity. Paper read at Inter-American Congress of Psychology, December 1967, Mexico City.

291. _____. 1969. "Personality Characteristics of a Nonconformist Youth Subculture: A Study of the Berkeley Nonstudent." JOURNAL OF SOCIAL ISSUES 25, no. 2:65-89.

SETTING, SUBJECTS, AND METHODS: See Whittaker and Watts Intro. Comparison of OPI data for nonstudents and student control group.

RESULTS: 82%-88% nonstudents judged "unconventional" in appearance vs. 15%-24% control group. Nonstudents discontinued education prematurely; are overrepresented in creative arts, fine arts, and humanities; underrepresented in business, engineering, biological and physical sciences; no difference in social sciences. Thirty percent nonstudents employed. Compared to male nonstudents, females have lived longer in Berkeley area, more often spend their childhoods in Bay Area. No major differences in SES noted, but nonstudents' fathers less often manager-owners, parents more often had high school education or less.

Nonstudents of both sexes score higher than same-sex students on OPI aestheticism, complexity, autonomy, impulse expression; lower on personal integration, masculinity-femininity, and response bias. Compared to same-sex students, nonstudent females score higher on religious liberalism and anxiety level, nonstudent males score lower on practical outlook. No differences on thinking introversion, theoretical orientation, social extroversion, or altruism. Overall, nonstudents appear more intellectually disposed than students, more antiauthoritarian, more disturbed socioemotionally (but within "normal" range), more repudiative of traditional sex roles and, for males, of practical-concrete success orientation. Authors conclude that compared to students, nonstudents are more maladjusted and have intellectual and creative disposition, but may lack the self-discipline necessary for achievement.

COMMENTS: Male and female nonstudents are very alike on OPI Scales. Study begins to define the "other" counterculture group that is contrasted with the more politically active group. Important questions about "normality" are raised and discussed briefly.

292. *_____ . 1971. "Personality Characteristics Associated with Activism and Disaffiliation in Today's College-Age Youth." JOURNAL OF COUNSELING PSYCHOLOGY 18, no. 3 (May):200-206.

SETTING, SUBJECTS, AND METHODS: See Whittaker and Watts Intro., Watts et al. 1969. Data analysis focuses primarily upon ACL, ACL compares activists, nonstudents, and student control group.

RESULTS: See Watts et al. 1969. Compared to cross section, activists and nonstudents both score higher on Anomia, autonomy, change and lability; lower on order, self-control and endurance. Activists are higher than nonstudents on aggression, dominance, achievement and self-confidence; lower on succorance, abasement, and number of negative adjectives checked. (These qualities differentiate within the nonconformist group.) Nonstudents score in the maladjusted direction on 6 out of 15 need scales; activists score maladjusted on 2 out of 15 need scales but all scores are within the normal range. Nonstudents differ from both groups on low achievement and dominance; activists differ from both groups on high aggression.

COMMENTS: Useful findings that help differentiate alienation from activism. Given nonconformity, choice of activism (vs. disaffiliation) seems determined by aggressive, dominant, achievement needs as opposed to self-abasement, neediness, and a negative self-conception.

293. Wiecking, Frederick A. 1969. "A Study of the Psychological Motives of the New Left." Bachelor's thesis, Wesleyan University, Connecticut. 61 pp. + App.

SETTING, SUBJECTS, AND METHODS: See Winter and Wiecking 1971, study group 1. More detailed discussion of methodology, only data from male Ss analyzed.

RESULTS: See Winter and Wiecking, 1971, study group 1. Further analysis of male achievement imagery shows that radicals more often stress instrumental activity, interpreted by author as orientation toward immediate action without evaluation of long-run significance. Excellent discussion of findings in terms of other N Ach and N Power research, and speculative discussion of changing motivations of American youth.

COMMENTS: A good undergraduate thesis examining achievement and power motivation in a small group of highly committed male radicals.

294. Williams, Douglas, Associates. 1969. "Cornell University Survey." Conducted for Special Trustee Committee. Cornell University, Ithaca, New York. 71 pp.

SETTING: July-Aug. 1969, Cornell University; take-over of Strought Hall by black students in April 1969.

SUBJECTS: 200 students, 100 faculty, 30 administrators, 300 alumni, 20 trustees, members of active faculty groups in Strought Hall controversy. Students and faculty sampled randomly with some stratifications, administrators drawn from organizational chart, alumni on every nth basis from computer lists, trustees Cornell graduates. SDS and black students not interviewed because of high refusal rate.

METHODS: Open-ended interviews averaging 45 minutes (students and alumni by telephone), coded with high reliability.

RESULTS: All groups see ground swell of student protest. Fifty-eight percent students approve protests that do not interfere with rights of others, 21% approve violent or disruptive protest under exceptional circumstances. Majority of all groups who were informed about black studies program approved, but 37% students, 59% alumni were uninformed. All groups think university should provide students an education and do research, but 38% of students think it should also promote social reform. Faculty most affirmative on academic freedom. Of on-campus groups, faculty most divided and conservative, administrators and students more liberal; alumni least informed and most conservative.

COMMENTS: Study conducted for Cornell trustees; describes attitudes of several constituencies in the aftermath of black students' protest. Note greater conservatism of faculty and alumni compared with students and administrators.

295. Williamson, E.G., and Cowan, John L. 1965. "The Role of the President in the Desirable Enactment of Academic Freedom for Students." EDUCA-TIONAL RECORD 46, no. 4 (Fall):351-72.

SETTING, INSTITUTIONS, METHODS, AND RESULTS: See Cowan 1966. Over 70% of deans and presidents support high student freedom to hear, criticize, express viewpoints on controversial issues, with support highest in New England, Mid-Atlantic and North Central states, in private nonsectarian universities, liberal arts colleges and public universities. Eighty-six percent presidents reported fairly permissive policies about modes of student expression; least free in permitting partisan political activity were large West Coast public universities. Student council can publicize resolutions with referendum on 86% of I's, without referendum at 46%; large public and private universities are most free. Fifteen percent of student editors reported censorship during 2½ years (none in Protestant or large public universities, vs. Catholic colleges). Student member on policy-making committees in 60% of I's, with highest voting membership in large public universities (vs. Catholic colleges). Student power related to freedom in topic discussion, speaker selection, and mode of expression. Student participation reported on the increase in all I's and most were favorable to it. Most presidents reported recent increase in student activism, especially at Catholic I's and private universities.

COMMENTS: See Cowan 1966. A descriptive report. Note high reported student participation in decision-making and increasing activism in 1961-64, finding that presidents' perception is closest to students.

296. _____. 1966. THE AMERICAN STUDENT'S FREEDOM OF EXPRES-
SION. Minneapolis: University of Minnesota Press. 193 pp.

SETTING, INSTITUTIONS, AND METHODS: See Cowan 1966, Williamson, and Cowan 1965. No study of institutional characteristics except type
and region.

RESULTS: Reported freedom for organized protest activity found greatest
at private and large public universities (vs. Catholic liberal arts and teachers'
colleges), in New England and Middle Atlantic (vs. Southern) states.

COMMENTS: Findings deal with reported freedom to protest, not actual
incidence of protest; but results are nonetheless similar.

297. Winborn, B.B., and Jansen, D.G. 1967. "Personality Characteristics of
Campus Socio-Political Action Leaders." JOURNAL OF COUNSELING
PSYCHOLOGY 14 (November):509-513.

SETTING, SUBJECTS, AND METHODS: See Jansen 1967. Analysis of
16PF findings: analysis of variance contrasting 5 groups by 2 sexes.

RESULTS: Compared to other leaders, sociopolitical leaders low on
superego strength, high on "autia" (unconcern for conventionality) and on
radicalism. No interactions with sex. Distinctiveness of sociopolitical
leaders is due primarily to liberals, who are lower on superego strength,
higher on autia and on radicalism, tend to be more sober and serious, more
emotionally sensitive, more forthright and unpretentious socially, more
confident and secure in daily life.

COMMENTS: See Jansen 1967. Interesting as a kind of Berkeley follow-up
at Indiana in 1966.

298. _____. 1968. "Perceptions of a University Environment by Social-Political
Action Leaders." PERSONNEL AND GUIDANCE JOURNAL, 47, no. 3
(November):218-222.

299. _____. 1969. "Profile of Social-Political Action Leaders." JOURNAL OF
COLLEGE STUDENT PERSONNEL 10 (January):7-11.

SUBJECTS, SETTING, METHODS, AND RESULTS: See Jansen 1967.
This paper emphasizes background data that differentiate all sociopolitical

leaders from other leaders; does not analyze differences between liberal and conservative leaders.

COMMENTS: See Jansen 1967.

300. *Winter, David G., and Wiecking, Frederick A. 1971. "The New Puritans: Achievement and Power Motives of New Left Radicals." BEHAVIORAL SCIENCE, 16, no. 6 (November):523-30.

SETTING: 1968-69, Wesleyan University (Conn.), occupation of president's office on May 5-6, 1969.

SUBJECTS: 3 groups: (1) 19 white males, 13 females, full-time workers in national offices of National Mobilization to End the War, War Resisters League, Catholic Peace Fellowship, etc. (All leaders with at least 1 year in the field). Control Group of 14 males, 19 females approximately matched on age (mean = 27) drawn from Vista volunteers, graduates and undergraduates, etc. (2) Ss taking 3 positions during occupation of the president's office: 19 occupiers, 36 repudiators, 82 neither. Repudiators signed statement repudiating opposition. Ss tested 3-15 months before building occupation. (3) 28 male students in introductory psychology course, divided into 13 who had peace posters and symbols in their rooms and 15 who did not.

METHODS: Administration of 5-picture modified TAT individually or in groups. Scored for N achievement, N affiliation, and N power (McClelland).

RESULTS: Group 1: male and female radicals scored higher on N ach than controls, male radicals lower on N power. Group 2: repudiators higher in N power and lower in N ach than occupiers and neutrals taken together. Group 3: those with peace posters scored lower in N power, did not differ in N ach. Authors suggest that radical socializing background produces high N ach, and that low N power is related to antiauthoritarianism of New Left. Historical discussion of relationship between N ach and N power.

COMMENTS: The only activism study that uses McClelland's need measures. Some question as to whether high N ach reflects leadership (activism) or ideology (leftism).

301. Wood, James L. 1971a. "The Role of Radical Political Consciousness in Student Political Activism: A Preliminary Analysis." Paper read at the American Sociological Association, September 1971, Denver. 31 pp.

SETTING, SUBJECTS, AND METHODS: See Somers 1967 and Wood 1971b. Questionnaires mailed to the parents of Ss in original sample, but no data from them included in report.

RESULTS: See Wood 1971b. Negative relationship between activism and belief that nonviolence will lead to racial equality, no relationship between activism and belief that American society is unjust but changes are possible; overall, activists believe American society is more unjust. Activists not distinguished by loneliness or belief that other students are unfriendly, or by overall draft status. Activism related to mothers in people-oriented occupations, left-wing mother's and father's political party, parents in liberal wing of party, high mother's education, humanities and social science major, religion (Jewish) and race (white); unrelated to family income (trend toward high income), father's education (but M.A.s and Ph.D.s high), father's occupation (but professionals high), year in college, sex, GPA. residence (fraternity and live-with-relatives low, apartment with friend or alone high), age, or marriage.

COMMENTS: See Wood 1971b. Compared with earlier Berkeley research, study shows lessened relationship to SES, lower relationship with most previous activism predictors, and suggests special maternal influence on activists.

302. ____. 1971b. "Student Political Activism." In Swift, David, ed. AMER-ICAN EDUCATION: A SOCIOLOGICAL PERSPECTIVE. Boston: Houghton Mifflin Co., forthcoming.

SETTING, SUBJECTS, AND METHODS: See Somers 1969. Reanalysis of Somers' data to test theories of student activism. Historical review of demonstrations, especially in Bay area. "Activists" are Ss who took part in student strike (December 1966 after ROTC conflict) or Oakland Induction Center demonstration (fall 1967) or Free Speech Movement (December 1964), N = about 136. Data reported in tables indicating percentage in various categories who are activists. Statistical methods unclear.

RESULTS: Activists overrepresented among Ss who oppose Vietnam involvement, believe revolutionary changes needed in America, criticize American democracy, support black power, and label selves socialist or other. (But in no case do activists represent a majority of those agreeing with "radical" positions.) Activists somewhat more critical of UCB because of large size, absence of student control, "factory," and mistrust of faculty and administration, but not more dissatisfied overall with UCB. Compared to nonactivists, activists do not differ with regard to closeness-distance vis-à-vis mother and father or status of parental marriage. Author concludes that data supports political consciousness theory.

COMMENTS: Study difficult to interpret because of incomplete reporting of data, but supports view that general political radicalism predicts activism better than does educational dissatisfaction. Findings also suggest low relationship between ideological radicalism and behavioral activism.

303. Zarit, Steven. 1971. "Studies in Political Participation." Bachelor's thesis, University of Michigan. 134 pp.

SETTING, SUBJECTS, AND METHODS: See G. Gurin 1971, study 2. Comparison of members of radical group, moderate group, and control Ss.

RESULTS: Largely the same as in G. Gurin 1971. Author emphasizes differences between male and female politically active Ss, importance of styles of group action in determining political participation, greater emphasis on moral questions for radicals than for moderate activists. Parents of radicals read more "high quality magazines"; fathers do more "serious reading." Radicals report more disagreement on political preferences and beliefs with both parents.

COMMENTS: An undergraduate thesis with an excellent critical review of literature on adult participation in regular party organizations.

Indexes

Author/Editor

Events, Groups, Institutions
and Settings Studied

Topic

Author/Editor

Aiken, M., 1, 43
Ailey, John S., 1
Allerbeck, Klaus R., 2
Altbach, Phillip, 106
American Council on Education (ACE), see
   A. Astin; Astin and Bayer; Bayer and
   Astin; Bayer, Astin and Boruch; Boruch
   and Creager; Bisconti; Bisconti and
   Astin; Royer.
Angel, Arthur, 148
Angell, Robert C., 55
Angres, Salma, 3, 60
Armistead, T.W., 3
Aron, William S., 4, 5
Ashmall, Roy, 98
Astin, Alexander W., 5–12, 21–24, 50, 147,
   178
Astin, Helen S., 10, 13, 15–17
Auger, Camilla, 17
Aya, R., 103

Baird, Leonard L., 18
Baker, Keith, 74
Barton, Allen H., 17–19
Bayer, Alan E., 6, 10, 12, 21–23, 147
Bellevita, Christopher, 74
Berkowitz, L., 146
Bisconti, Ann S., 6, 10, 17, 23–24
Blau, Peter, 24
Block, Jeanne H., 25–27, 81–84, 157
Blume, Norman, 29
Boruch, Robert F., 6, 22–23, 29
Bowers, William J., 30, 96
Braungart, Margaret M., 34–35
Braungart, Richard G., 30–35, 190–191
Brehm, Mary L., 102
Bresnahan, Daniel M., 53
Brown, S.R., 35
Bureau Social Science Research (BSSR),
   see H. Astin; A.S. Bisconti

Cabin, Seymour, 42
Cameron, William Bruce, 106
Carnegie Commission on Higher Education,
   91, 176
Carns, Donald E., 156
Centra, J.A., 138, 141
Cherniss, Cary, 36, 183
Christie, Richard, 37, 71
Clarke, J.W., 37
Coles, Robert, 38–40
Collins, John N., 40
Cook, S.W., 8
Covington, M., 147

Cowan, John L., 40, 198–199
Creager, John A., 6, 29
Crisp, Lloyd E., 43

Dan, Alice J., 43, 60
Davis, J.A., 149
Demerath, N.J. III, 1, 43
Denisoff, R. Serge, 45
Derber, C., 46, 60–61
Dockett, D.A., 122
Donaldson, Robert H., 47
Donovan, J.M., 47
Doress, Irvin, 48
Drew, David E., 50
Dunlap, Riley, 51–53

Egan, J., 37
El-Assal, M., 153
Epstein, Yakov M., 53
Erikson, Erik, 39
Everson, David H., 54–55
Ezekiel, Ralph, 55

Fenton, J. H., 55
Finney, Henry C., 56
Fisher, Larry, 148
Fishkin, James, 57
Fishman, Jacob R., 58, 160–163
Flacks, Richard E., 43, 46, 59–62, 118,
   150, 174, 175
Foster, Julian, 10, 18, 62, 86, 112–113, 132,
   190
Frank, J.D., 63–64
Freeman, J.L., 64
Friedman, Lucy N., 37, 71

Gagnon, John H., 155–156
Gale, Richard P., 51–53
Gales, K.E., 65, 164
Gamson, Z.F., 66, 73
Gastwirth, Donald, 66
Gaylin, Willard, 67
Gelineau, Victor, A., 68
Geller, Jesse D., 42, 68
Gergen, K.J., 69
Gergen, M.K., 69
Gleason, G., 55
Gold, Alice R., 37, 71
Gold, Carol Hancock, 74
Goldsmid, Paula, 60, 72
Goldsmith, Jeff C., 72
Goodman, J., 66, 72
Gore, P.M., 73
Gottlieb, David, 74, 166

Events, Groups, Institutions
and Settings Studied

Topic

Categories that refer to student characteristics are followed by (S).

213

About the Author

Kenneth Keniston is a graduate of Harvard College (B.A.) and of Oxford University (D.Phil.), where he was a Rhodes Scholar. He is the author of *Uncommitted: Alienated Youth in American Society* (1965); *Young Radicals: Notes on Committed Youth* (1968); and *Youth and Dissent: The Rise of a New Opposition* (1971)—all published by Harcourt Brace Jovanovich. He is and has been a member and/or chairman of a large number of public and private, local, state, and national committees, boards, and commissions in his fields of youth and psychiatry. He has received honorary degrees from Notre Dame and Colgate. Dr. Keniston is Professor of Psychiatry at Yale Medical School, and is currently on a leave of absence to be Chairman and Executive Director of the Carnegie Council on Children.